Revised second edition

Don Pedro
presents...

POLITICS & PROTEST

A decade of subvertising, graffiti and other photographs

This book is dedicated to Will Brown, 1959-2010.
A genuine-to-the-core political activist and artist,
and much missed.

Introduction to the 2nd edition

I'm a serial photographer — over time images accumulate into series, and this is one of them: politics and protest.

Here you'll photographs from 1999 to 2011 - featuring subvertising*, graffiti, posters and stickers, speaking directly to anyone who's looking.

Most of the images were taken in Bristol, as I moved around on foot or by bike. I document images whether they match my own view of the world or not, and irrespective of offensiveness. I'm interested in anything placed into public view without permission - a political act in itself.

The categories I've used in this book just provide a loose structure. Many images could easily fit into several categories. Those in 'And the rest...' didn't reach a critical mass to merit categories of their own.

Don Pedro

'Don Pedro' is the only respectful nickname my daughters have given me. When they were little they asked what Pete was in Spanish. On hearing Pedro, they added the 'Don' without realising that it's a courteous form of address. They've since dropped the Don, but I haven't. When I had to come up with a name for my photos hosted on Flickr, it was the first thing I thought of.

Flickr

At www.flickr.com/photos/donpedro you can see these images and the hundreds that didn't make it into the book, plus thousands of other street photos and more. Find the 'Sets' page to see images grouped into series.

The recent political landscape

At the time of the book's inception (summer 2009) MPs had been uncovered misbehaving with their expenses (Tony Blair's expenses were shredded 'by mistake'), Labour were entering their 13th and final year in power, and the banks had been bailed out after helping create a global financial crisis.

By the time the book was first published in November 2010 the Conservative and Liberal Democrat coalition government was under way, with the promise of large-scale cuts in public spending.

At the time of writing (October 2011), the trade unions are promising industrial action over changes to public sector pensions, and the government (amongst other things) continue with plans to make fundamental changes to the health service, to devolve power to local communities, and to change countryside planning laws. Watch this space...

Amongst its 16 extra pages, this second edition features hand-made signs from the big anti-cuts demonstration in March 2011, new anti-cuts and anti-government images, plus a timeline to give a flavour of the last decade.

Don Pedro (aka Pete Maginnis)

*Subvertising is the practice of subverting an existing advert by adding letters or images to change its meaning. Or the creation of a new advert which surprises by using a familiar appearance to say something unexpectedly different.

My thanks to the St Just Mob, whose subvertising features strongly throughout the book.

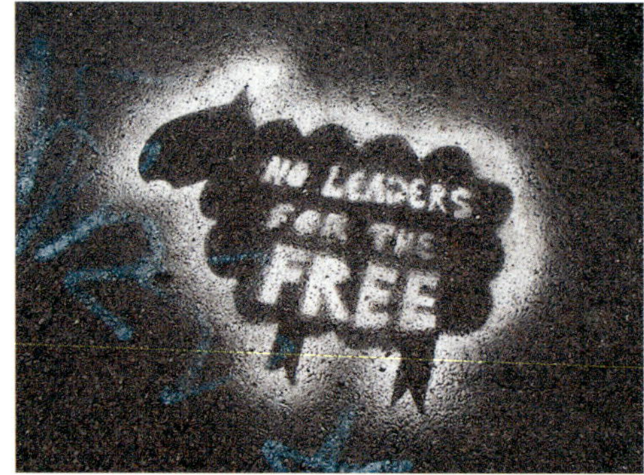

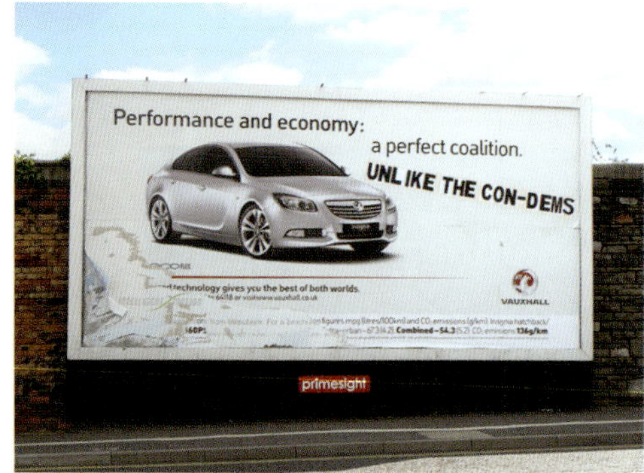

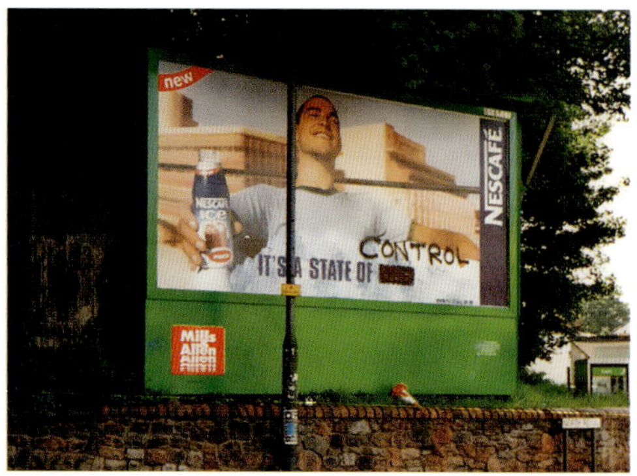

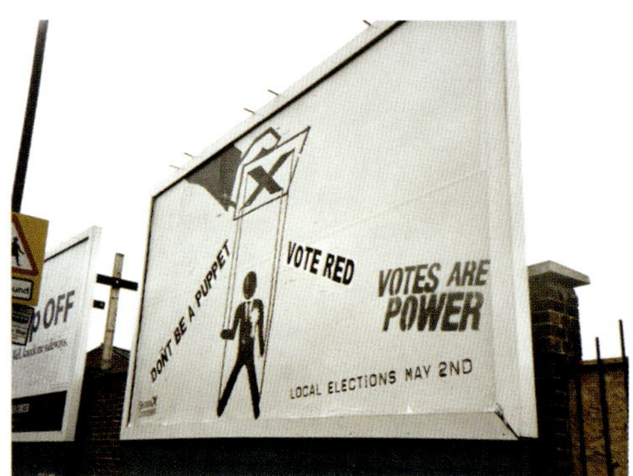

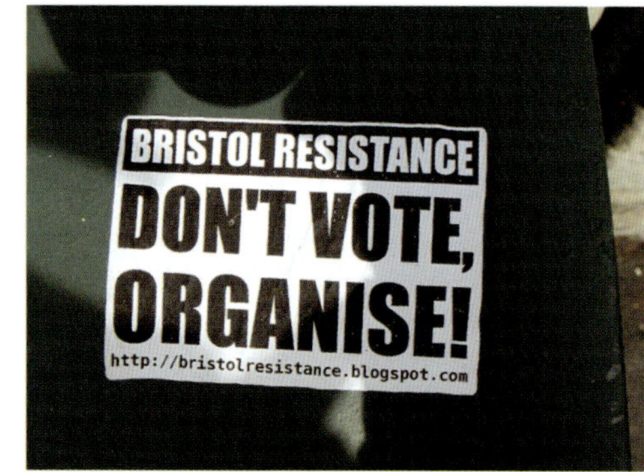

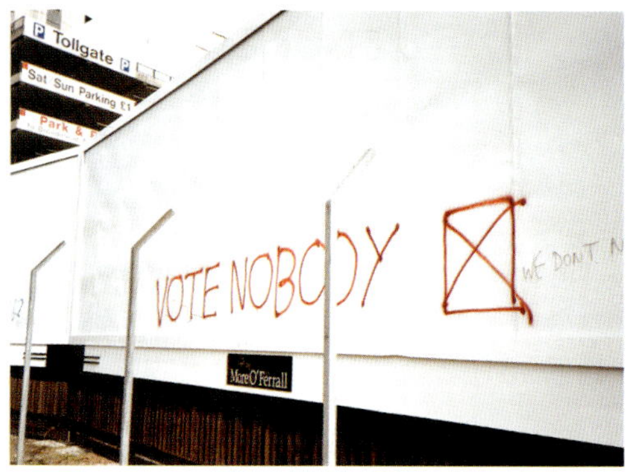

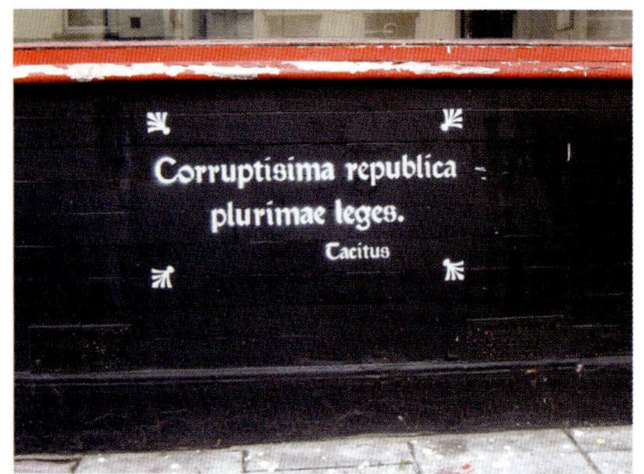

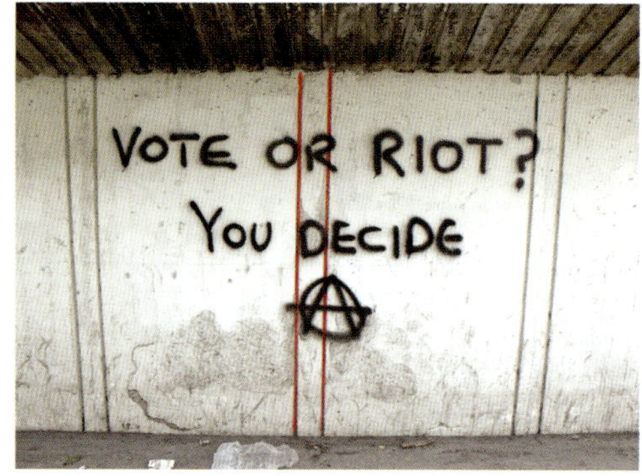

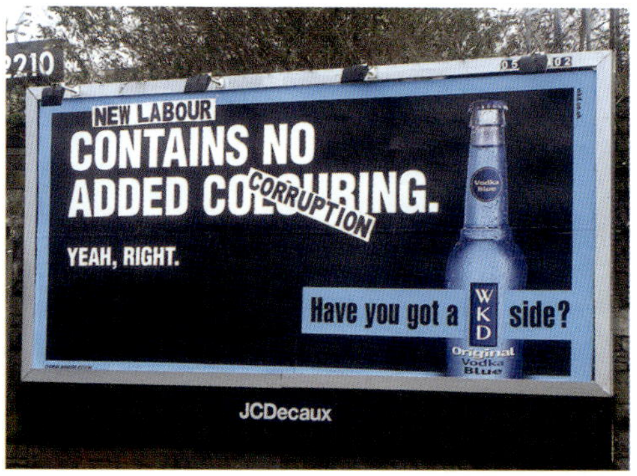

Top row from left – 2005: No leaders for the free | 2010: A perfect coalition — unlike the Con-Dems | 2000: It's a state of control | Middle row — 2002: Don't be a puppet vote red | 2010: Don't vote, organise! | 2001: Vote nobody | Bottom row — 2009: Corruptisima republica plurimae leges [the quote from Roman historian Tacitus translates as 'The more corrupt the state the more numerous the laws'] | 2010: Vote or riot? You decide | 2006: New Labour contains no added corruption |

Government...

I like this quote from Tony Benn on the nature of political struggle. The sentiment is echoed in images throughout this book.

"Every generation had to fight the same battles as their ancestors had to fight, again and again, for there is no final victory and no final defeat. Two flames have burned from the beginning of time – the flame of anger against injustice and the flame of hope..."

Tony Benn, Letters to my Grandchildren

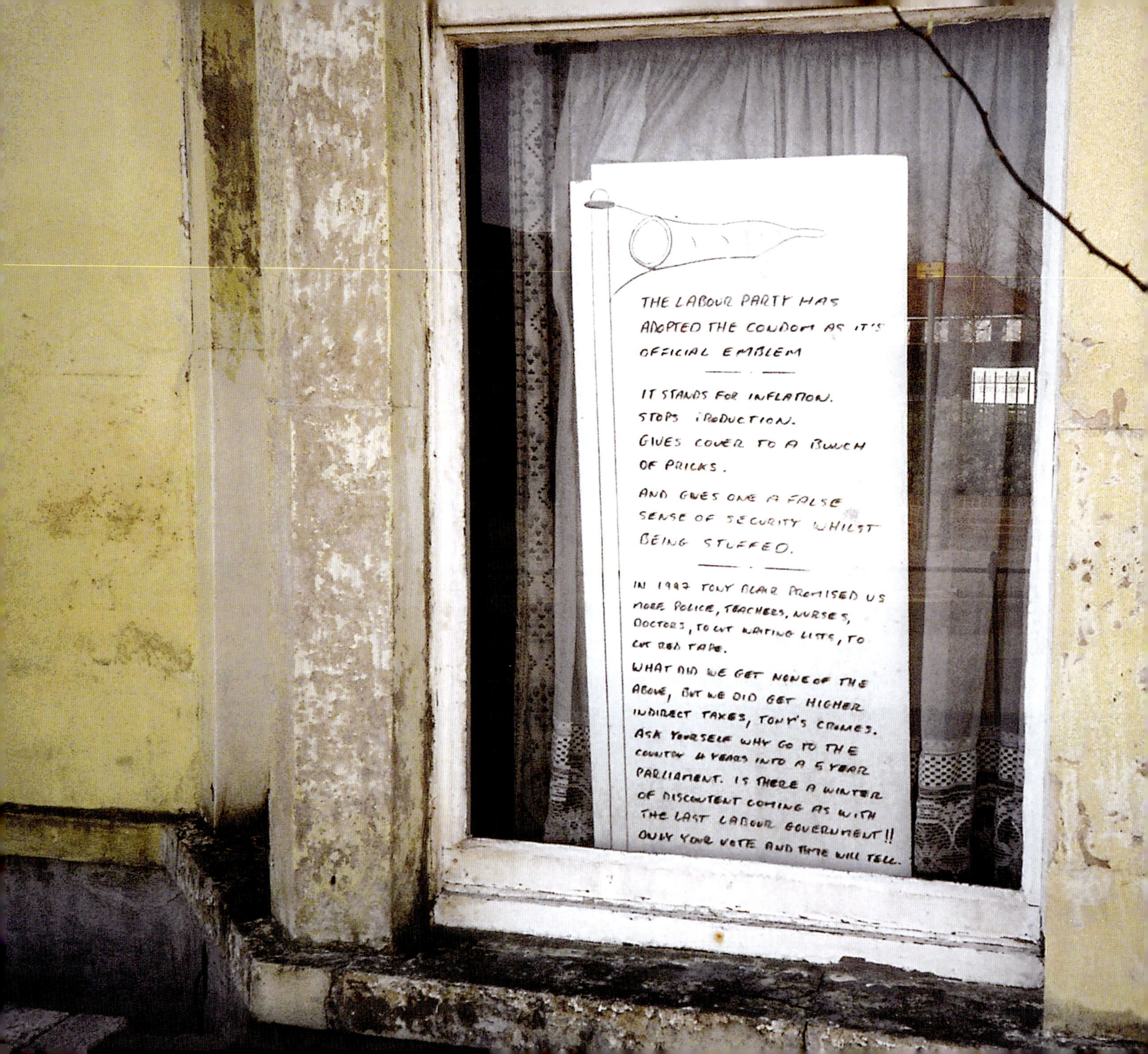

THE LABOUR PARTY HAS
ADOPTED THE CONDOM AS IT'S
OFFICIAL EMBLEM

IT STANDS FOR INFLATION.
STOPS PRODUCTION.
GIVES COVER TO A BUNCH
OF PRICKS.

AND GIVES ONE A FALSE
SENSE OF SECURITY WHILST
BEING STUFFED.

IN 1997 TONY BLAIR PROMISED US
MORE POLICE, TEACHERS, NURSES,
DOCTORS, TO CUT WAITING LISTS, TO
CUT RED TAPE.
WHAT DID WE GET NONE OF THE
ABOVE, BUT WE DID GET HIGHER
INDIRECT TAXES, TONY'S CRONIES.
ASK YOURSELF WHY GO TO THE
COUNTRY 4 YEARS INTO A 5 YEAR
PARLIAMENT. IS THERE A WINTER
OF DISCONTENT COMING AS WITH
THE LAST LABOUR GOVERNMENT!!
ONLY YOUR VOTE AND TIME WILL TELL.

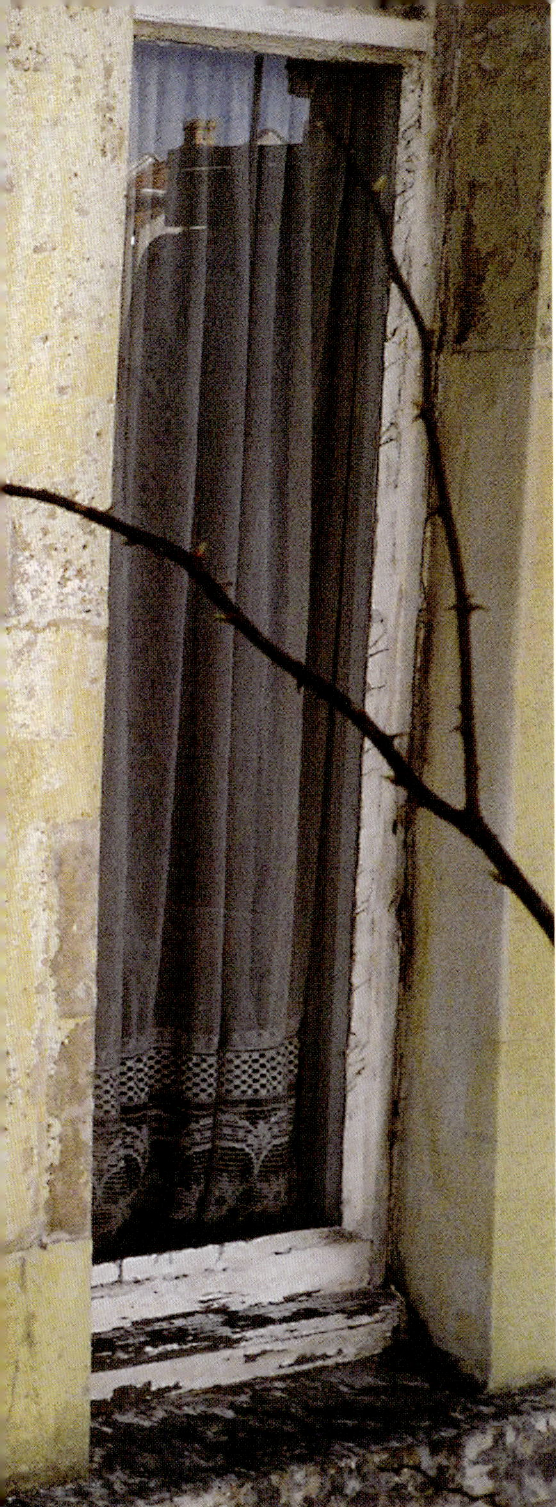

2004: The Labour Party has adopted the condom as it's official emblem.

It stands for inflation. Stops production. Gives cover to a bunch of pricks.

And gives one a false sense of security whilst being stuffed.

In 1997 Tony Blair promised us more police, teachers, nurses, doctors, to cut waiting lists, to cut red tape.

What did we get none of the above, but we did get higher indirect taxes, Tony's cronies. Ask yourself why go to the country 4 years into a 5 year Parliament. Is there a winter of discontent coming as with the last Labour government!! Only your vote and time will tell.

[The Winter of Discontent was in 1978—1979, when local authority trade unions went on strike for better pay whilst the Labour government of James Callaghan sought to hold a pay freeze to control inflation]

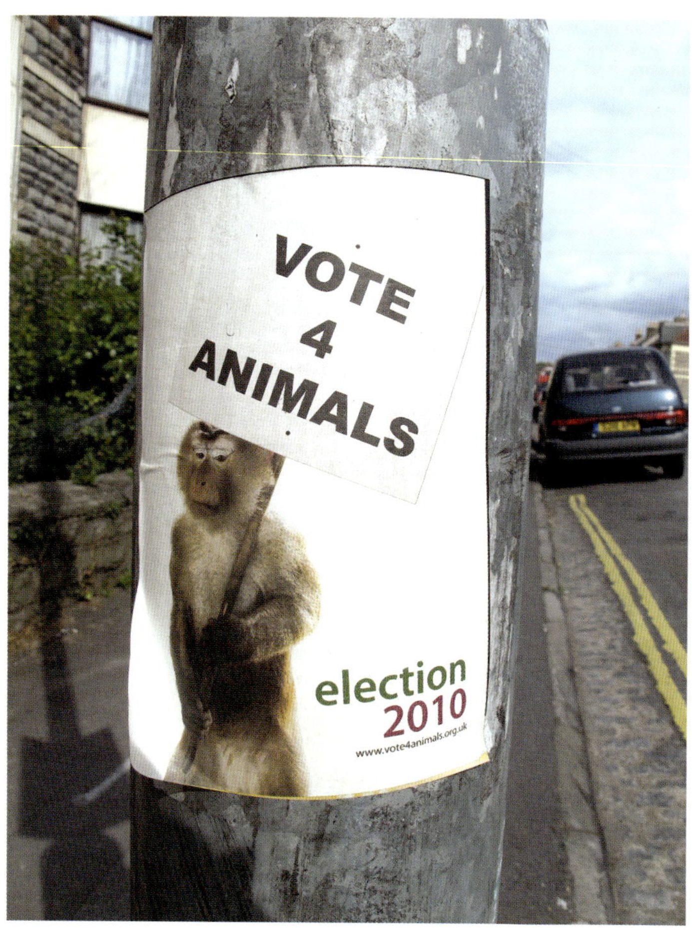

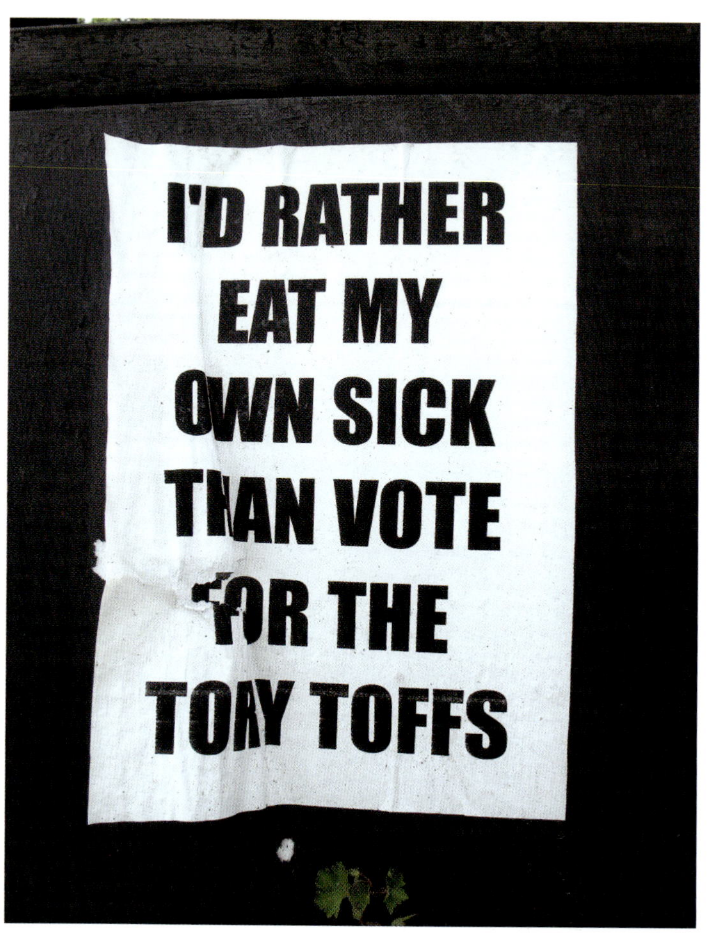

Vote 4 animals [www.vote4animals.org.uk]

All from 2010 in the run up to the general election.

I'd rather eat my own sick than vote for the Tory
toffs

Government...

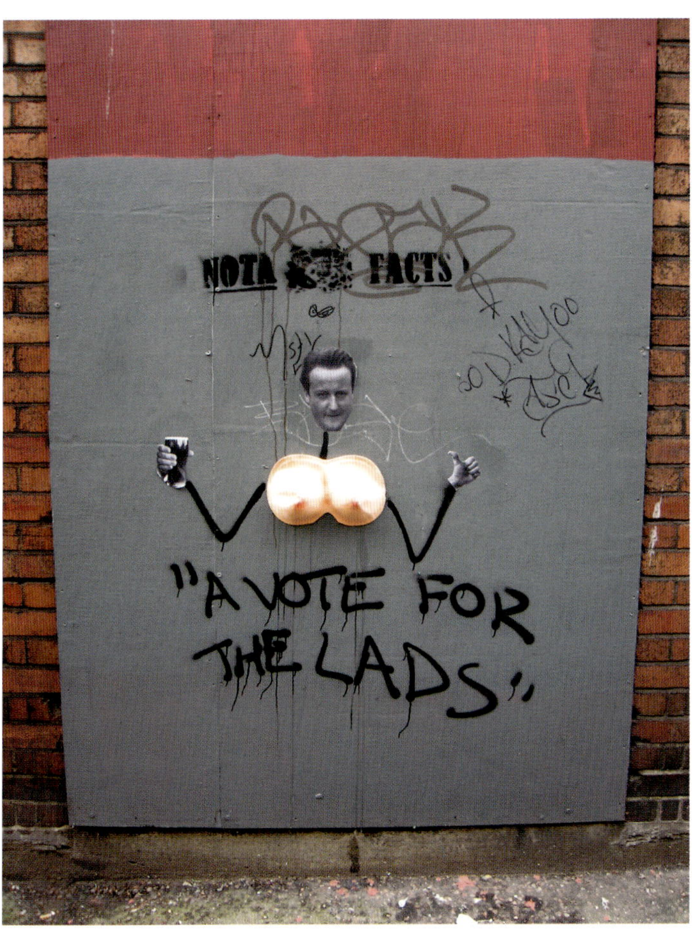

A vote for the lads [Nota Facts produced some unusual and memorable 2010 election commentaries]

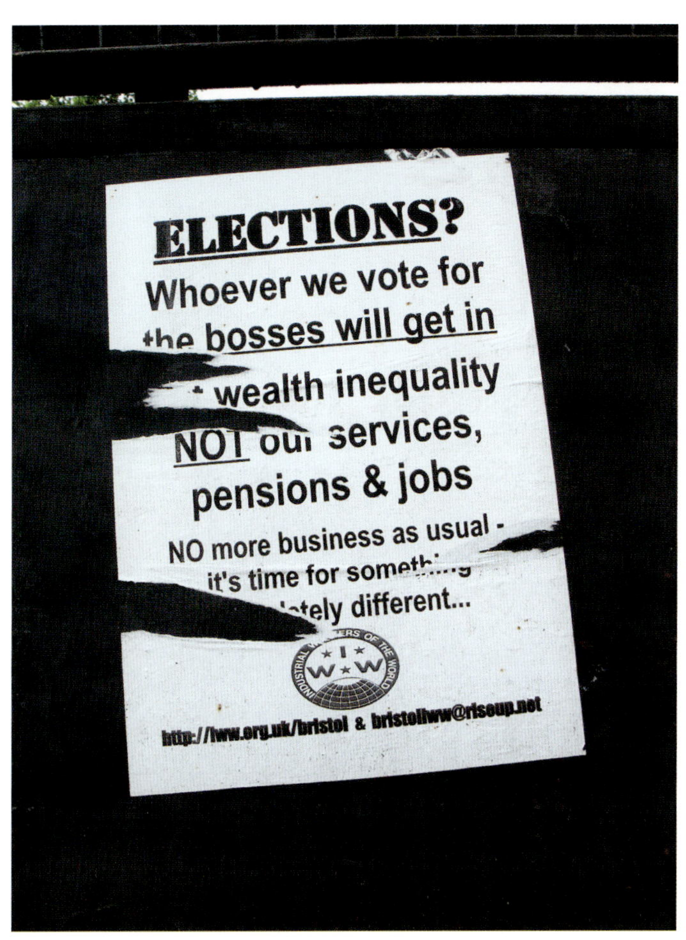

Elections? The Industrial Workers of the World [http://iww.org.uk/bristol]

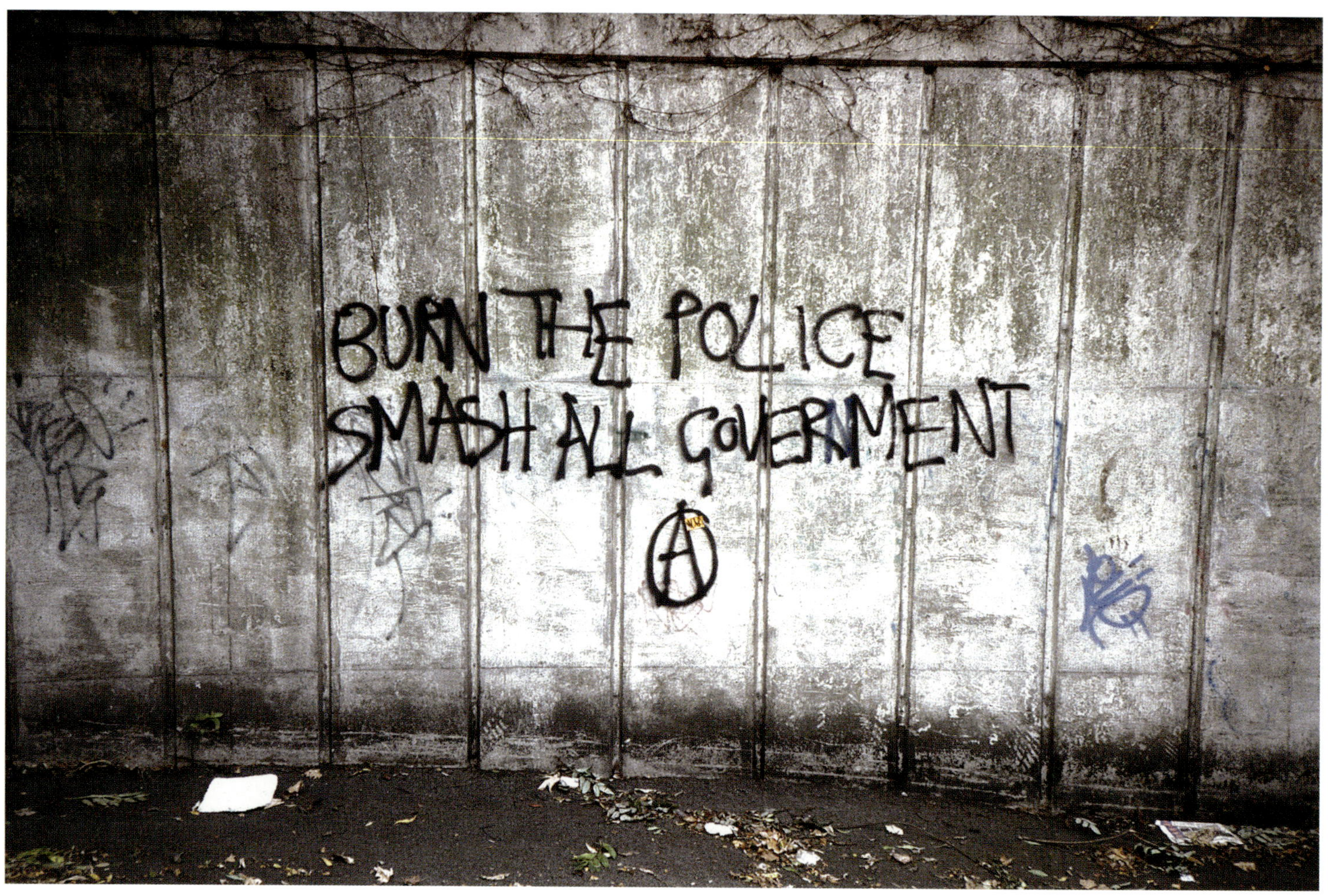

2003: Burn the police smash all government

Government...

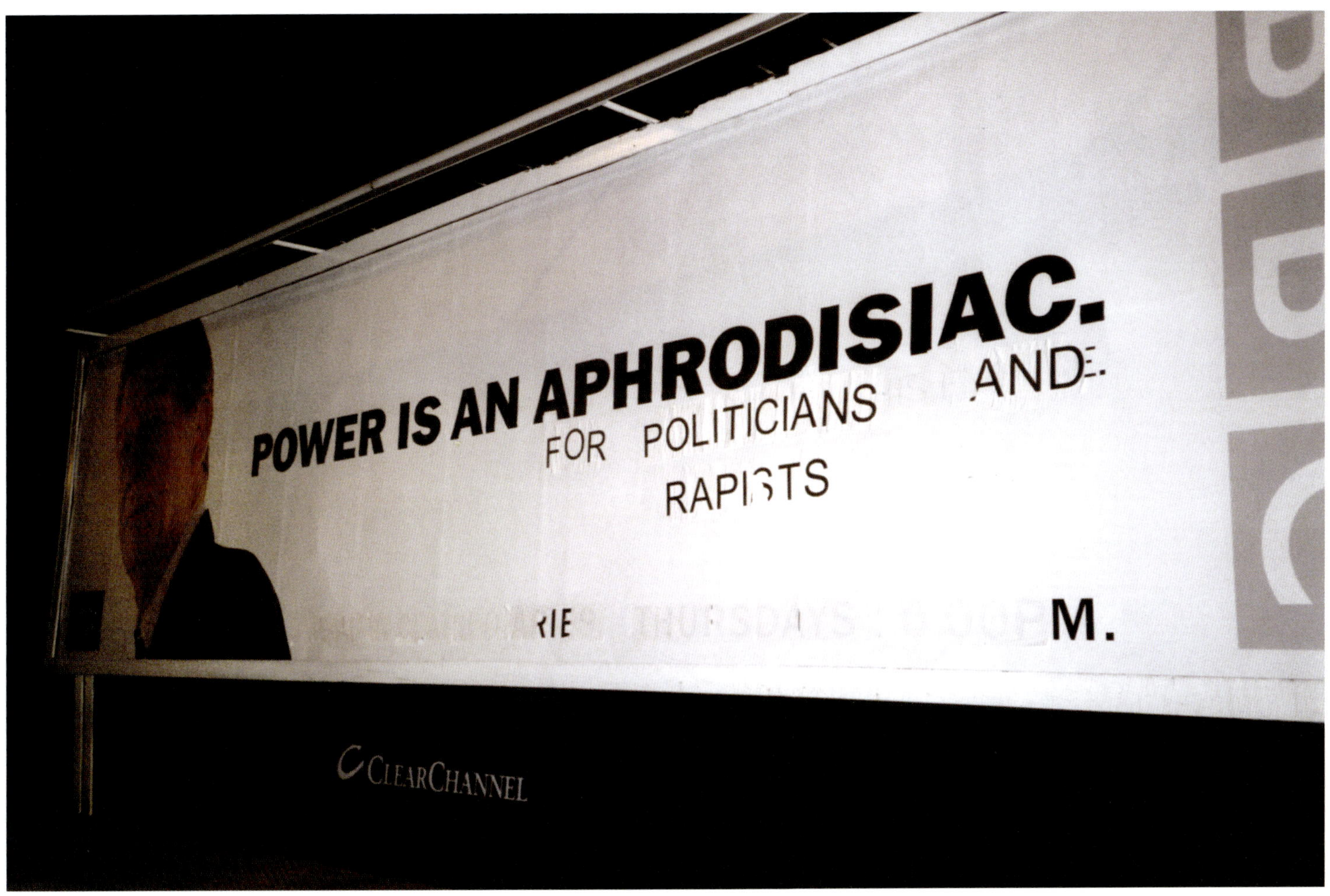

2004: Power is an aphrodisiac for politicians and rapists

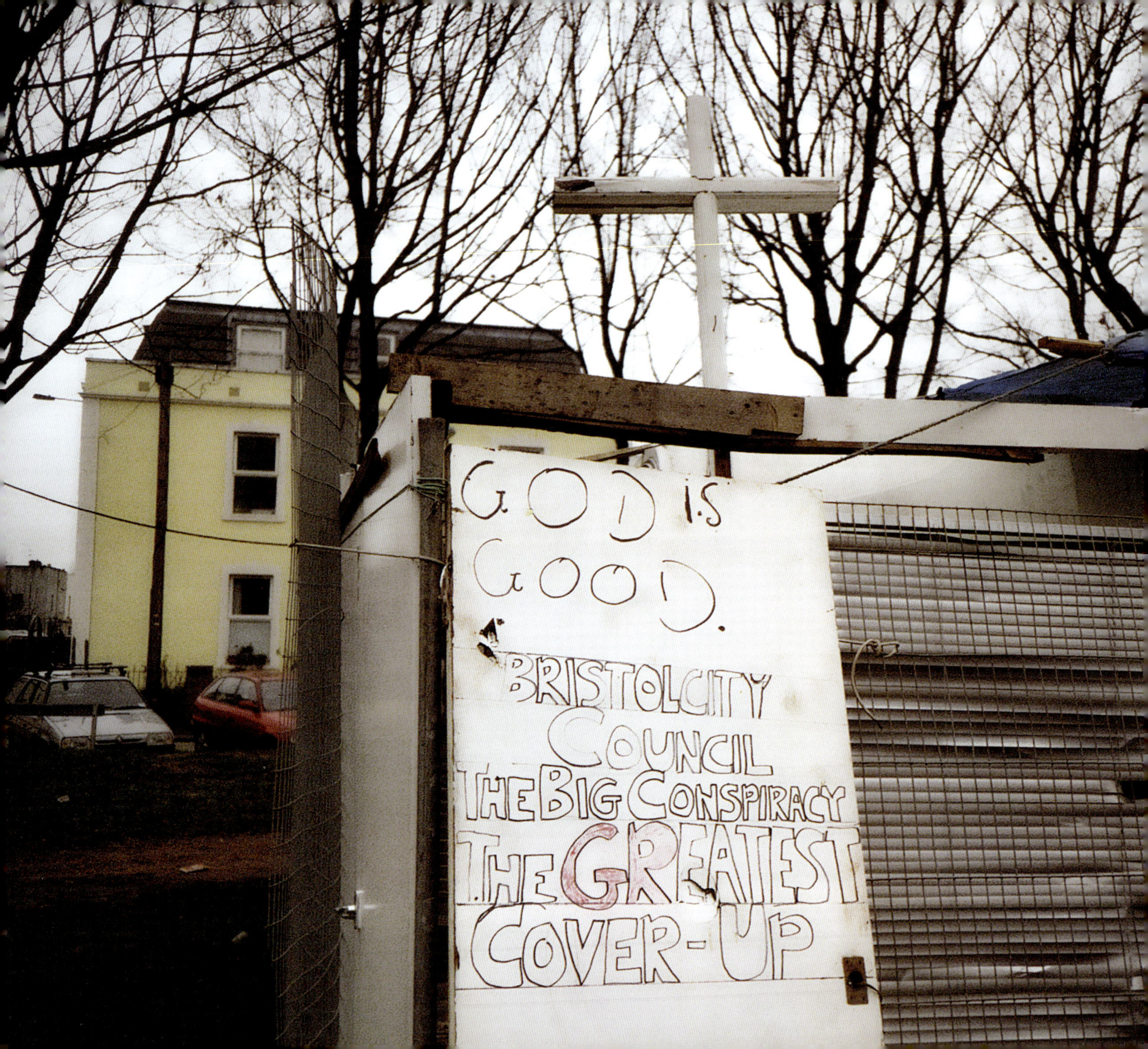

G O D IS
G O O D.
BRISTOL CITY
COUNCIL
THE BIG CONSPIRACY
THE GREATEST
COVER-UP

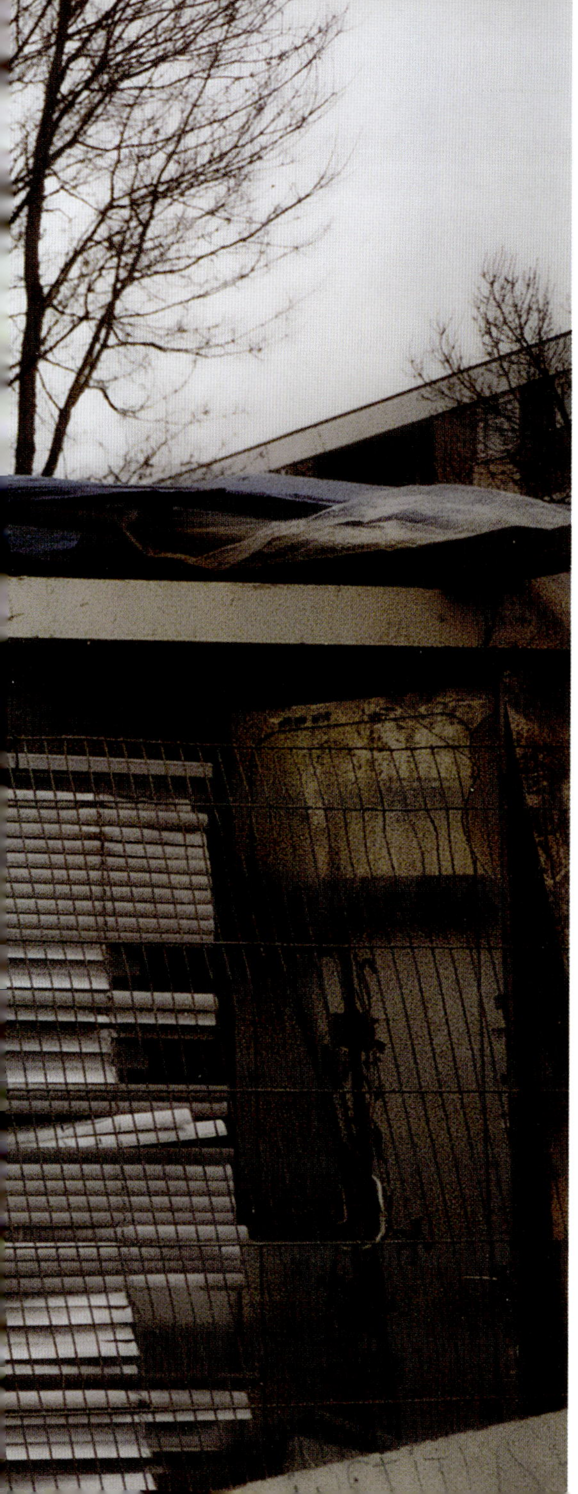

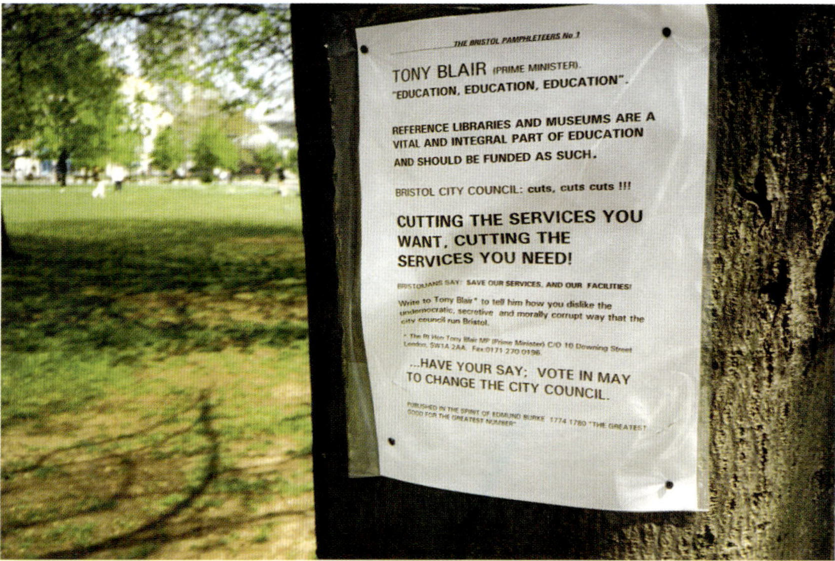

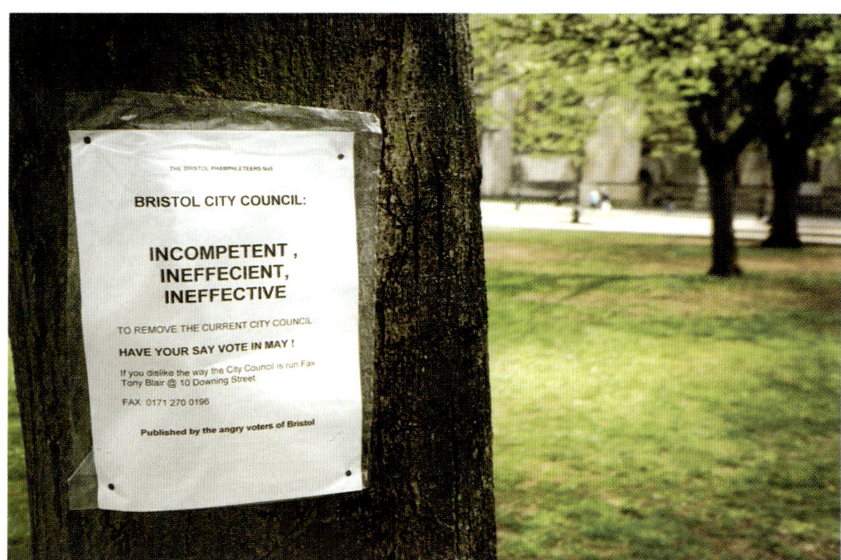

1999: The council under attack

Left – 2003: I'm told that a man in dispute with the council over the loss of his council house lived in this structure for several years.

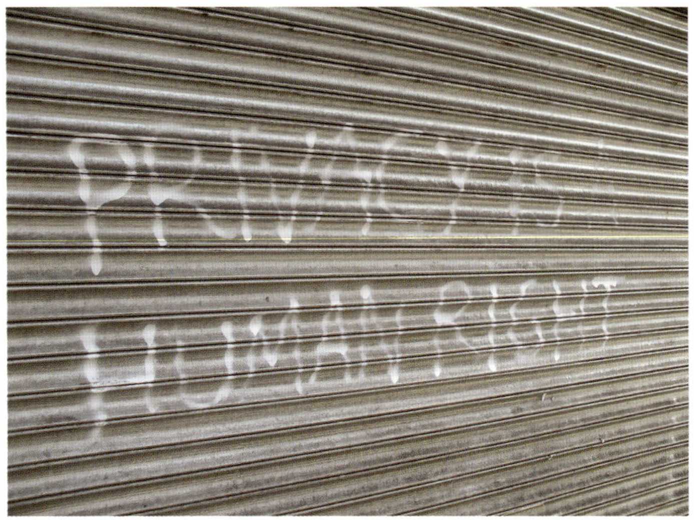

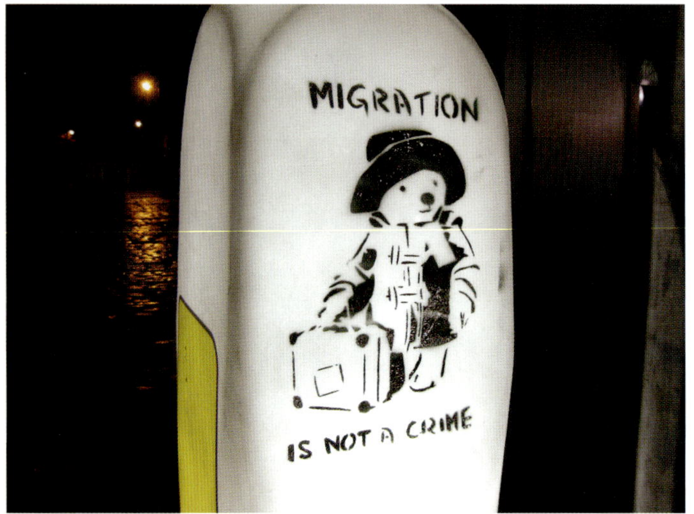

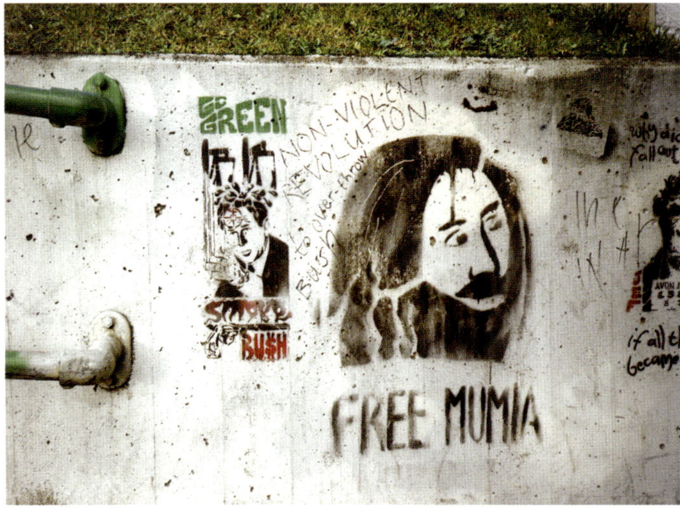

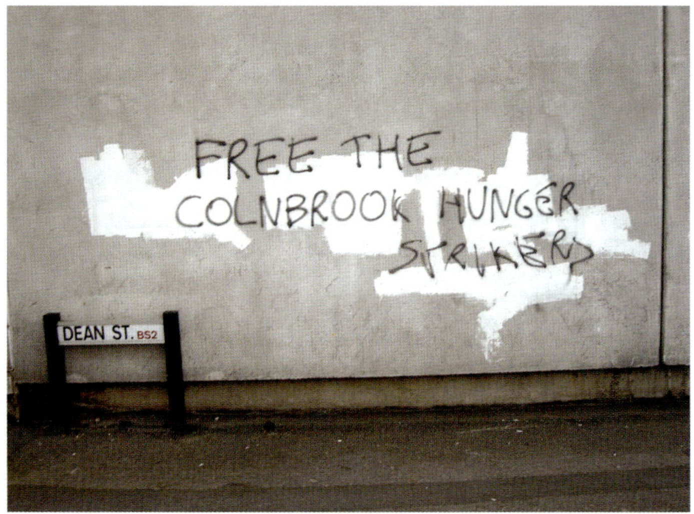

Clockwise from top left – 2006: Privacy is a human right | 2007: Migration is not a crime | 2006: free the Colnbrook hunger strikers [Up to 150 detainees at Colnbrook, a detention centre for asylum seekers, went on hunger strike in protest against their likely deportation] | 2002: Free Mumia [Mumia Abu-Jamal has been on death row in Pennsylvania for almost 3 decades. His sentence is still under review] |

Human rights...

Human rights...

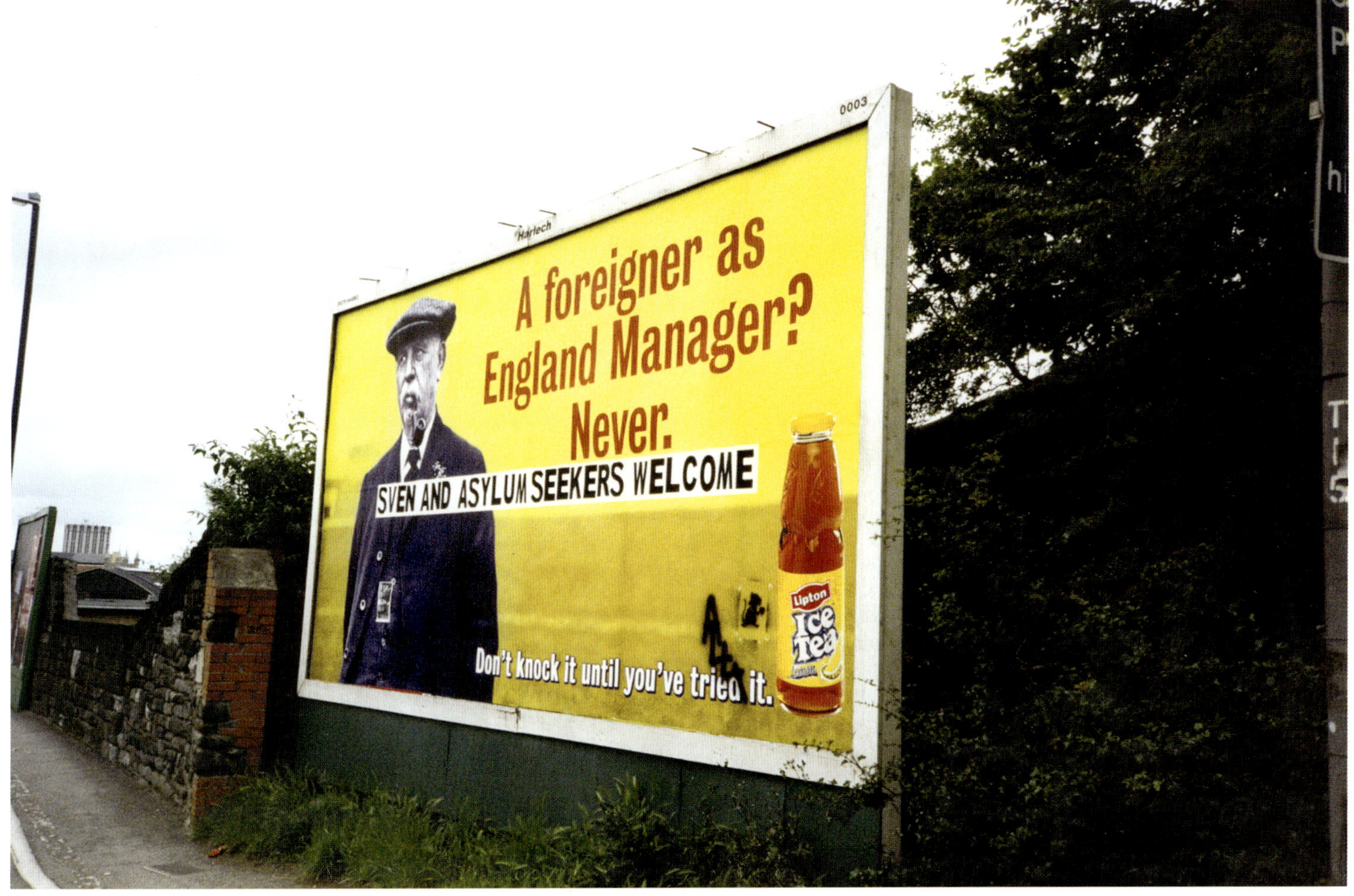

2002: Sven and asylum seekers welcome [Sven-Goran Eriksson became the first foreign manager of the England football team in 2001]

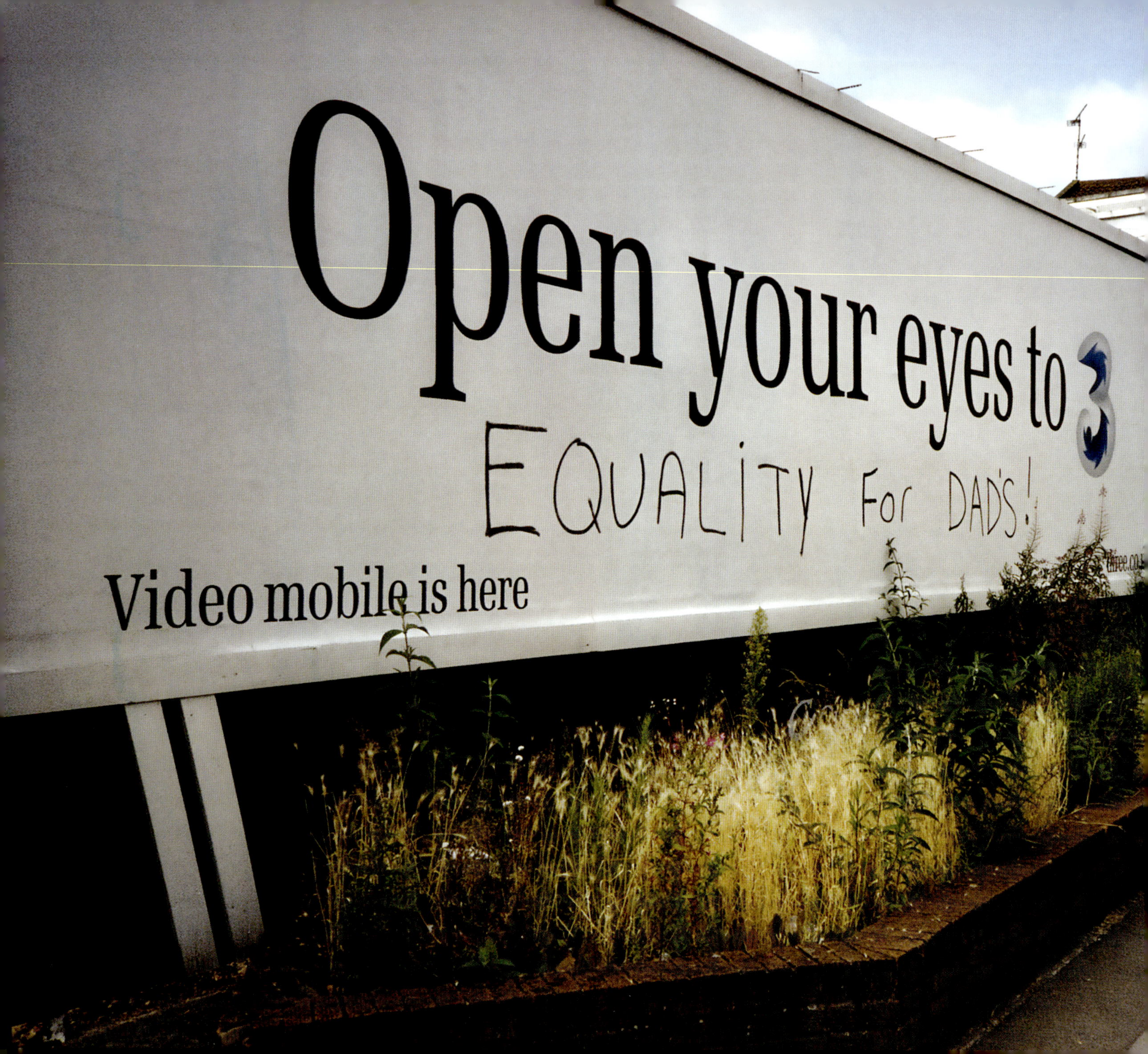
Open your eyes to 3
EQUALITY For DAD'S!
Video mobile is here

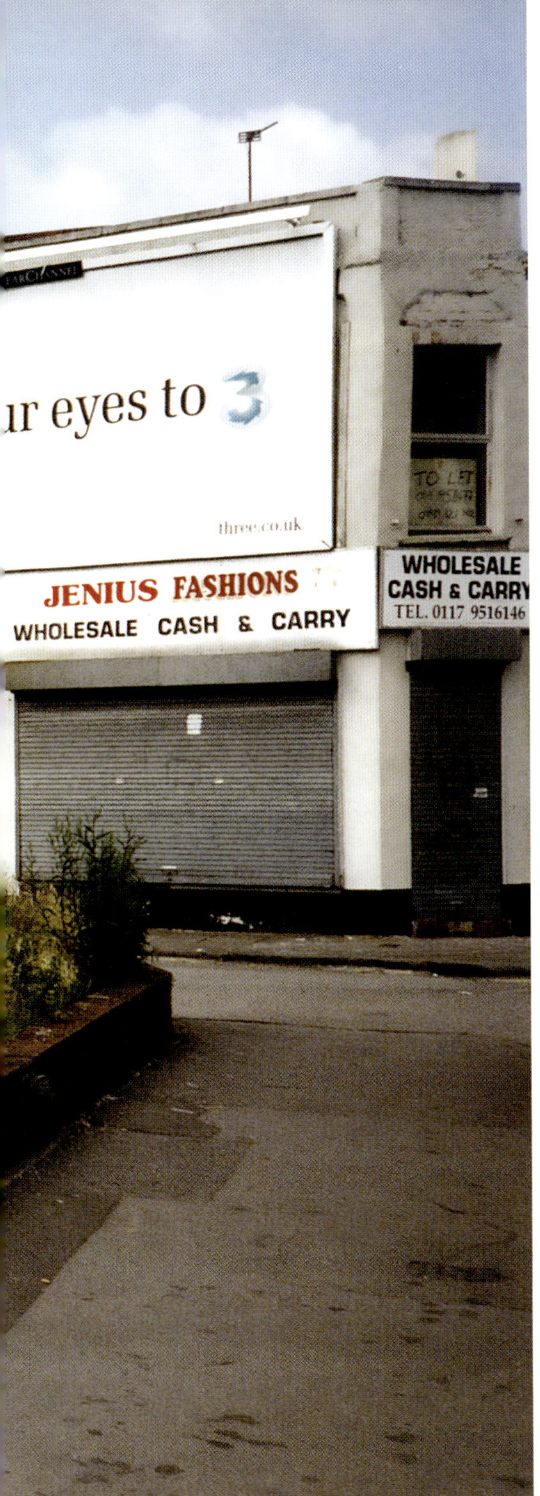

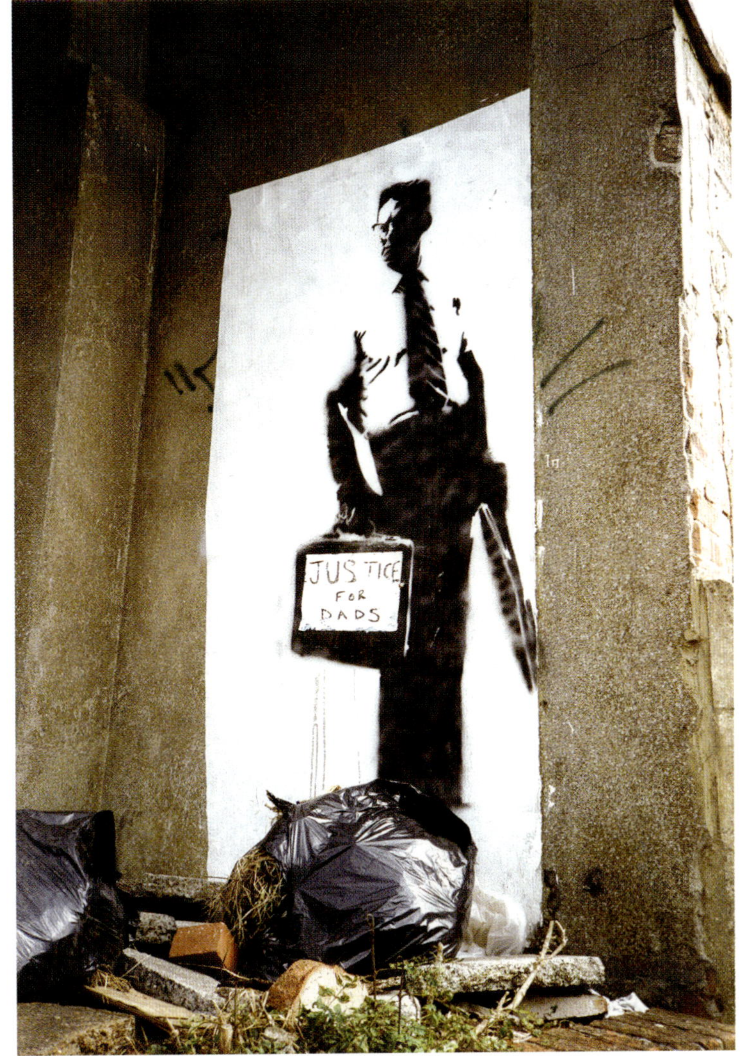

2003: Justice for dads

Left — 2003: Equality for dads

[Fathers 4 Justice were active at this time. In one 2003 incident two campaigners scaled the Royal Courts of Justice, dressed as Batman and Robin. The stencil shows Michael Douglas in the film 'Falling Down', about to go on a violent rampage having been pushed to his limits]

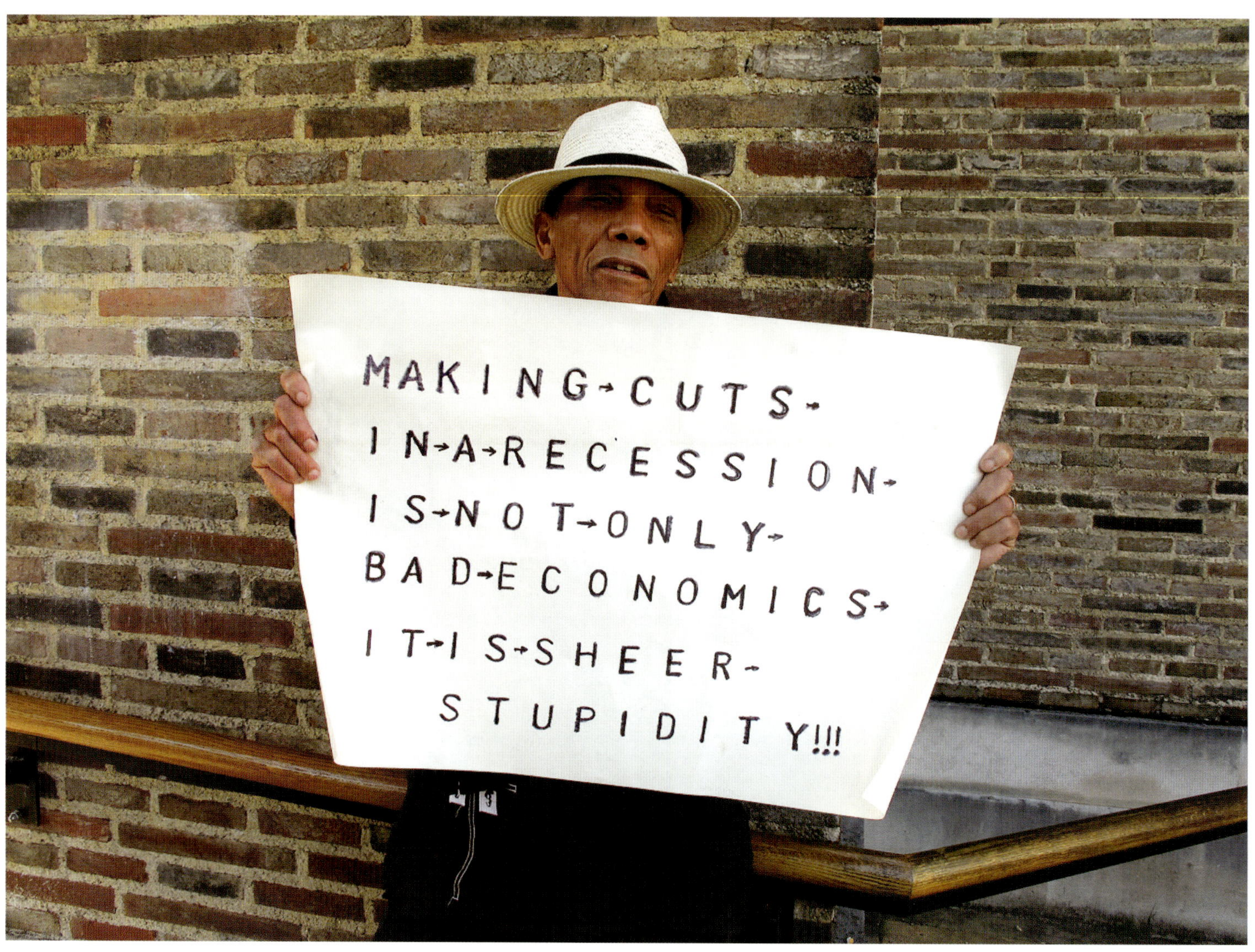

2010: Making cuts in a recession [This gentleman also made the point that the lower socio-economic classes (C, D, E) were paying for the mistakes of classes A and B]

Human rights...

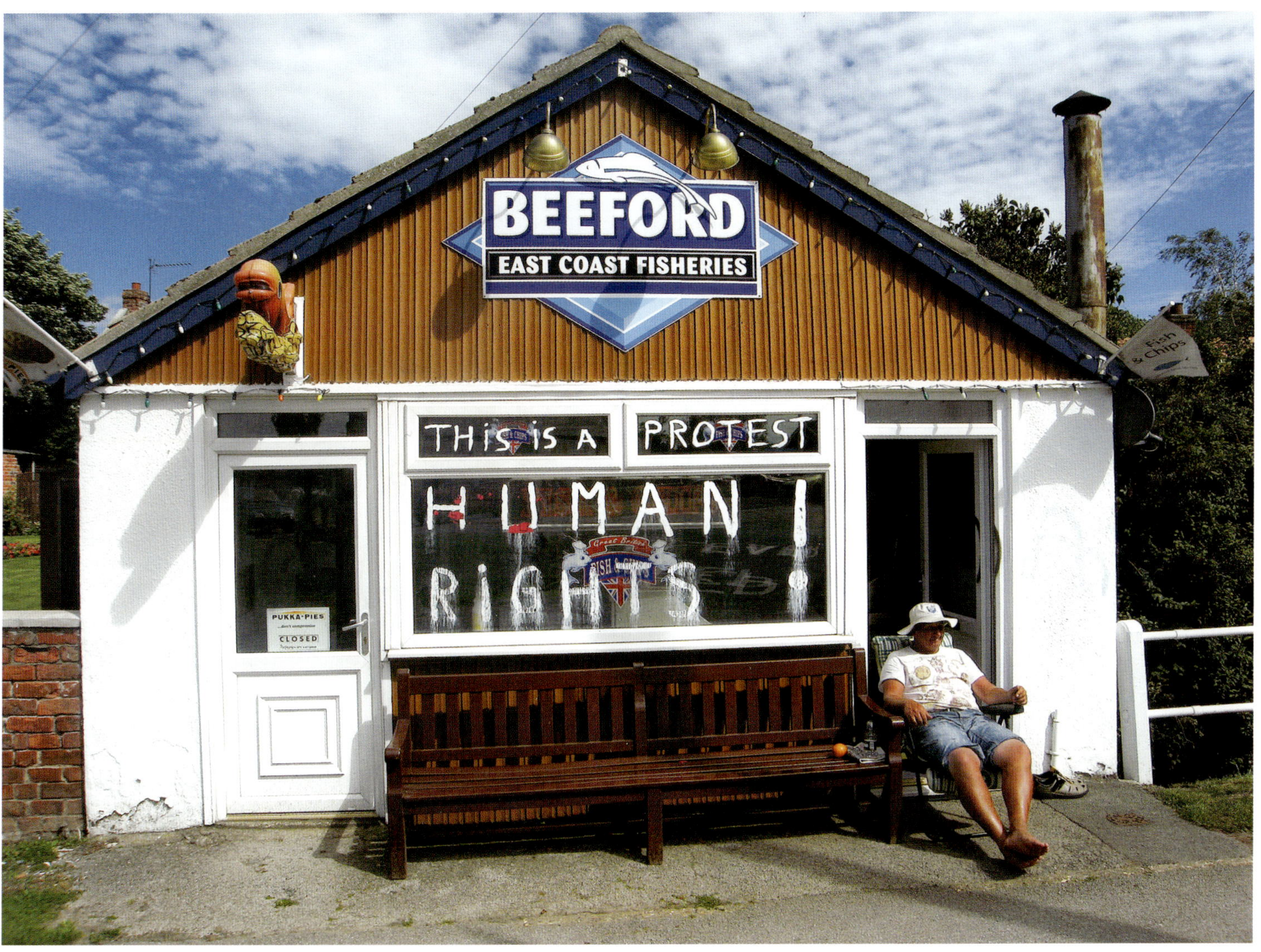

2010: This is a protest – human rights! [This gentleman told me that he had been under 24 hour surveillance for the last 4 years by the government, who had forced him to close his chip shop. He maintains a daily protest]

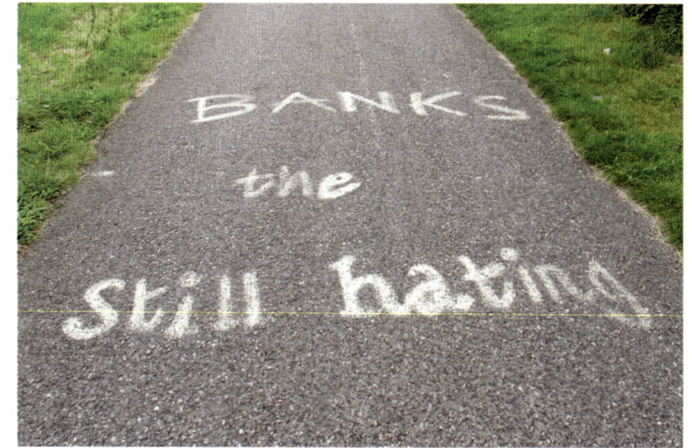
BANKS
the
still hating

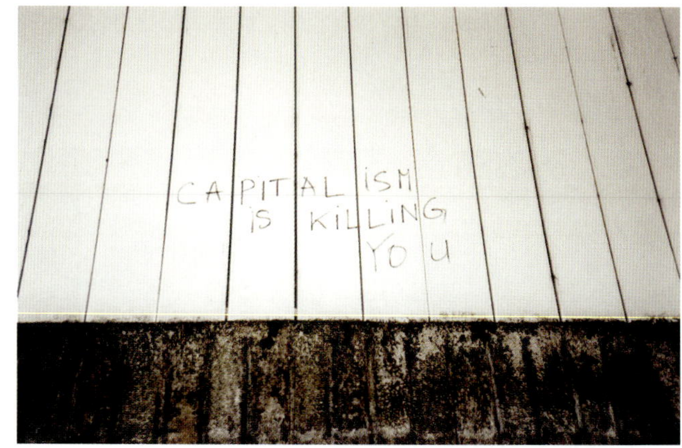
CAPITALISM
IS KILLING
YOU

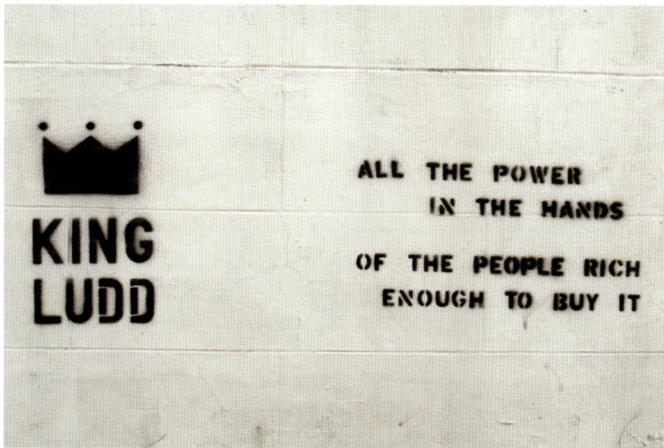
KING
LUDD
ALL THE POWER
IN THE HANDS
OF THE PEOPLE RICH
ENOUGH TO BUY IT

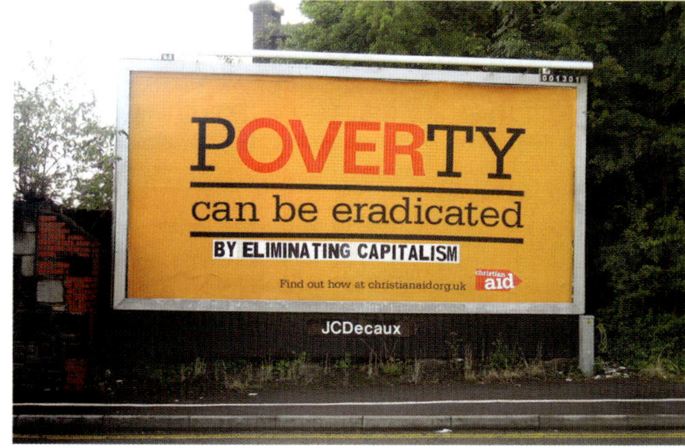
POVERTY
can be eradicated
BY ELIMINATING CAPITALISM
Find out how at christianaid.org.uk
christian aid
JCDecaux

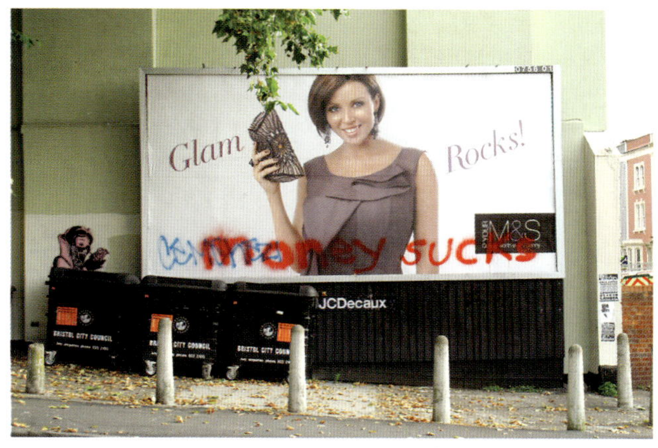
Glam
Rocks!
M&S
money sucks
JCDecaux
BRISTOL CITY COUNCIL

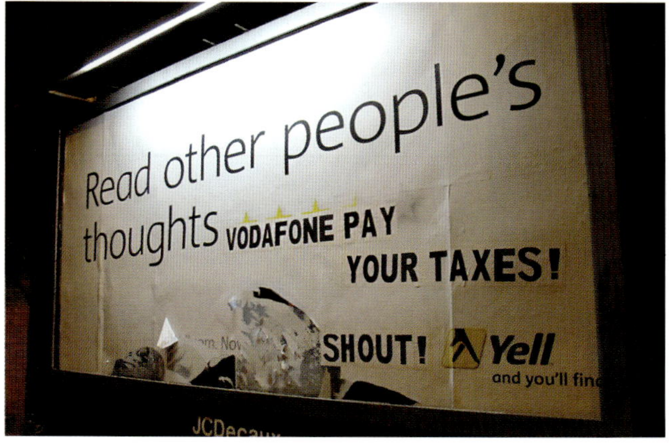
Read other people's
thoughts VODAFONE PAY
YOUR TAXES!
SHOUT! Yell
and you'll find
JCDecaux

Capitalism...

Capitalism in its present form requires continuous generation of profit and economic growth, resulting in conflicts with our long-term needs. How can the environment cope with the effects of present levels of consumption? How can a value system which is motivated by profit produce outcomes that are good for the planet and for all?

Banks are an essential part of the capitalist infrastructure, so it's no surprise they come in for particular attention, especially since their role in the current economic crisis.

Some multinational companies possess budgets that exceed some nations' GDPs (Gross Domestic Product, a measure of wealth), and consequently exert considerable power in local and world economies. They too are identified as part of the problem.

Clockwise from top left – 2011: Still hating the banks | 2001: Capitalism is killing you | 2009: Poverty can be eradicated by eliminating capitalism | 2010: Read other people's thoughts – Vodaphone pay your taxes! | 2010: Glam rocks! Money sucks | 2011: All the power in the hands of the people rich enough to buy it |

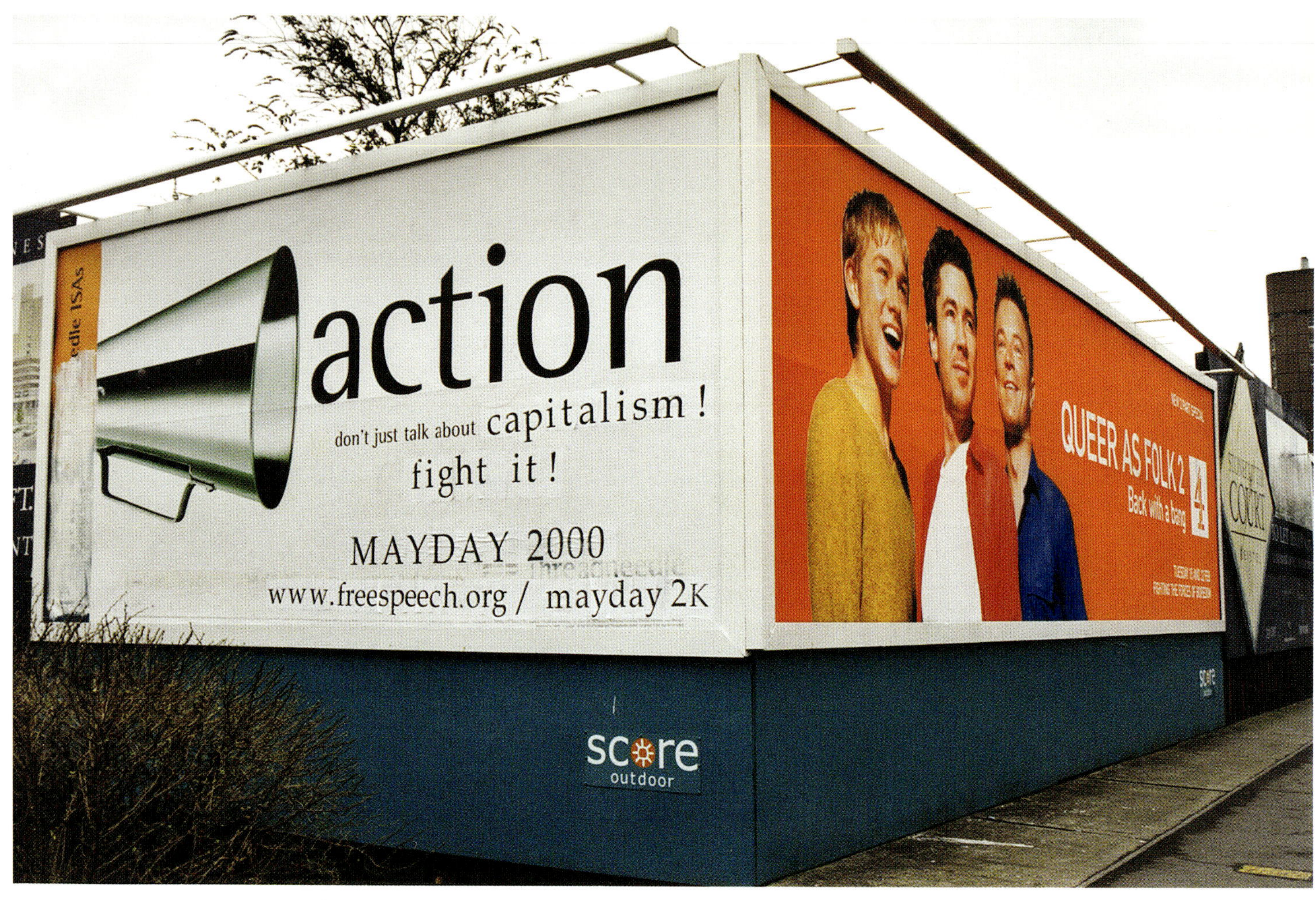

2000: Don't just talk about capitalism! Fight it!

Capitalism...

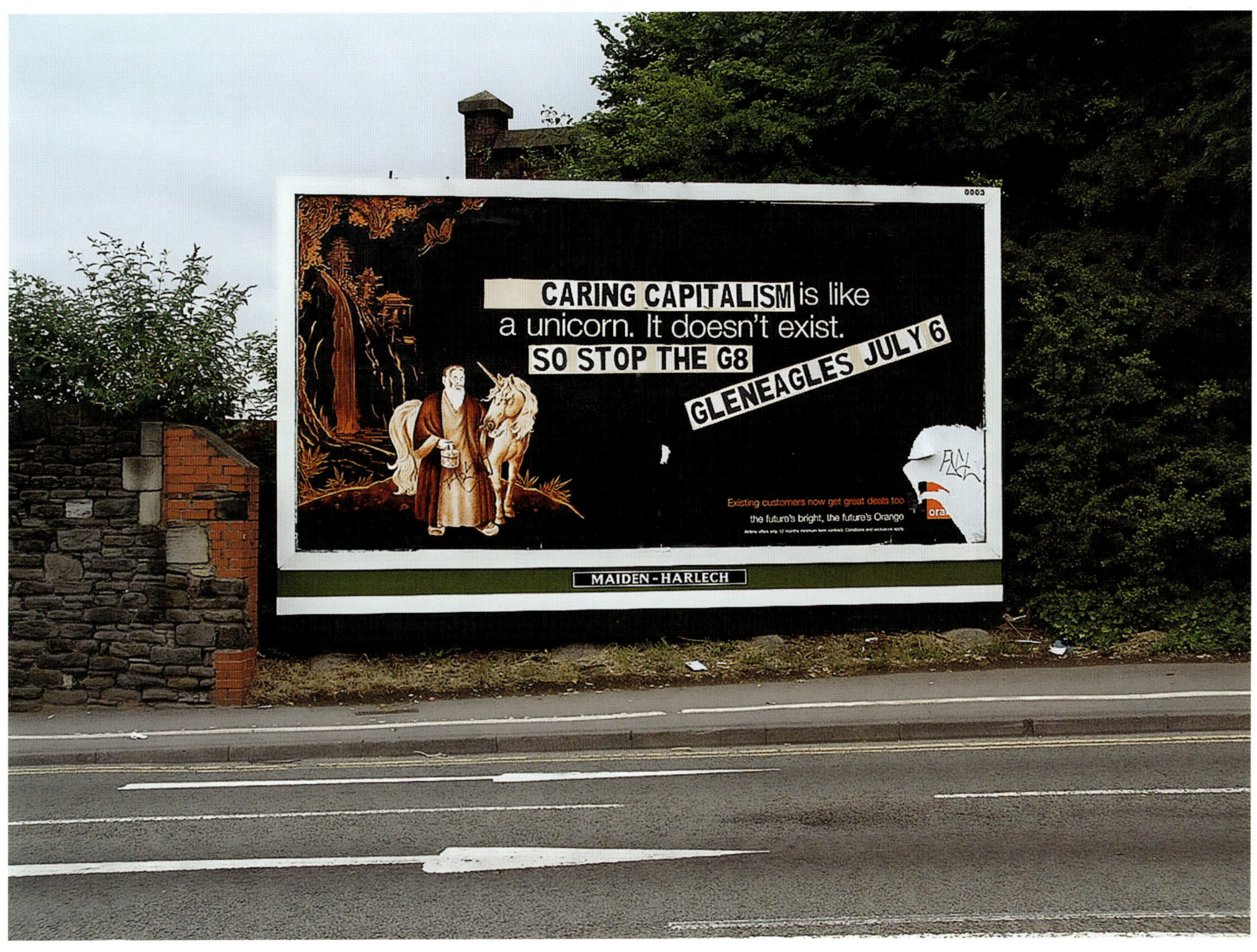

2005: Caring capitalism is like a unicorn. It doesn't exist

Next page — 2009: Find out why millions of people across Britain are unemployed

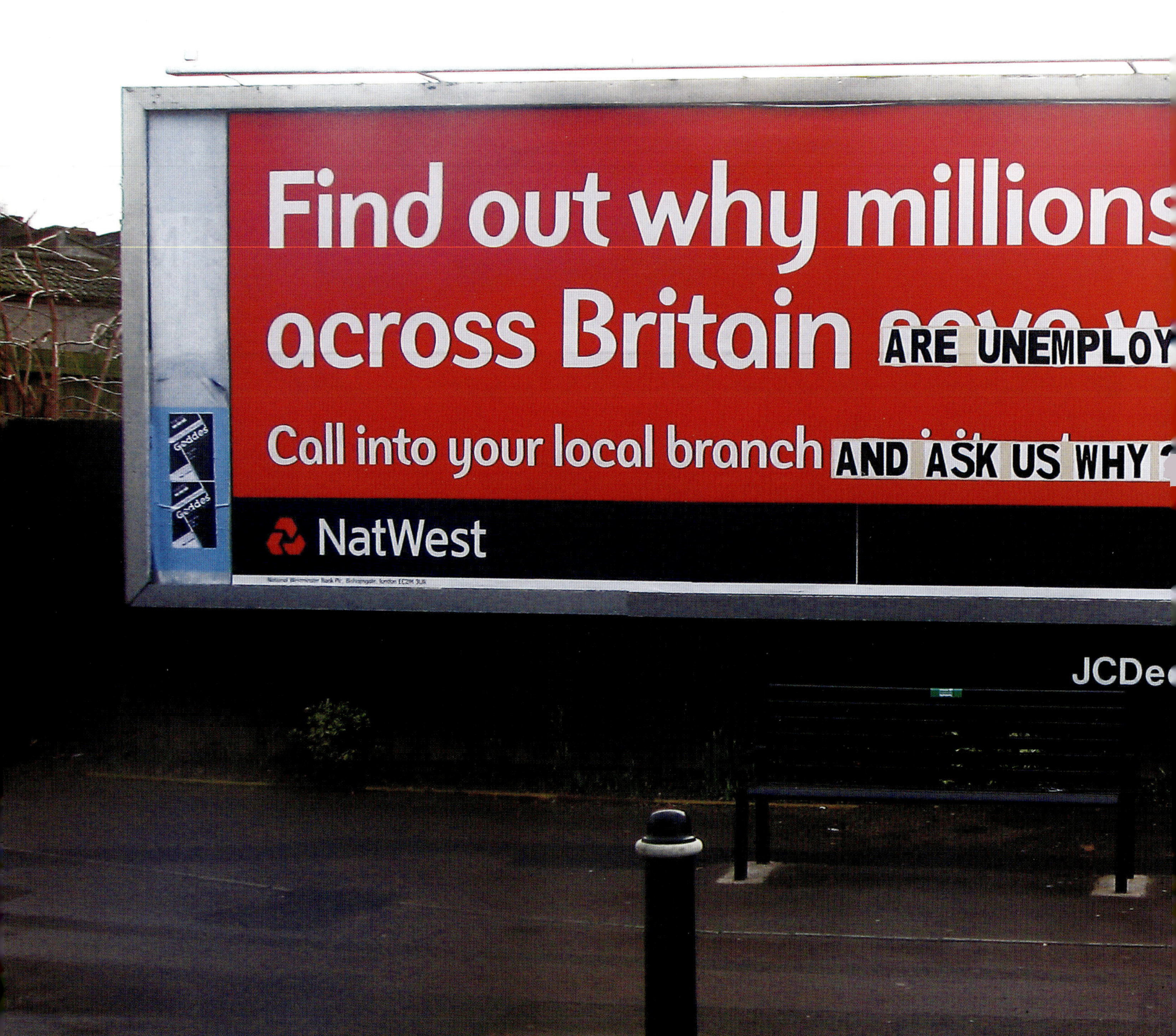

Find out why millions
across Britain ARE UNEMPLOY
Call into your local branch AND ASK US WHY ?
NatWest
JCDe

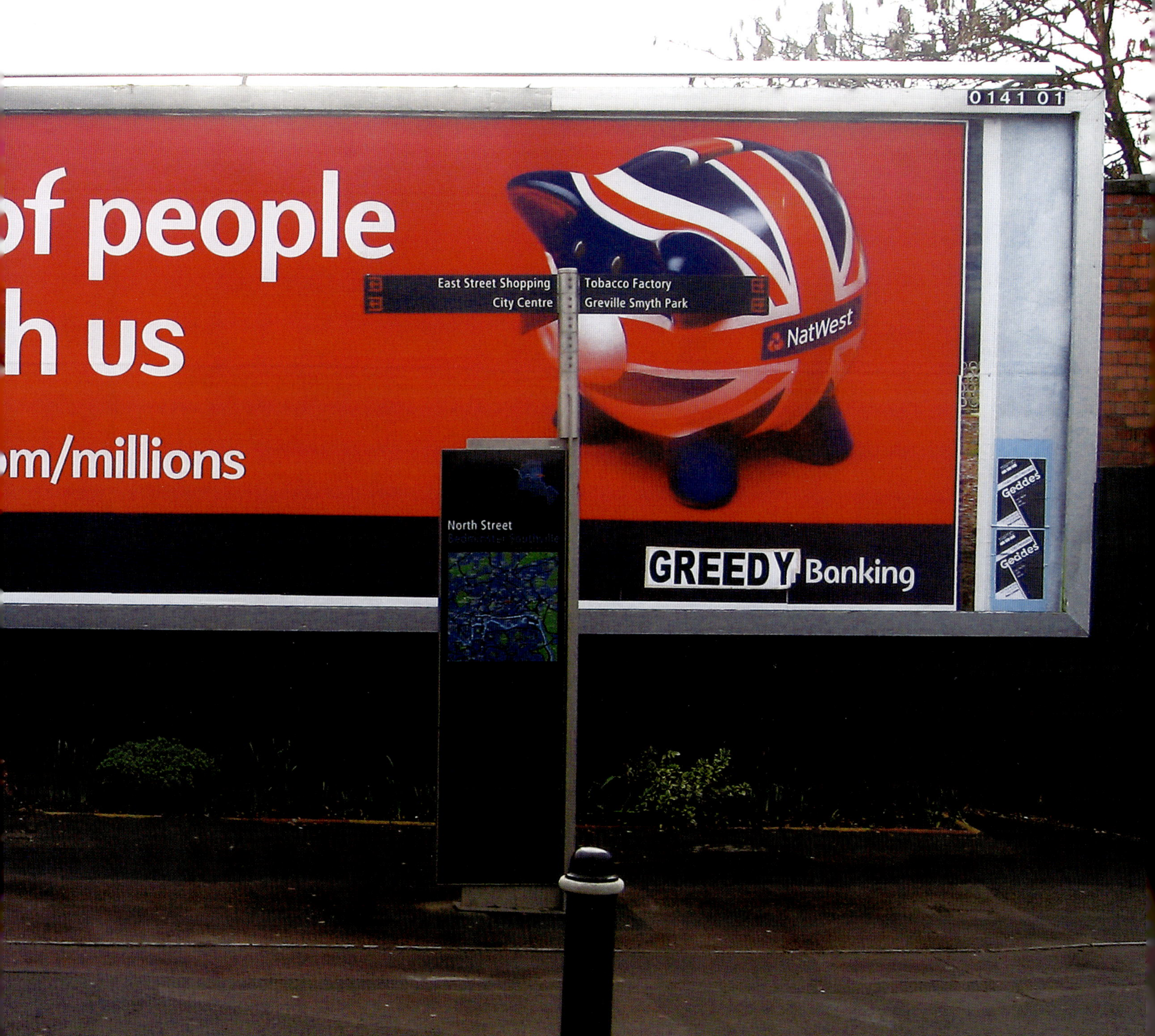
of people
h us
m/millions
East Street Shopping
City Centre
Tobacco Factory
Greville Smyth Park
NatWest
GREEDY Banking
North Street
Bedminster Southside
Geddes
Geddes
0141 01

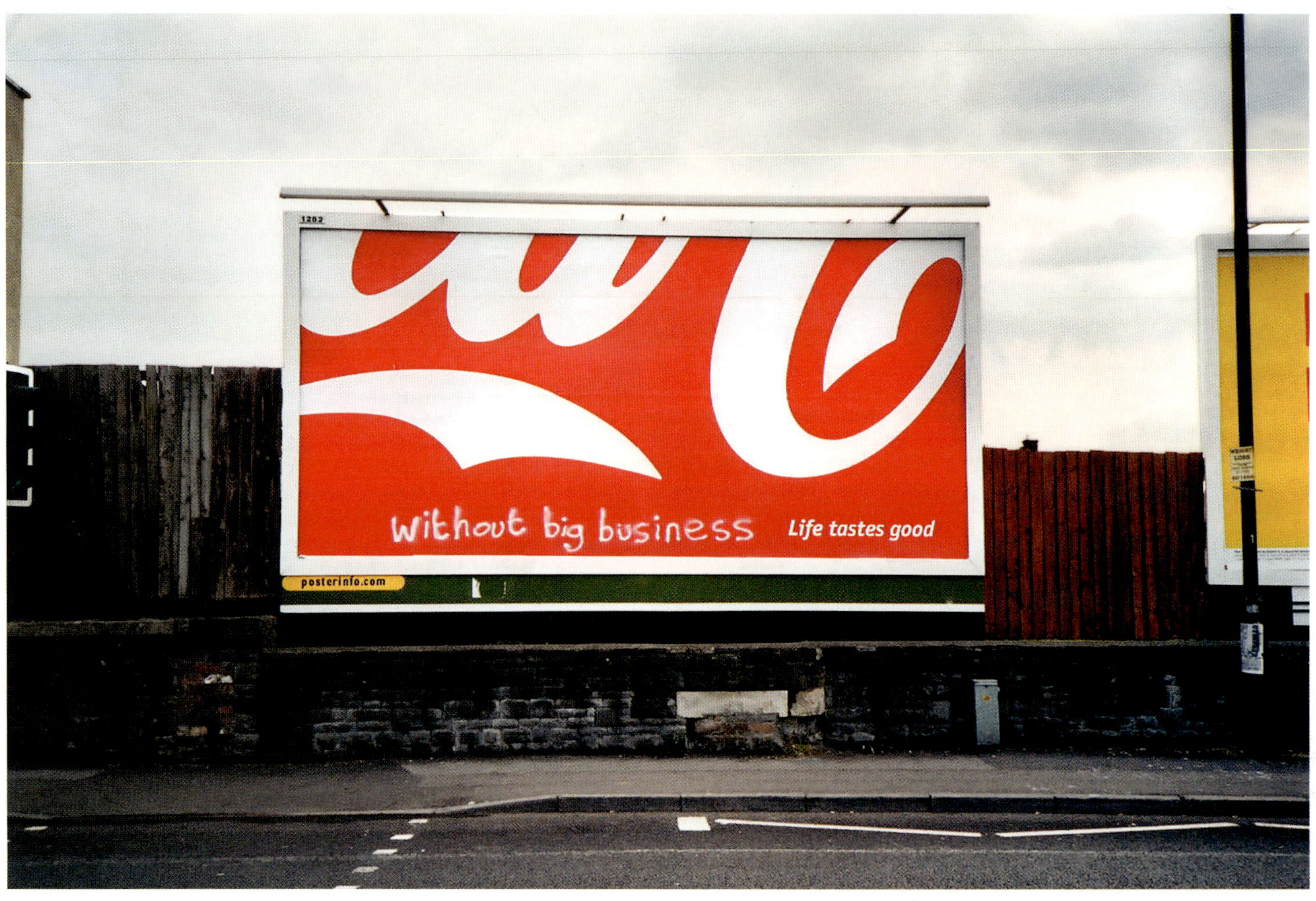

2001: Without big business life tastes good

[Amongst global companies Coca Cola, MacDonalds and Nestlé adverts are most frequently targeted]

Capitalism...

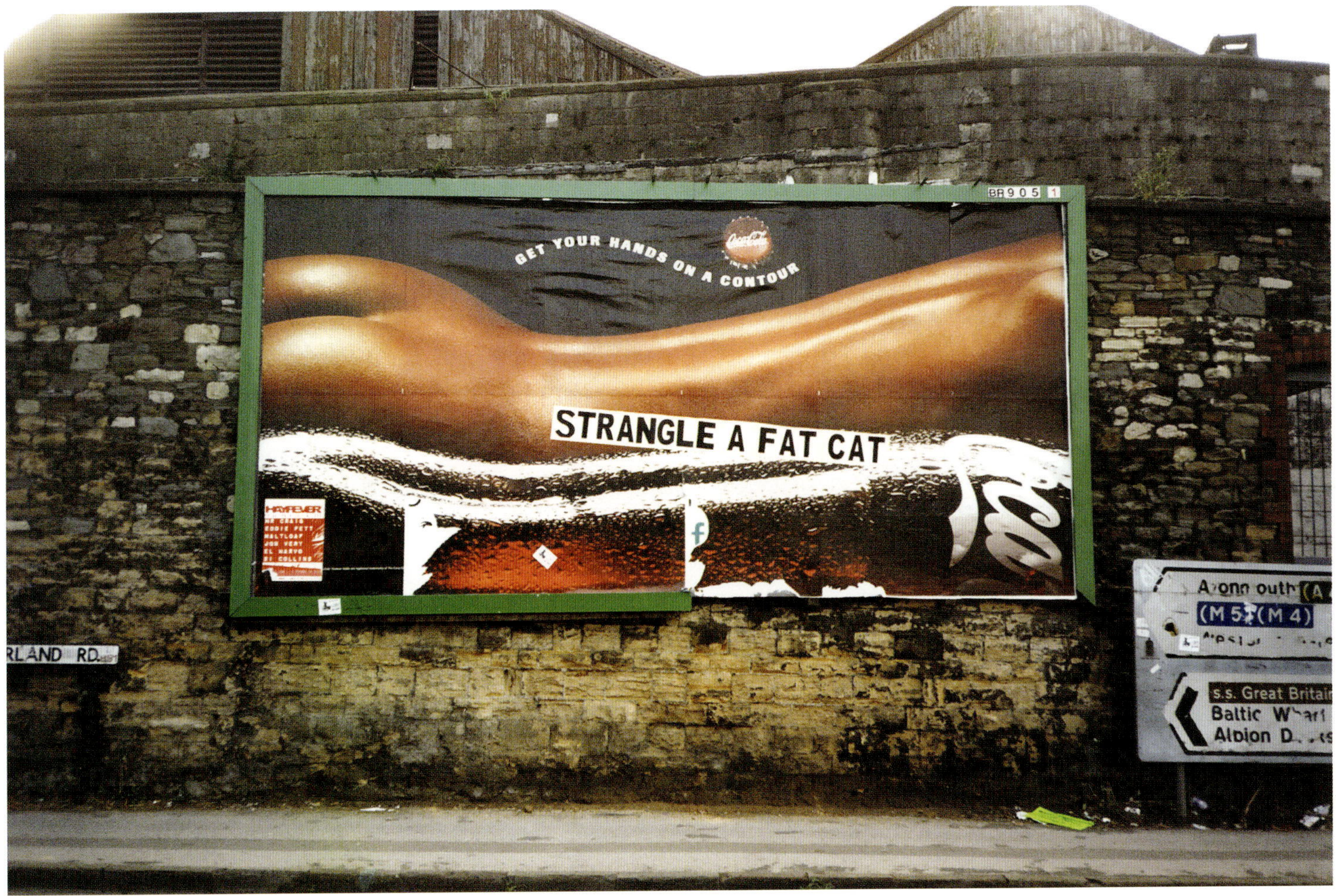

2002: Get your hands on a contour – strangle a fat cat

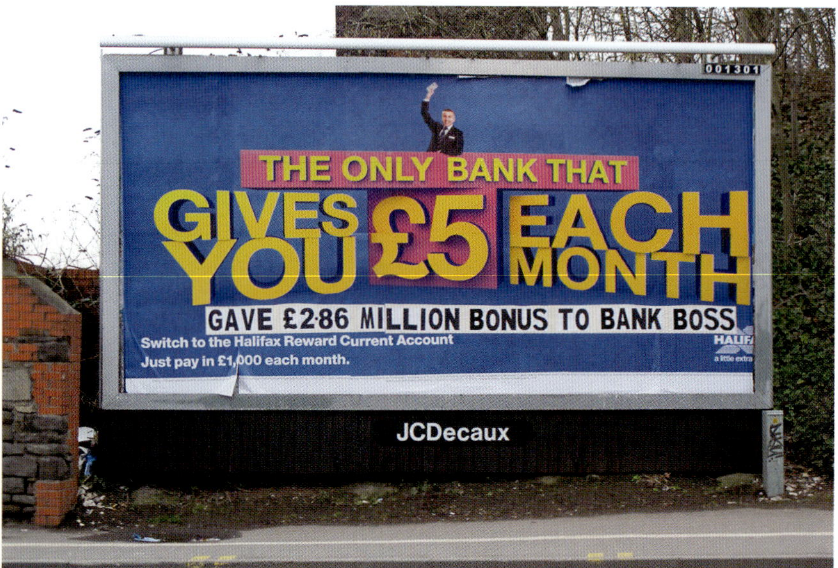

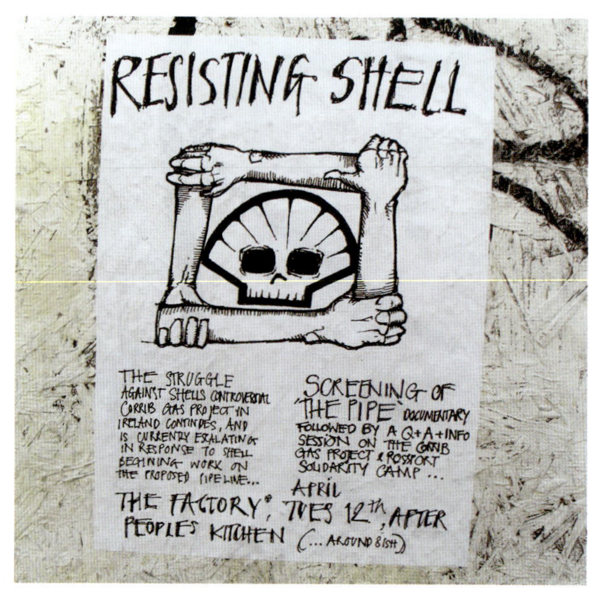

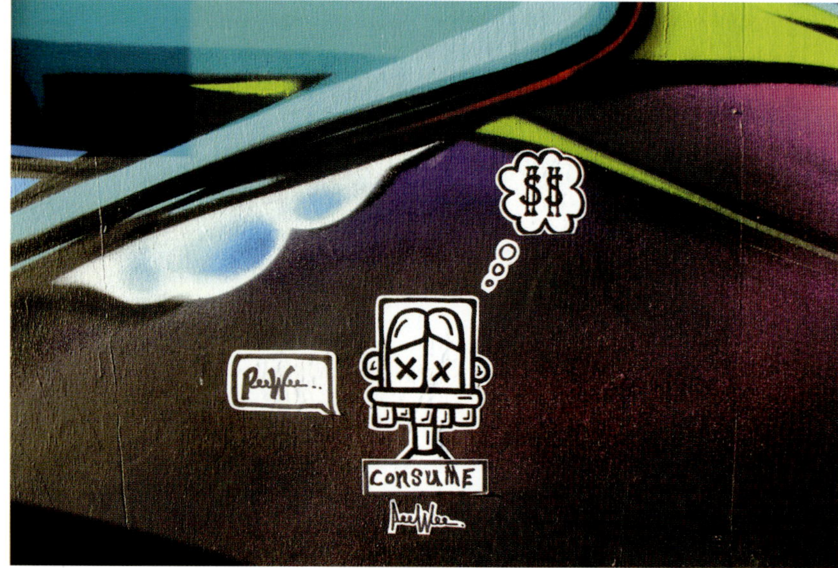

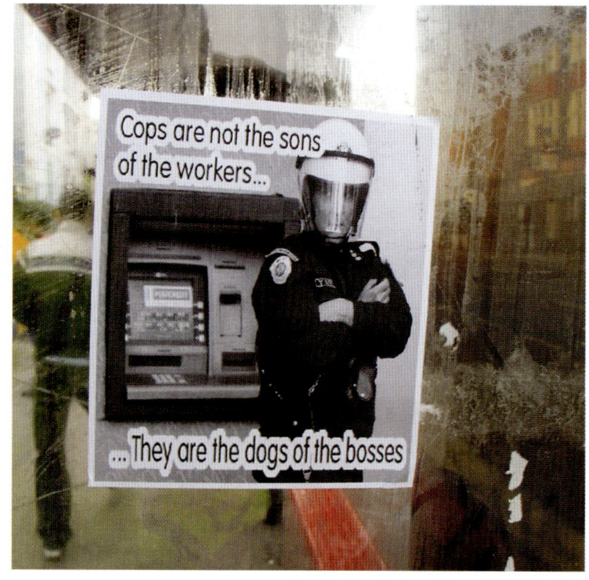

All 2011. Clockwise from top left – The only bank that gave £2.86 million bonus to bank boss | Resisting Shell | Cops are not the sons of the workers... they are the dogs of the bosses | PeeWee... consume |

Capitalism...

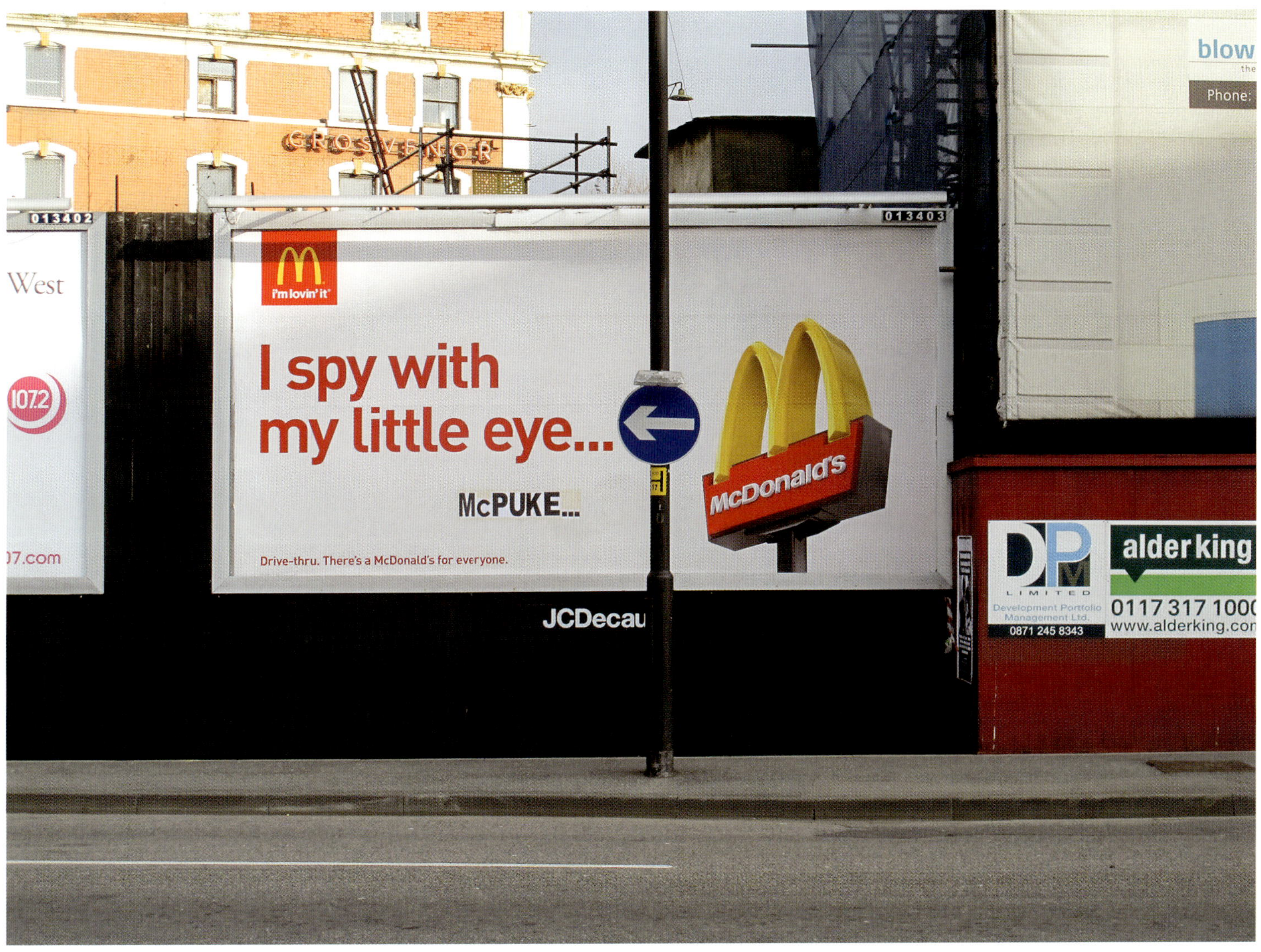

2011: I spy with my little eye... McPuke...

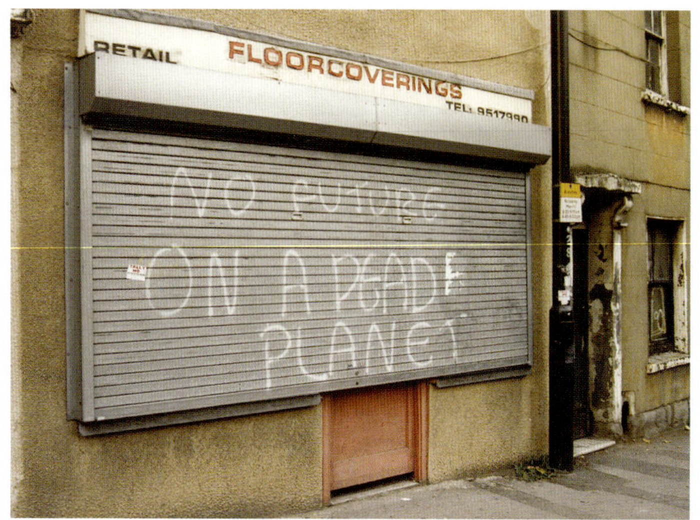

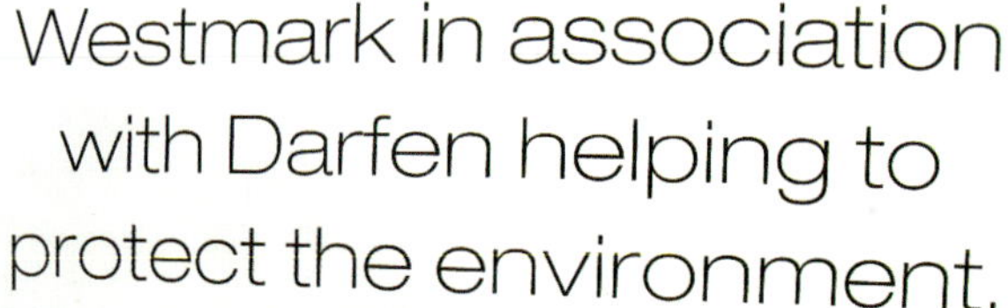

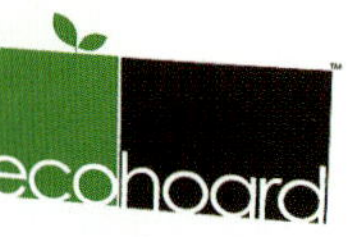

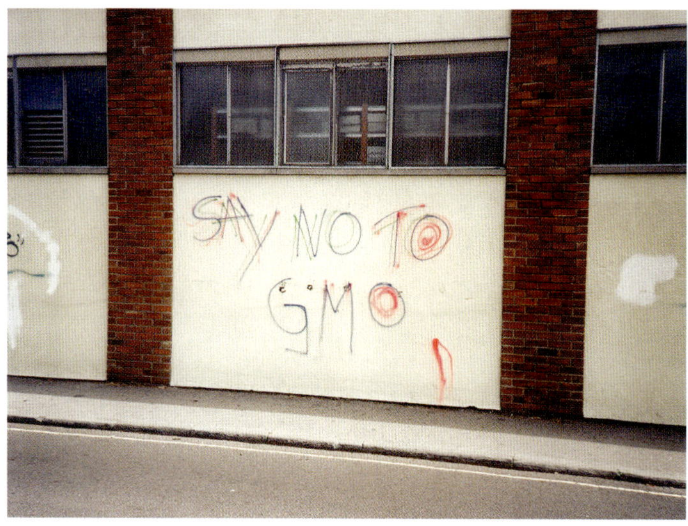

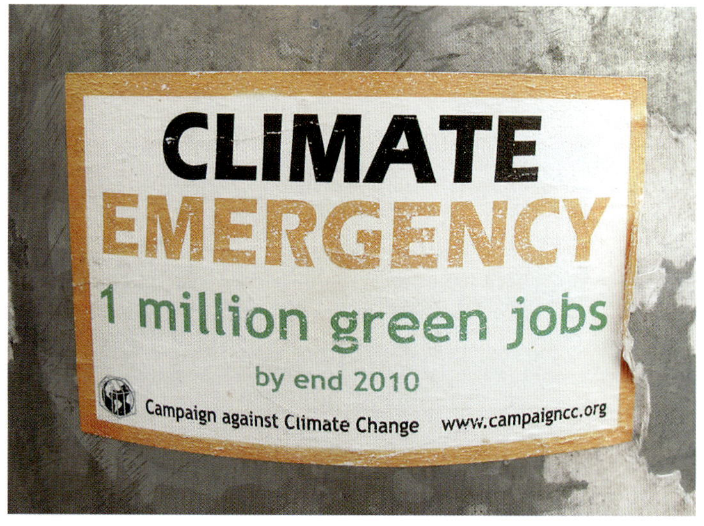

Clockwise from top left: 2000: No future on a dead planet | 2009: The 70 yr old plane tree that once stood here would disagree... | 2010: Climate emergency [www.campaigncc.org] | 2001: Say no to GMO [Genetically Modified Organism] |

Environment...

We need a fundamental shift in our value systems, in order to bring ecological imperatives to the centre of our commerce and our actions.

Otherwise we're risking our collective future through the adverse effects of climate change (habitat destruction and species loss, water shortages, rising sea levels, desertification, spread of disease, disruption of climactic balance, mass migrations and conflict) as well as pollution and overconsumption.

World Bank chief economist Nicholas Stern, author of the Stern Review on the economics of climate change, describes the changes now under way in Earth's atmosphere as "the greatest and widest-ranging market failure ever seen."

"We should be practicing a sustainable approach to economics that takes advantage of the ability of markets to allocate scarce resources while explicitly recognizing that our economy is dependent on the broader ecosystem that contains it."
Worldwatch Institute president Christopher Flavin
(Source: www.worldwatch.org/node/5571)

We're finding out just how smart and adaptable we really are, but time is not on our side.

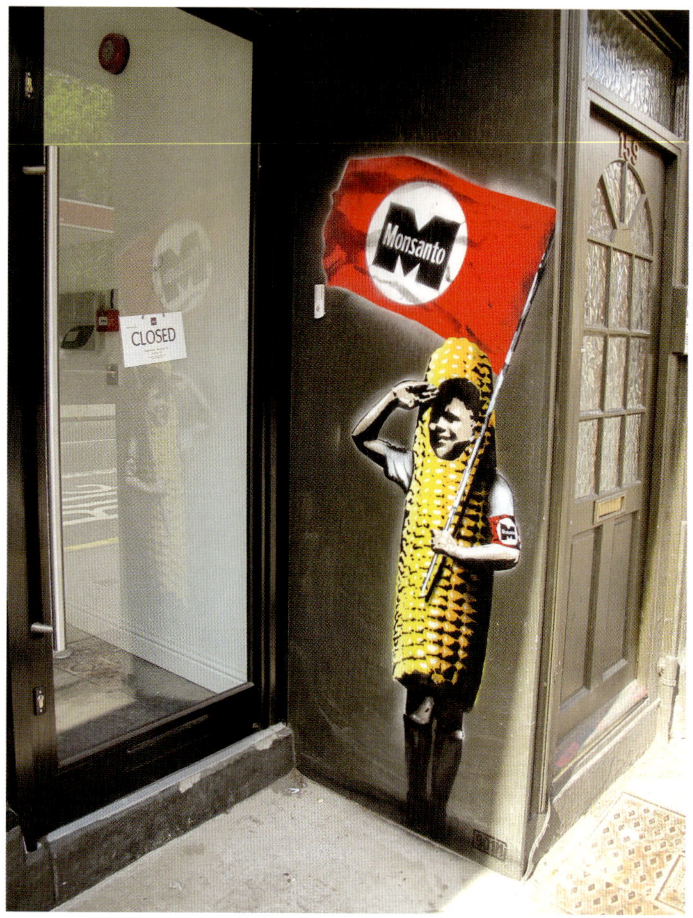

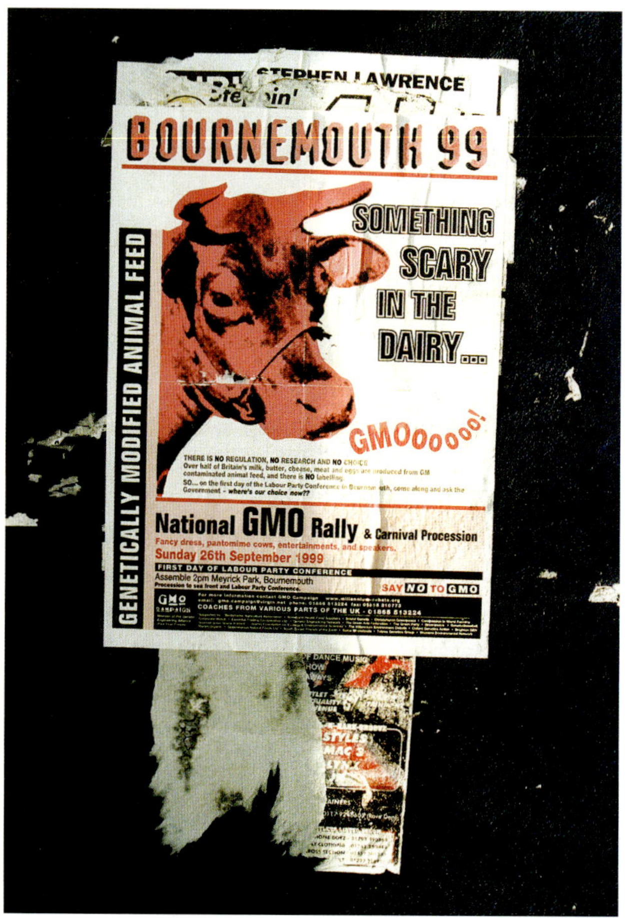

2010: Monsanto

1999: Something scary in the dairy, GMOOOooo

[Monsanto's development and marketing of genetically engineered seed and bovine growth hormone, as well as its aggressive litigation, political lobbying practices, seed commercialization practices and "strong-arming" of the seed industry have made the company controversial around the world]

Source: Wikipedia

Environment...

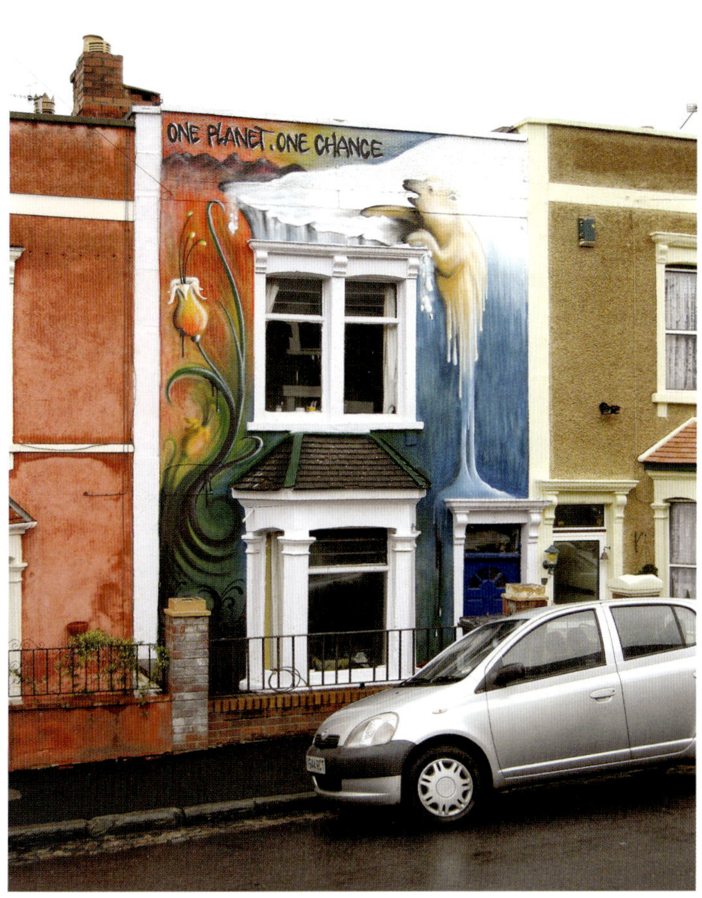

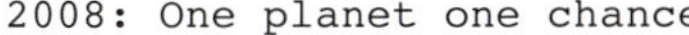

2008: One planet one chance

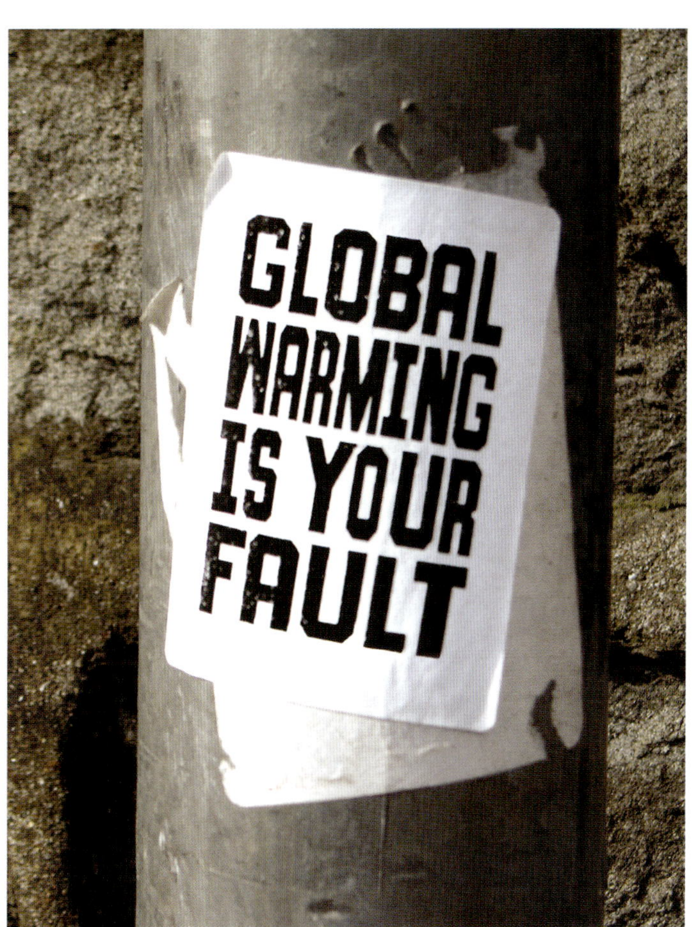

2008: Global warming is your fault

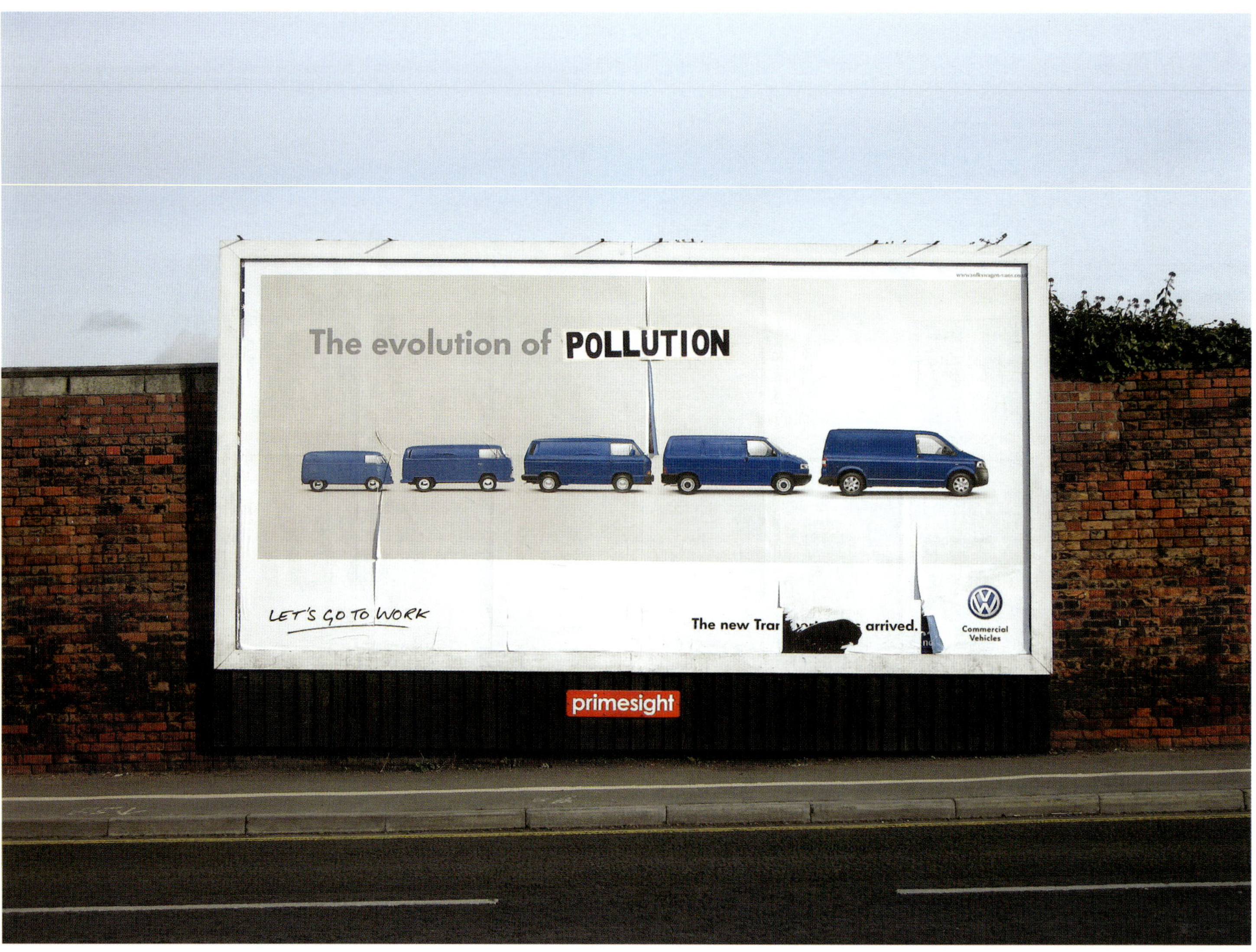

2010: The evolution of pollution

Environment...

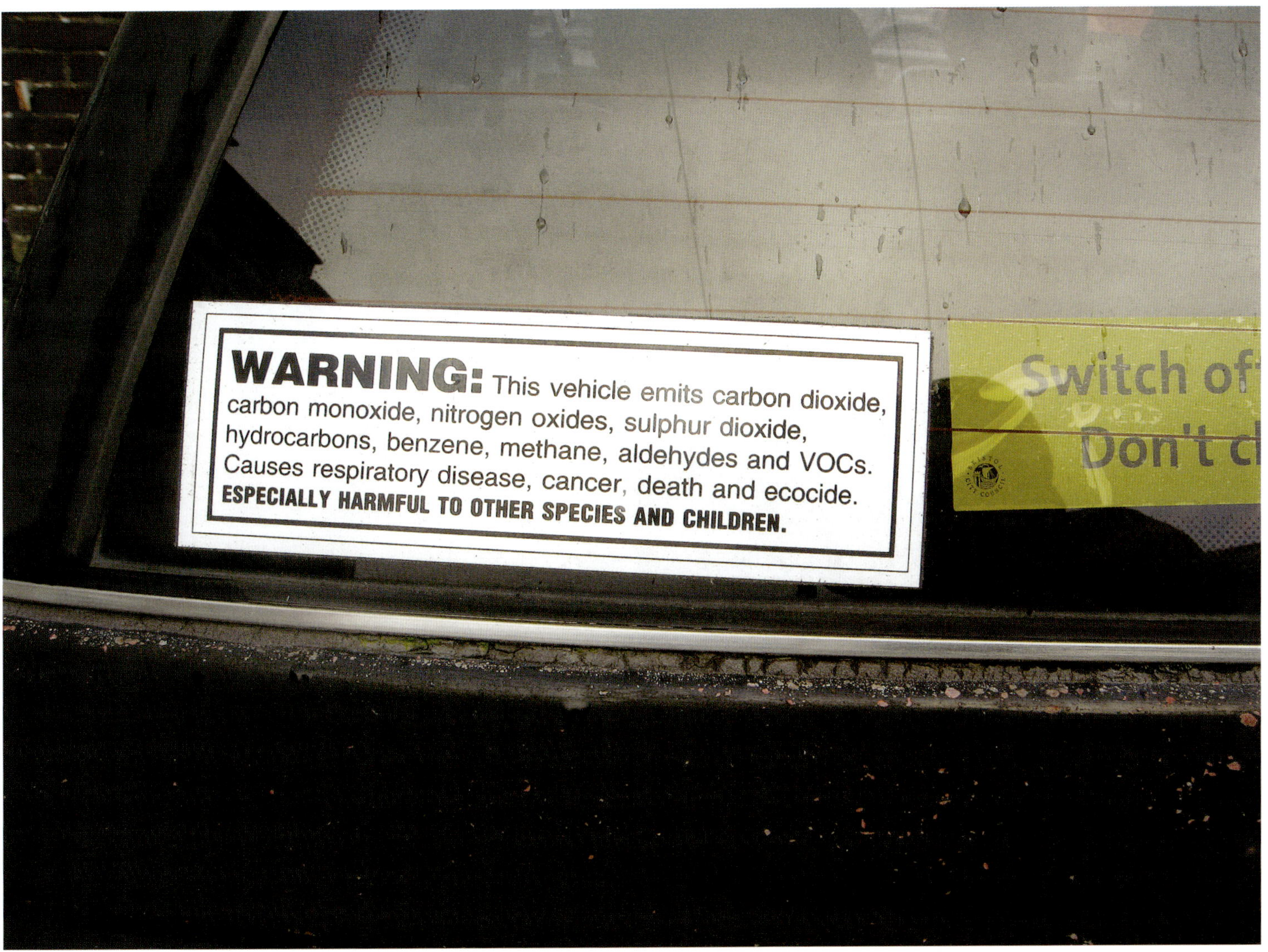

2007: Warning: This vehicle emits carbon dioxide…

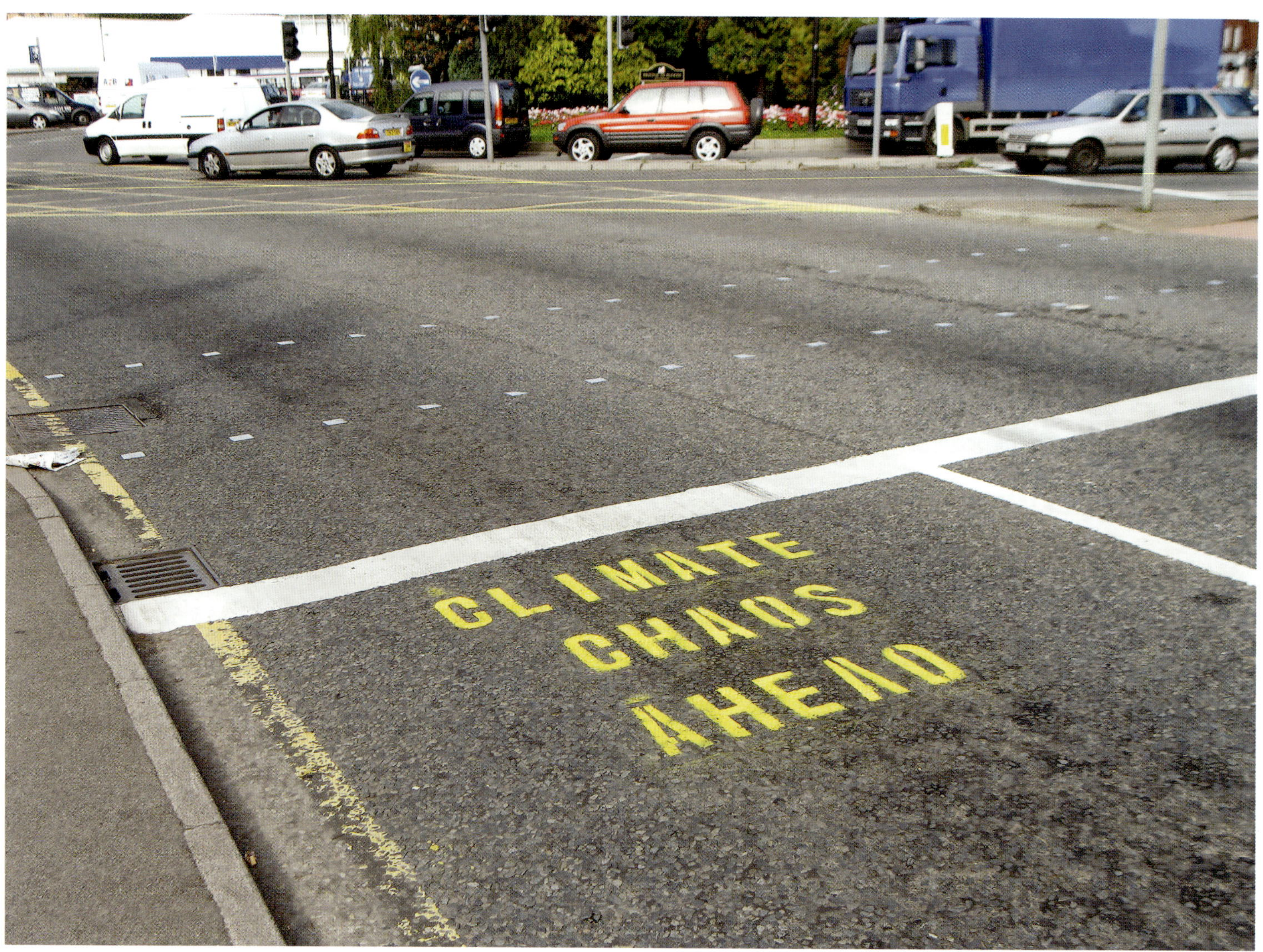

2006: Climate chaos ahead

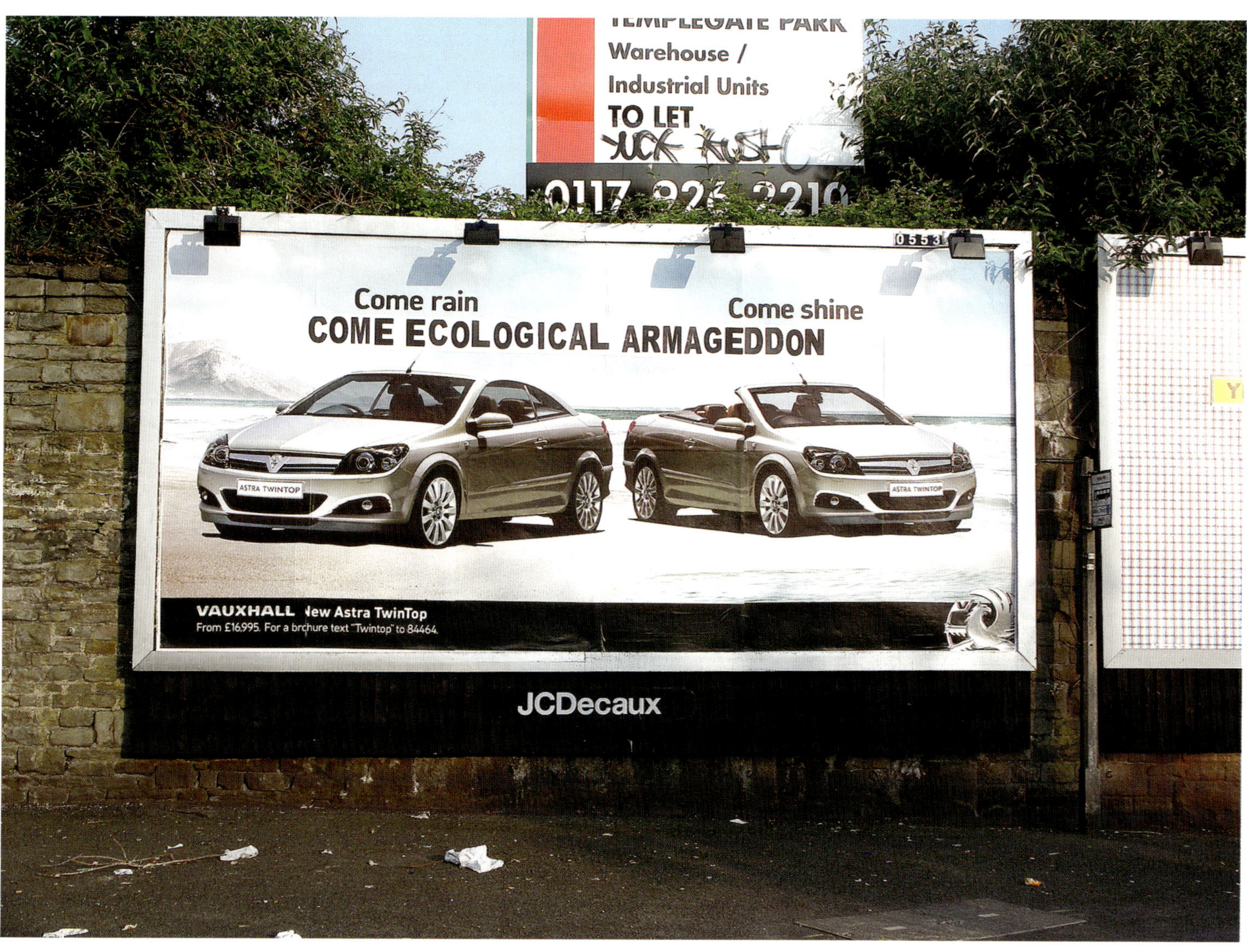

2006: Come rain, Come shine, Come ecological Armageddon

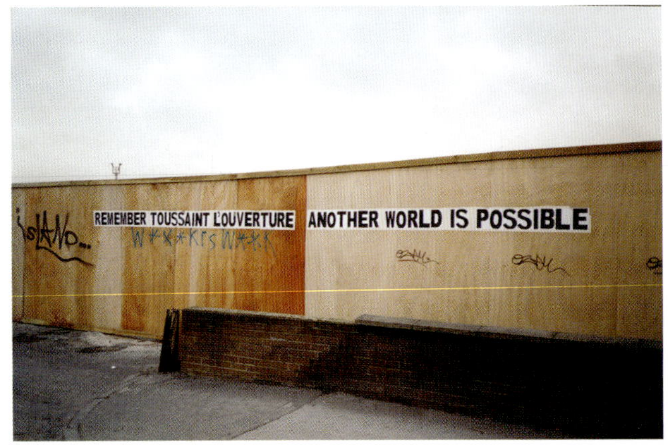
REMEMBER TOUSSAINT L'OUVERTURE   ANOTHER WORLD IS POSSIBLE

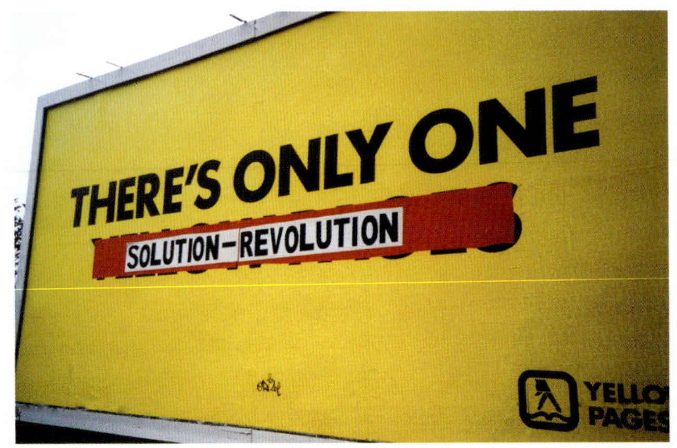
THERE'S ONLY ONE
SOLUTION - REVOLUTION
YELLOW PAGES

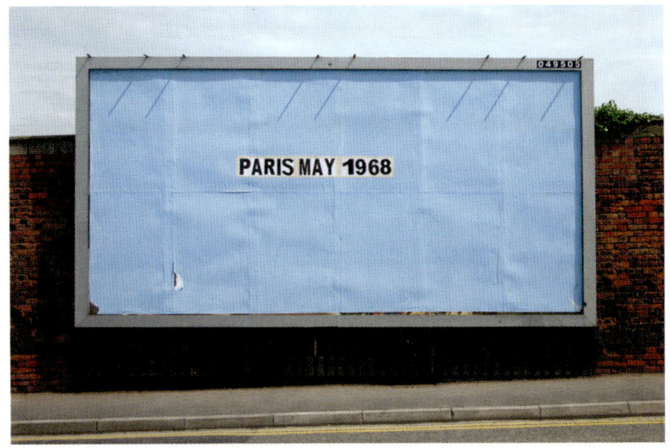
PARIS MAY 1968

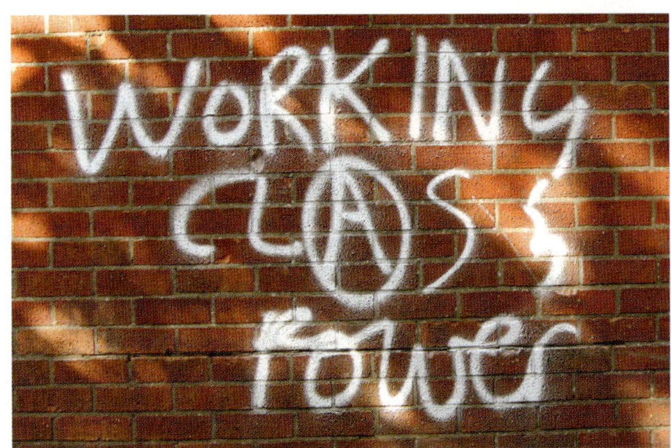
WORKING CLASS power

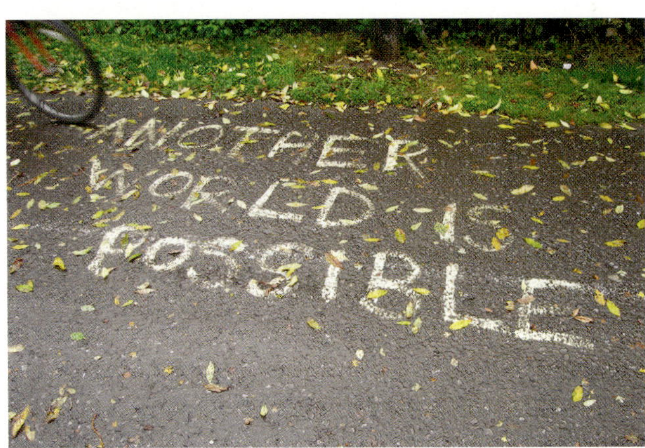
ANOTHER WORLD IS POSSIBLE

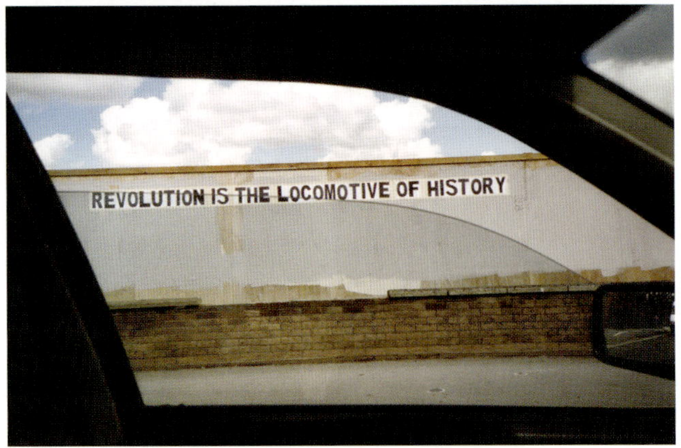
REVOLUTION IS THE LOCOMOTIVE OF HISTORY

Left and right...

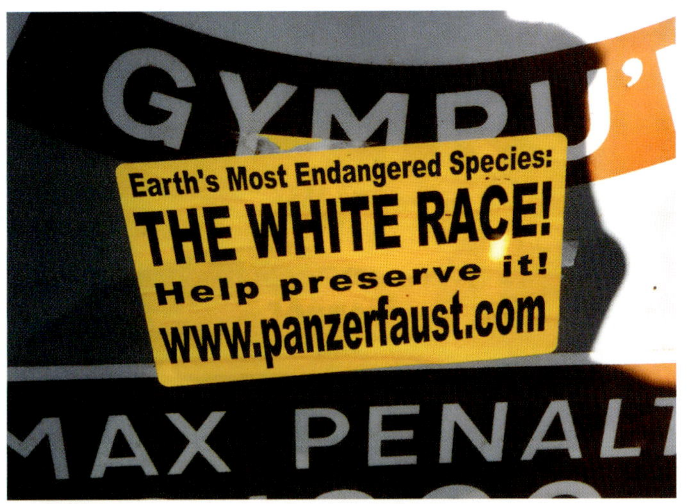

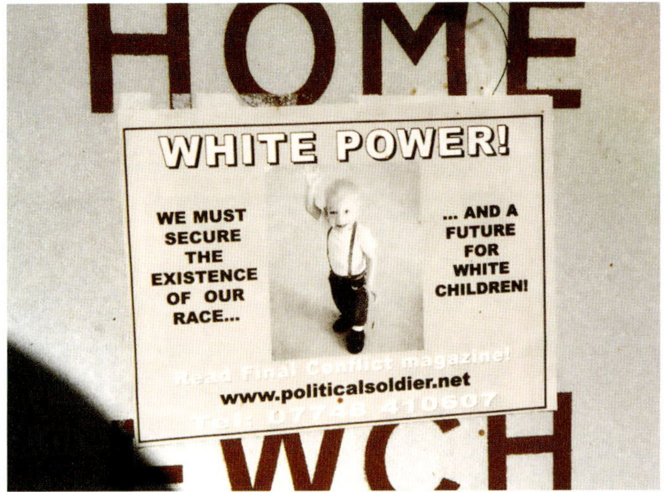

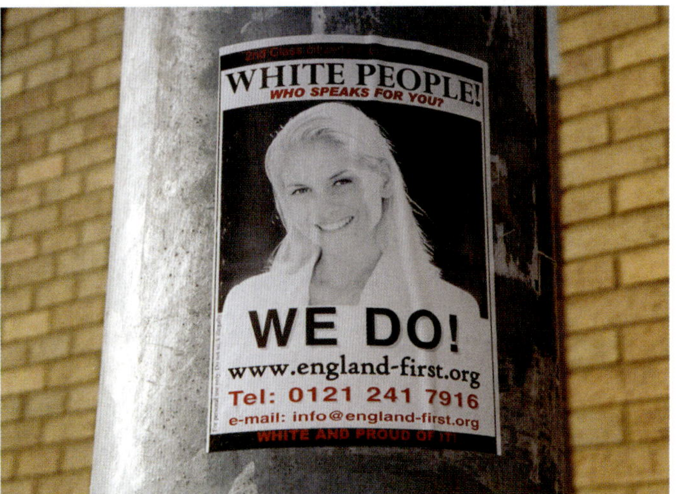

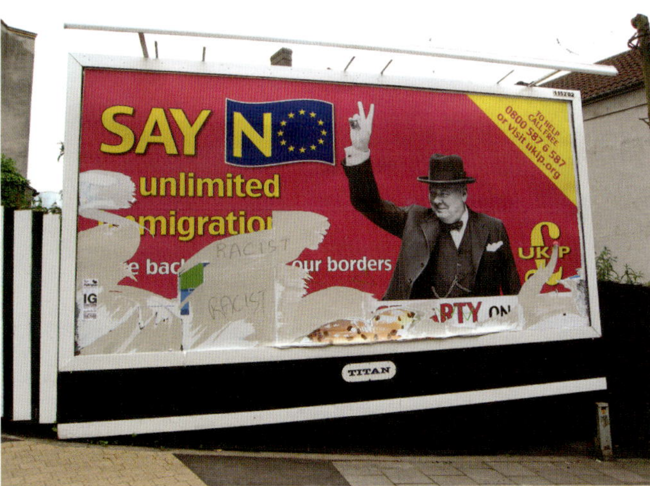

Above. Clockwise from top left – 2004: Earth's most endangered species [www.panzerfaust.com] | 2004: White power! [www.politicalsoldier.net] | 2009: Say no to unlimited immigration [UKIP] | 2004: White people who speaks for you? [www.england-first.org] |

Previous page. Clockwise from top left — 2004: Remember Toussaint L'Ouverture another world is possible [black leader of Haitian revolution in the 1790s] | 2004: There's only one solution - revolution | 2007: Working class power | 2004: Revolution is the locomotive of history | 2007: Another world is possible | 2008: Paris May 1968 [student protests, general strike, revolution in the air] |

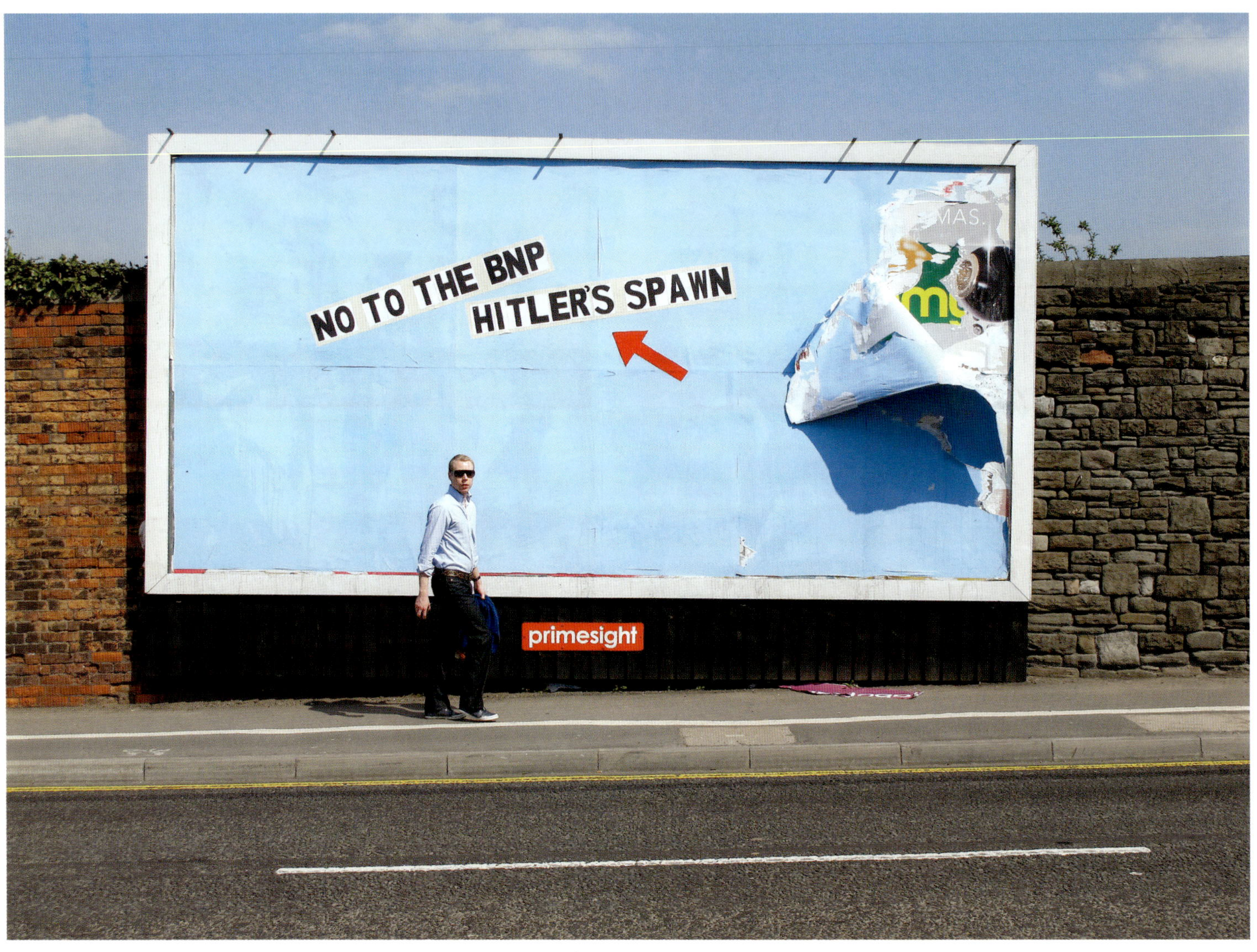

2010: No to the BNP, Hitler's spawn

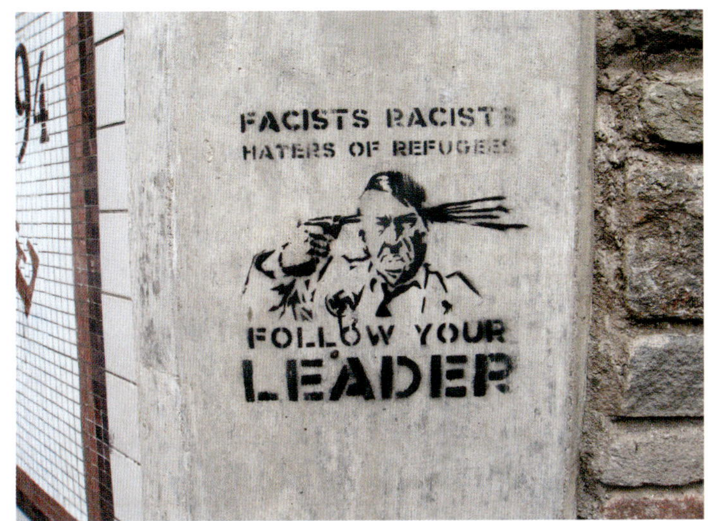

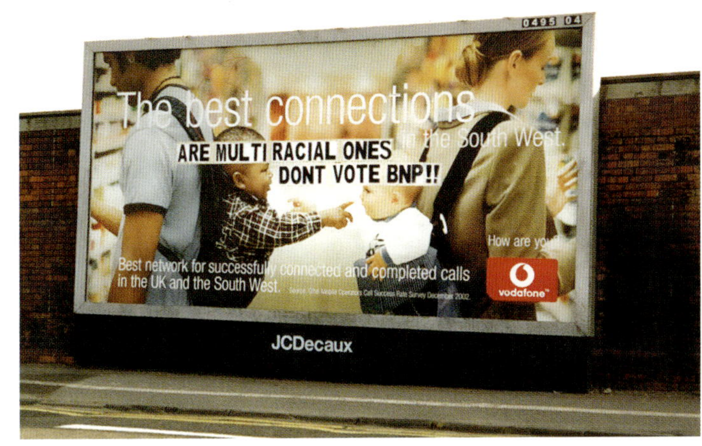

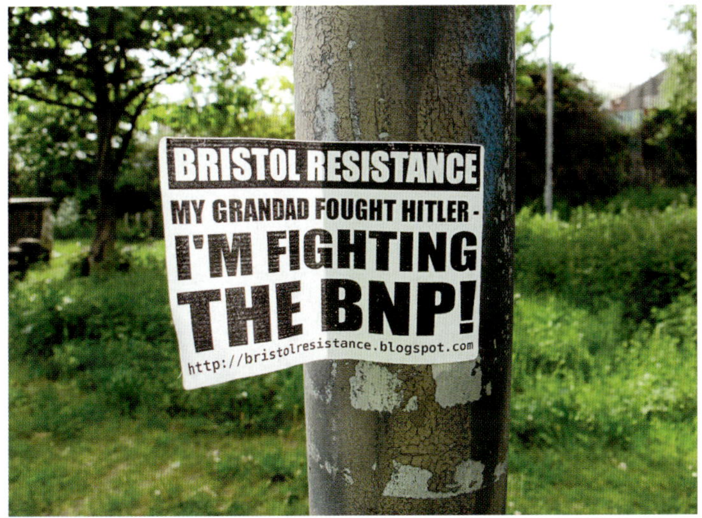

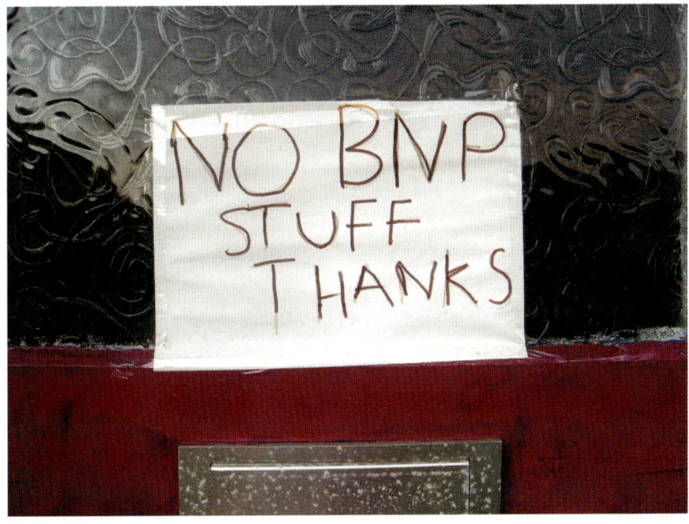

Clockwise from top left – 2007: Facists racists haters of refugees follow your leader | 2003: The best connections are multiracial ones, don't vote BNP | 2009: No BNP stuff thanks | 2010: Bristol Resistance my grandad fought Hitler |

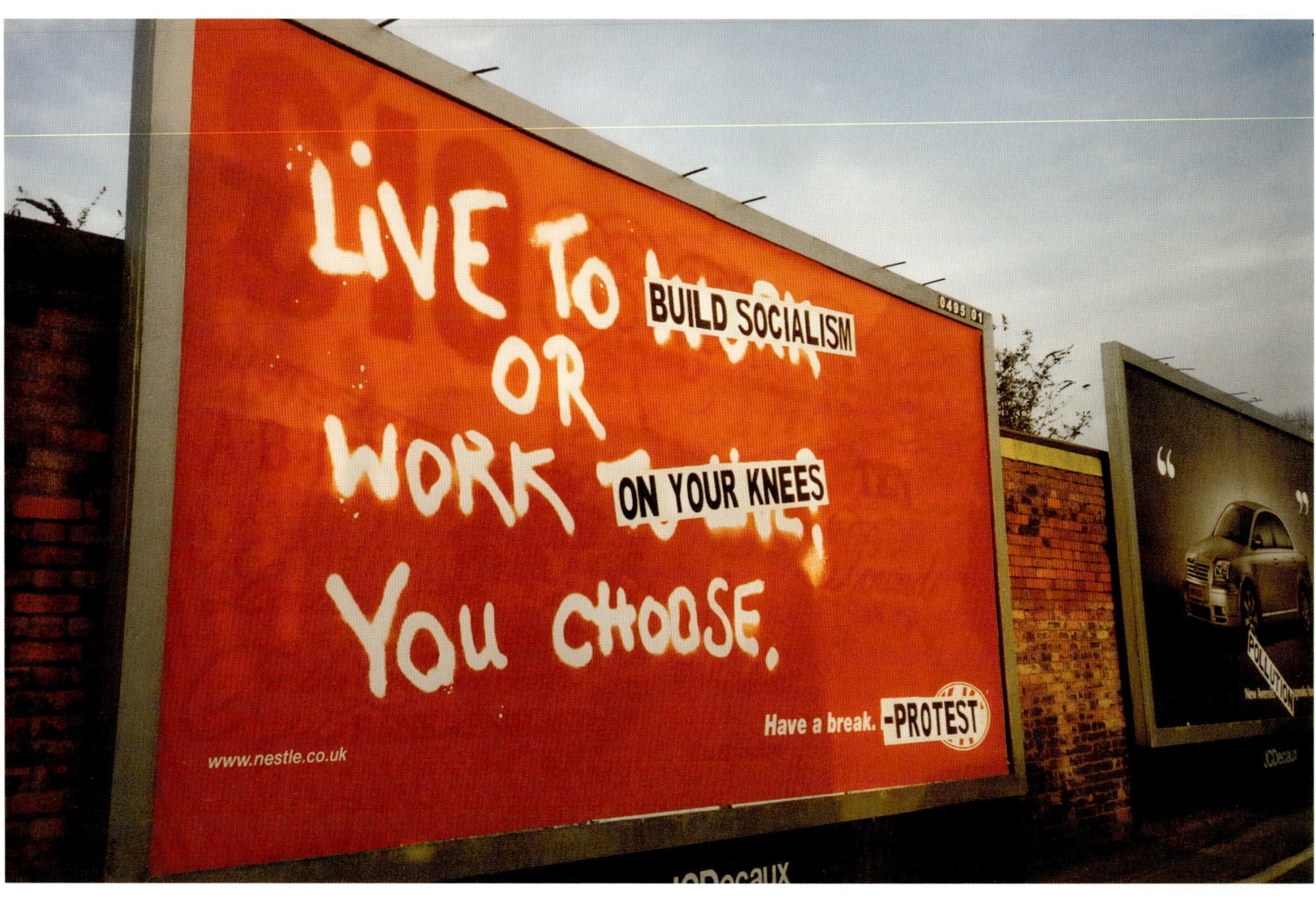

2003: Live to build socialism

Left and right...

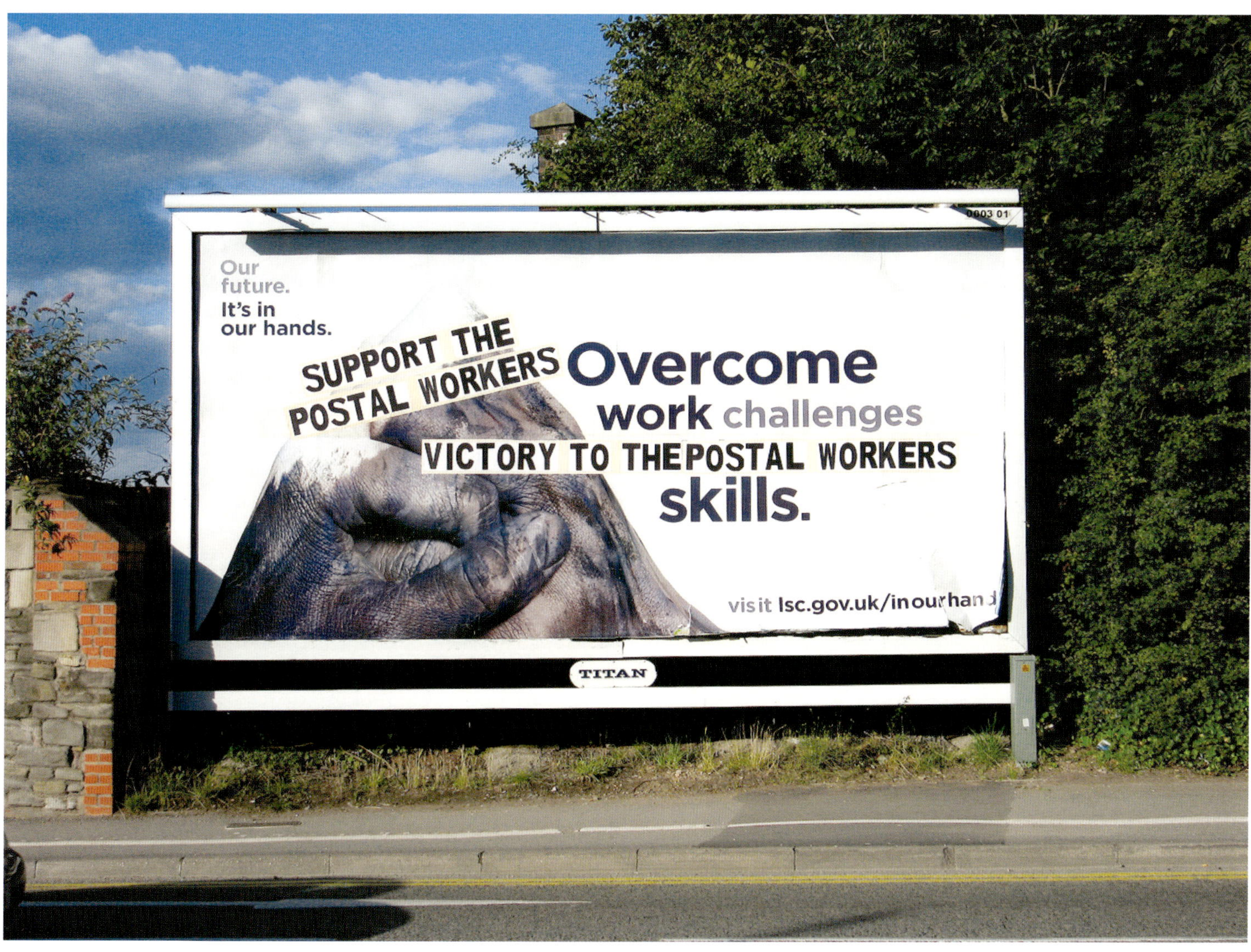

2007: Support the postal workers

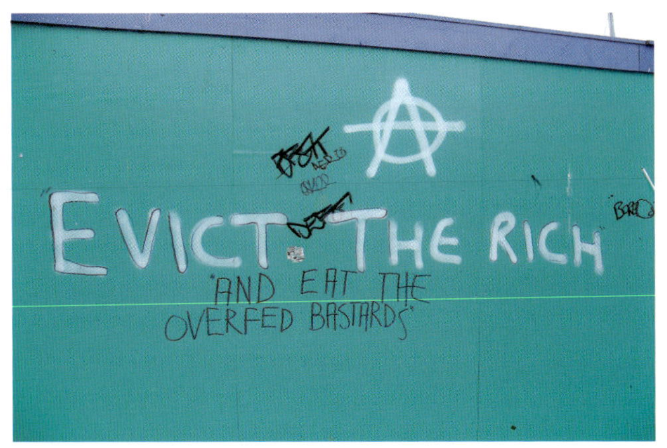
EVICT THE RICH
'AND EAT THE
OVERFED BASTARDS'

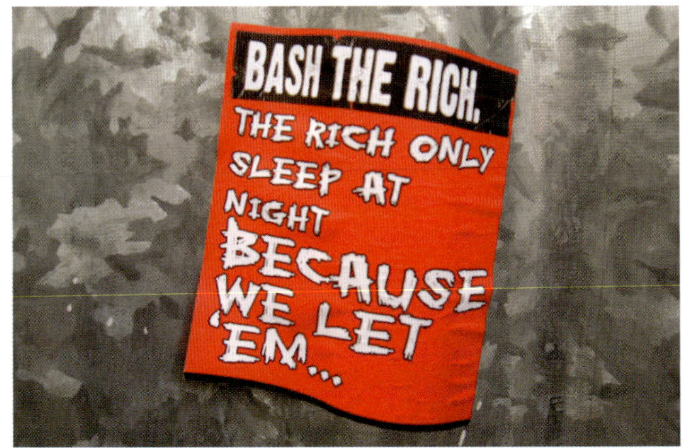
BASH THE RICH.
THE RICH ONLY
SLEEP AT
NIGHT
BECAUSE
WE LET
'EM...

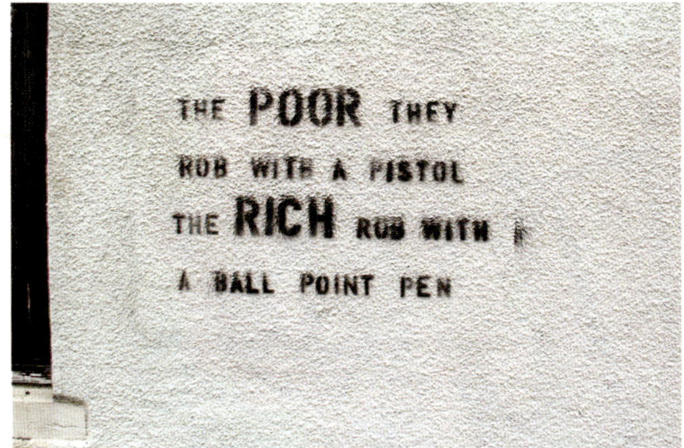
THE POOR THEY
ROB WITH A PISTOL
THE RICH ROB WITH
A BALL POINT PEN

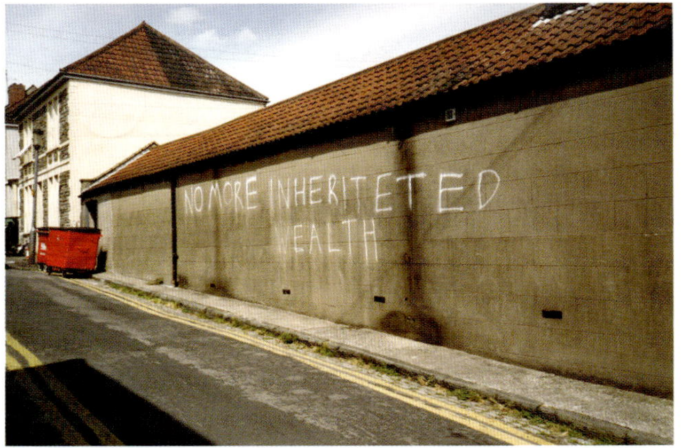
NO MORE INHERITETED
WEALTH

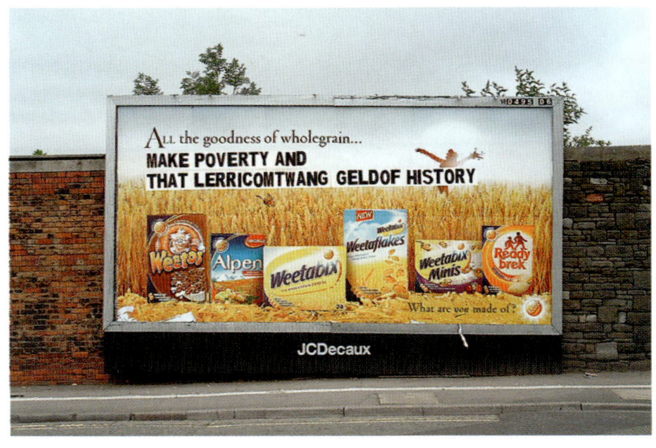
ALL the goodness of wholegrain...
MAKE POVERTY AND
THAT LERRICOMTWANG GELDOF HISTORY
Weetos
Alpen
Weetabix
Weetaflakes
Weetabix Minis
Ready brek
What are you made of?
JCDecaux

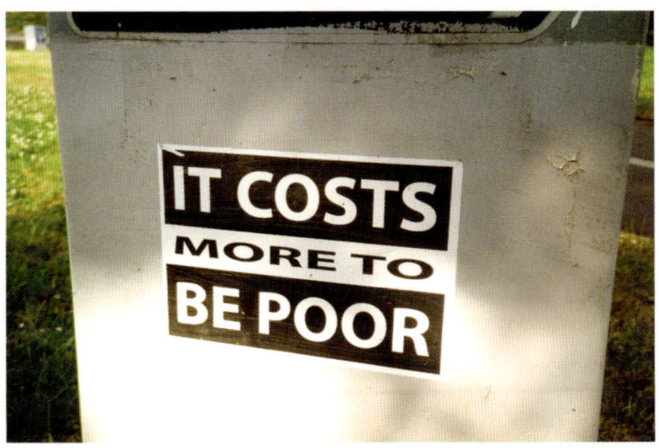
IT COSTS
MORE TO
BE POOR

Rich and poor...

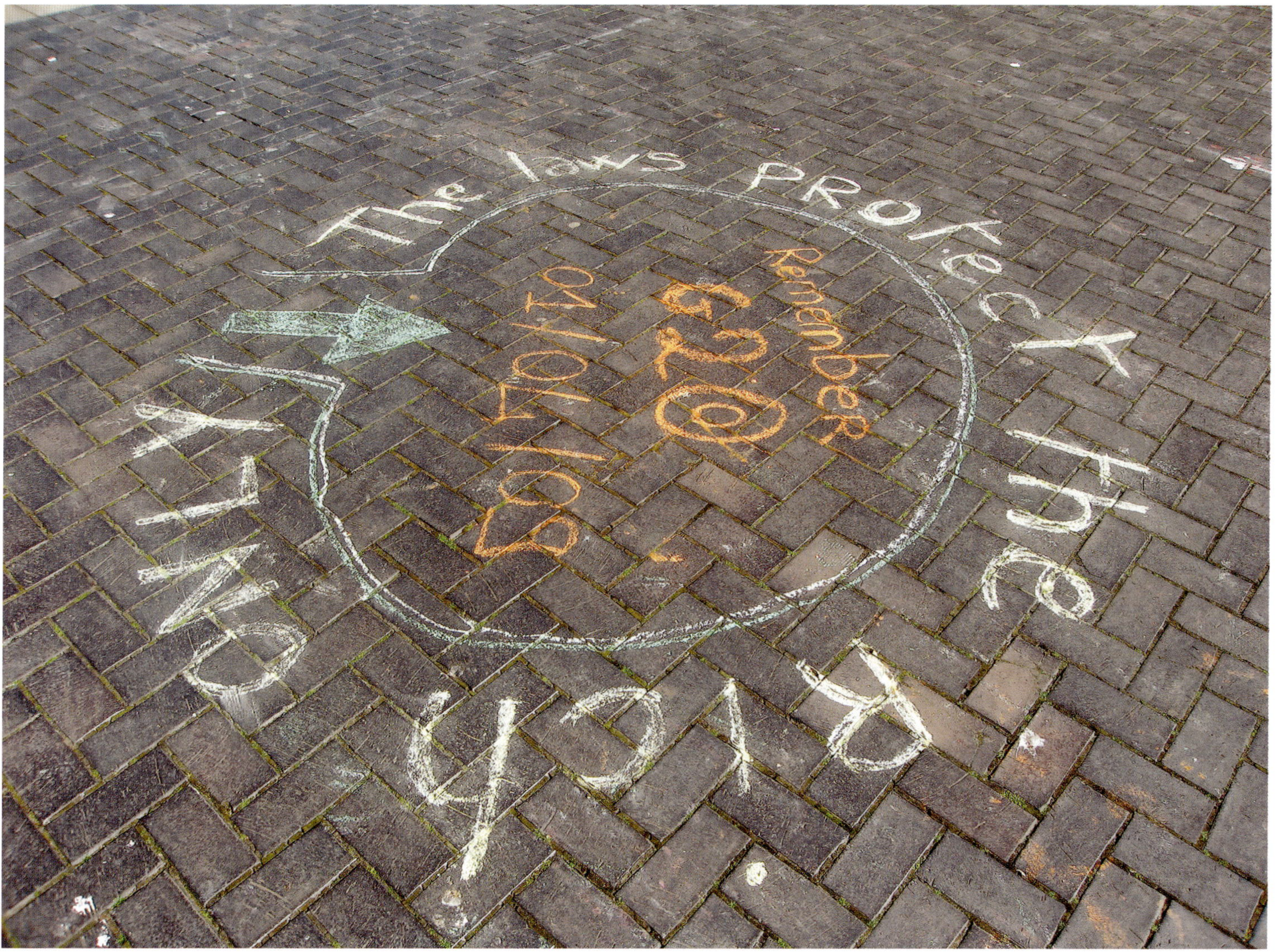

Above – 2009: The laws protect the rich only

Previous page. Clockwise from top left – 2006: Evict the rich | 2008: The rich only sleep at night because we let 'em | 2004: No more inheriteted wealth | 2004: It costs more to be poor | 2004: Make poverty and that lerricomtwang Geldof history [Bob Geldof was behind Band Aid and Live Aid raising money for poverty-stricken African countries] | 2011: The poor they rob with a pistol |

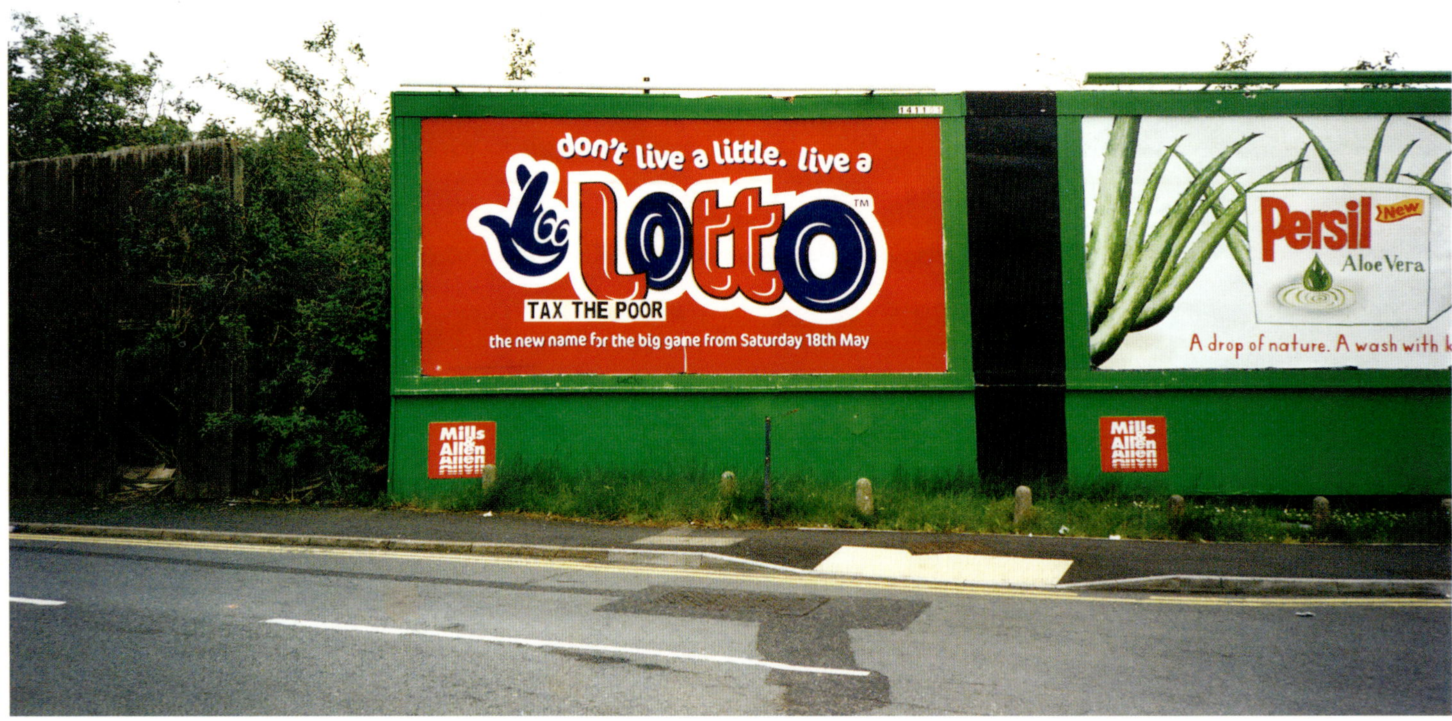

2002: Lotto - tax the poor

Rich and poor...

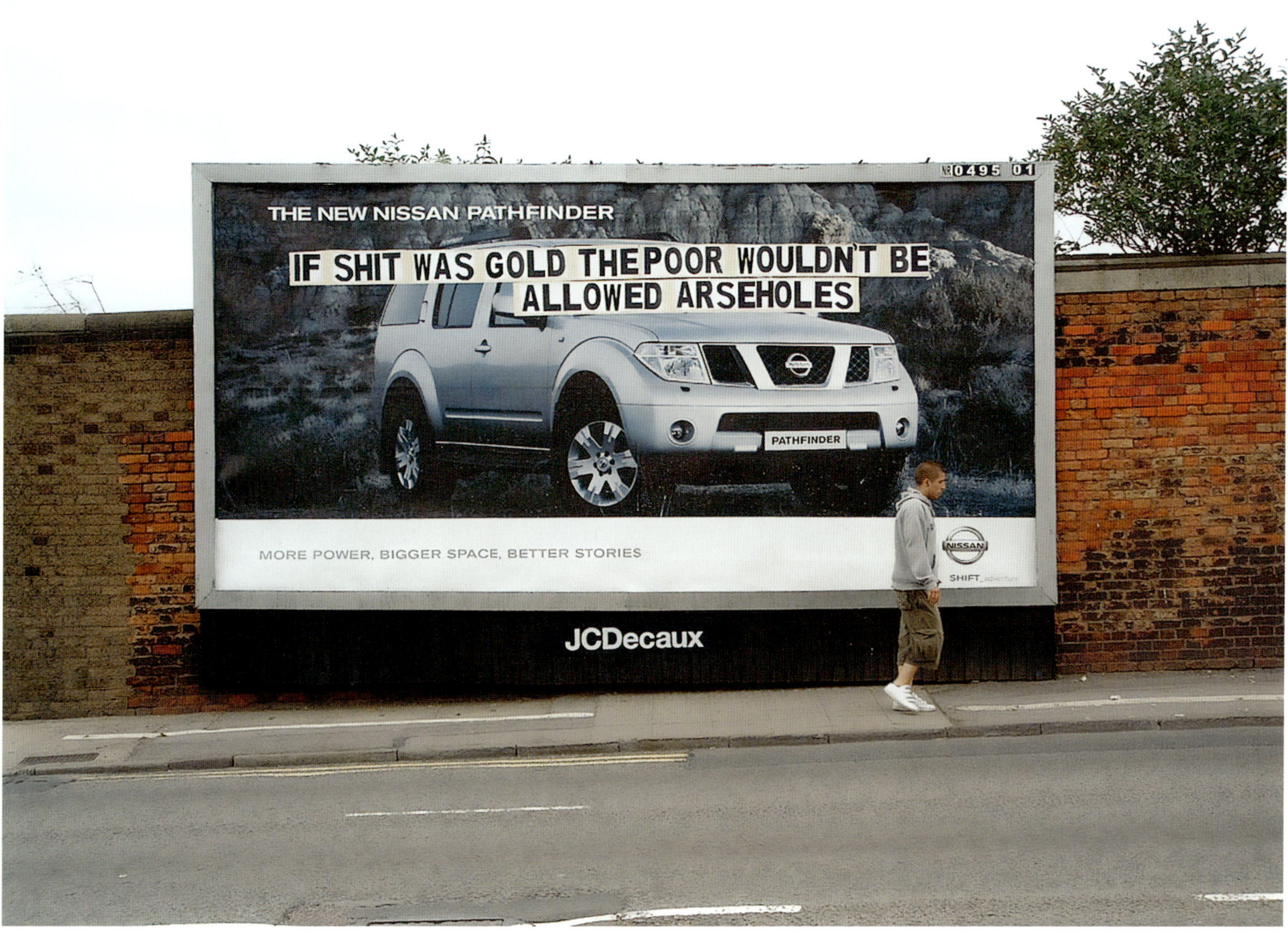

2004: If shit was gold the poor wouldn't be allowed arseholes

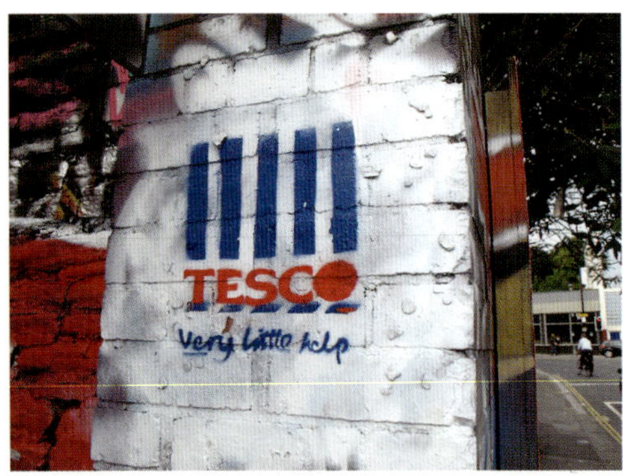

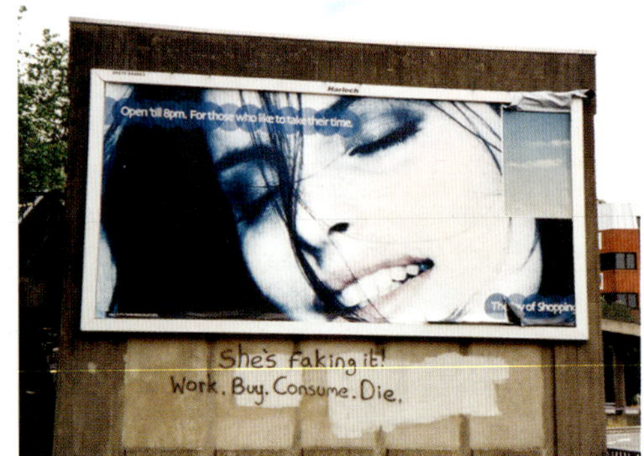

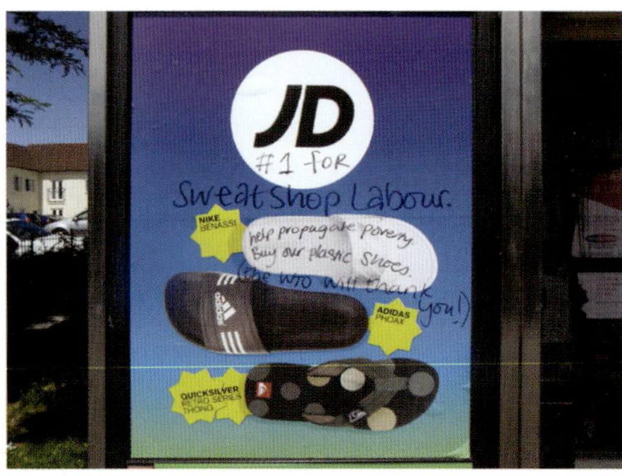

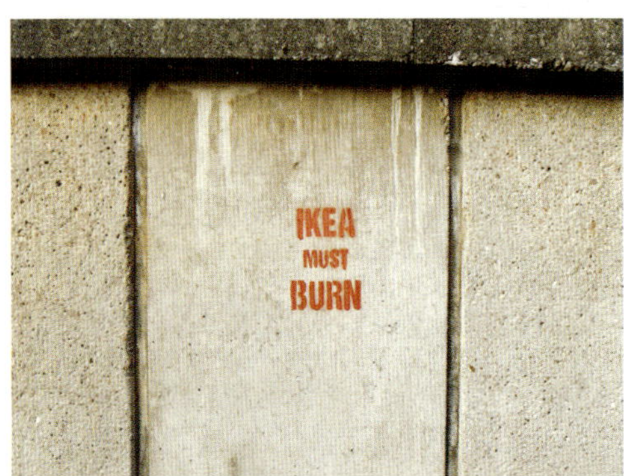

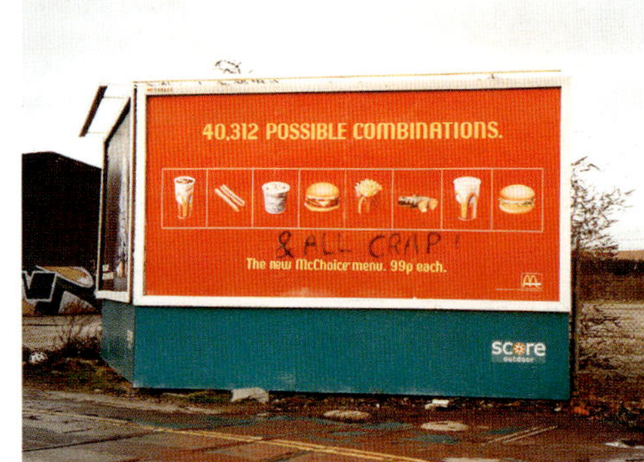

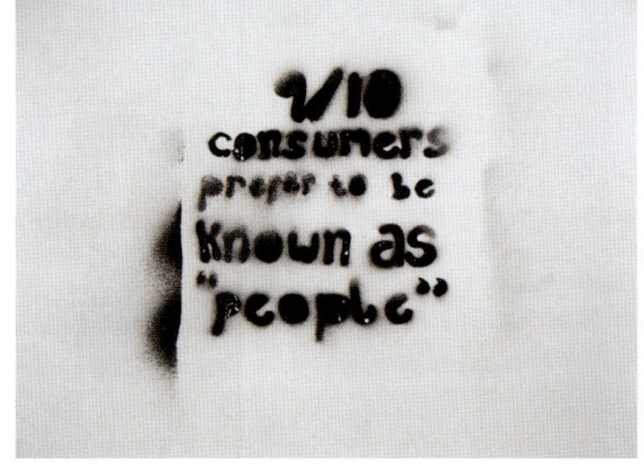

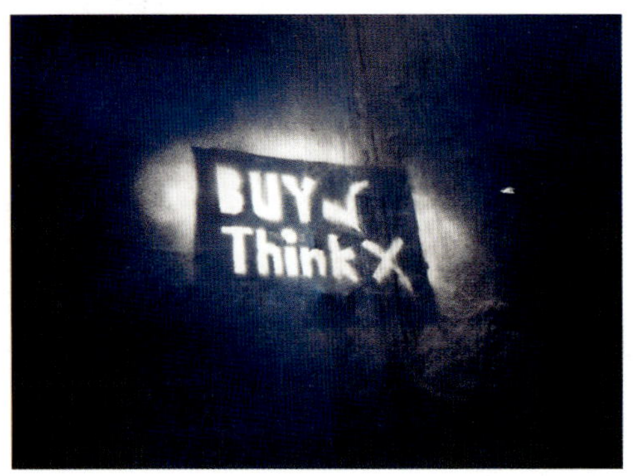

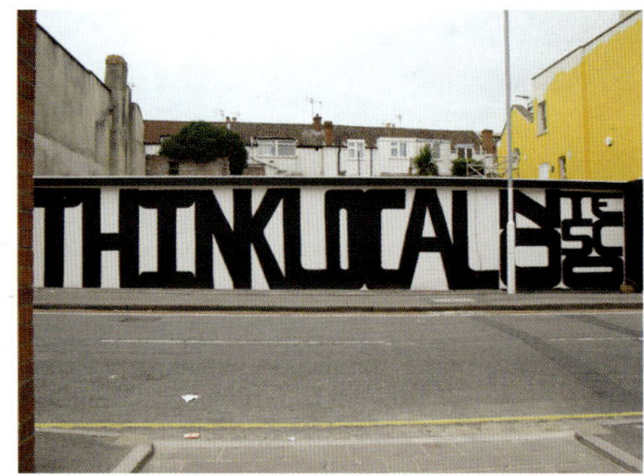

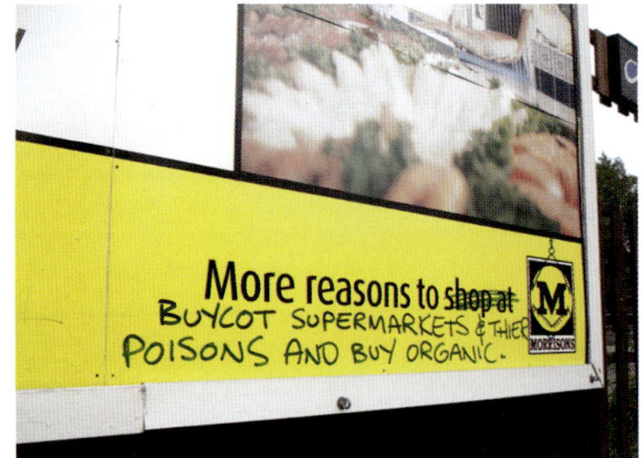

Top row from left – 2011: Tesco. Very little help | 2002: She's faking it! Work. Buy. Consume. Die. | 2005: JD #1 for sweatshop labour | Middle row from left – 2001: Ikea must burn | 2002: 40,312 combinations & all crap! | 2009: 1/10 consumers prefer to be known as "people" | Bottom row from left – 2002: Buy think | 2010: Think local no Tesco | 2005: Buycot supermarkets & thier poisons and buy organic |

Shop/consume...

Socrates (c.470 BC — 399 BC): "How many things I have no need of"

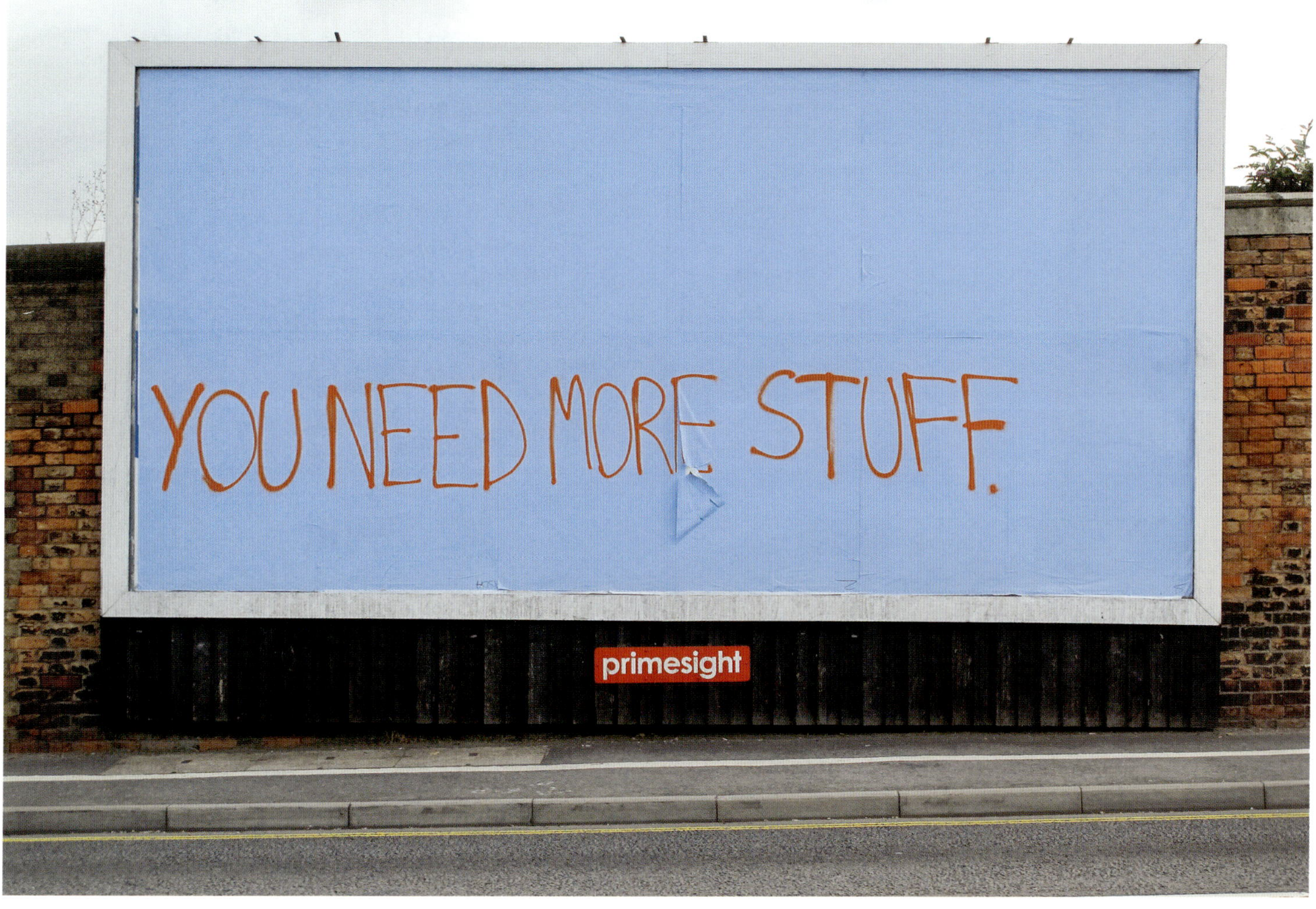

2010: You need more stuff

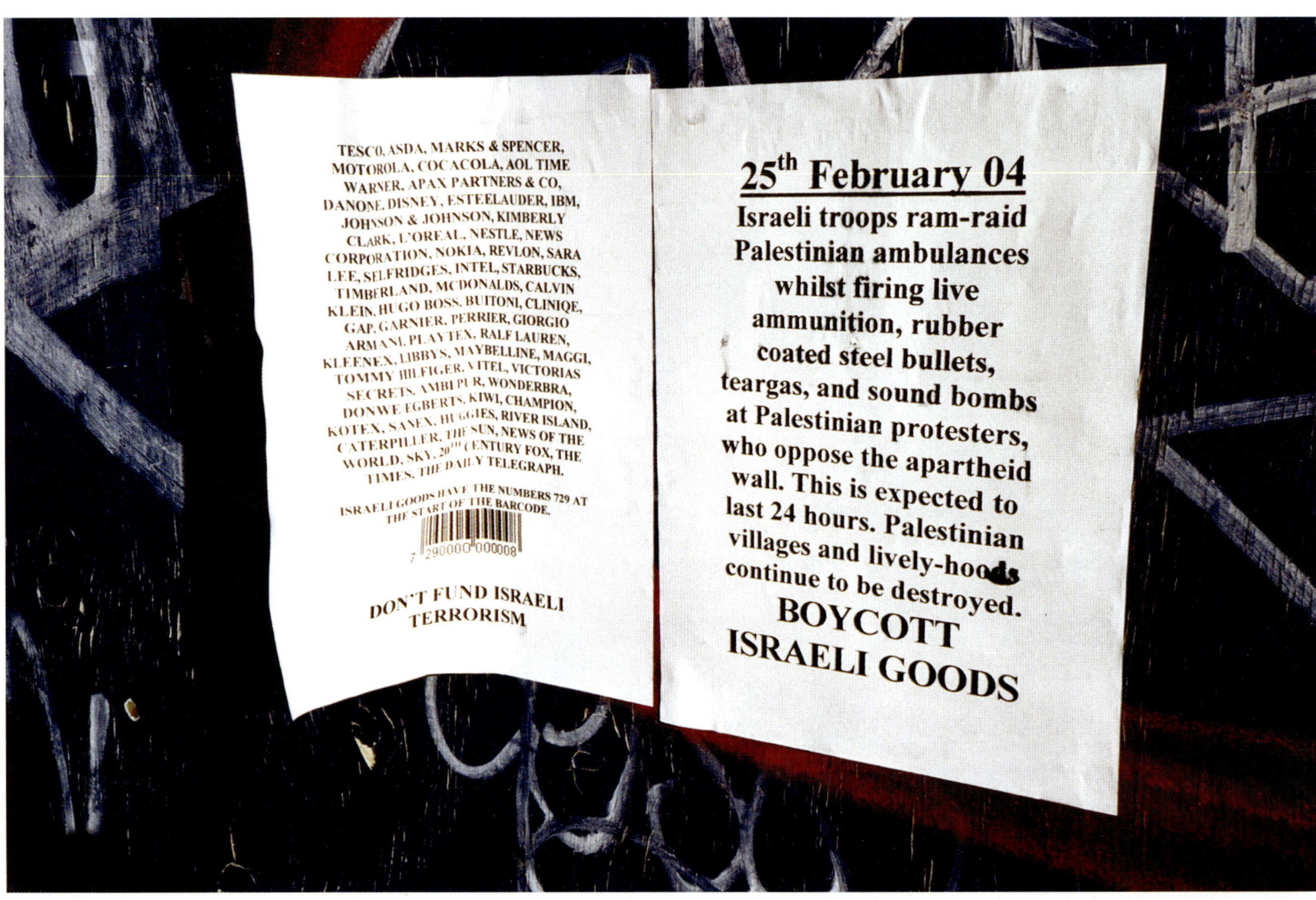

2004: Boycott Israeli goods

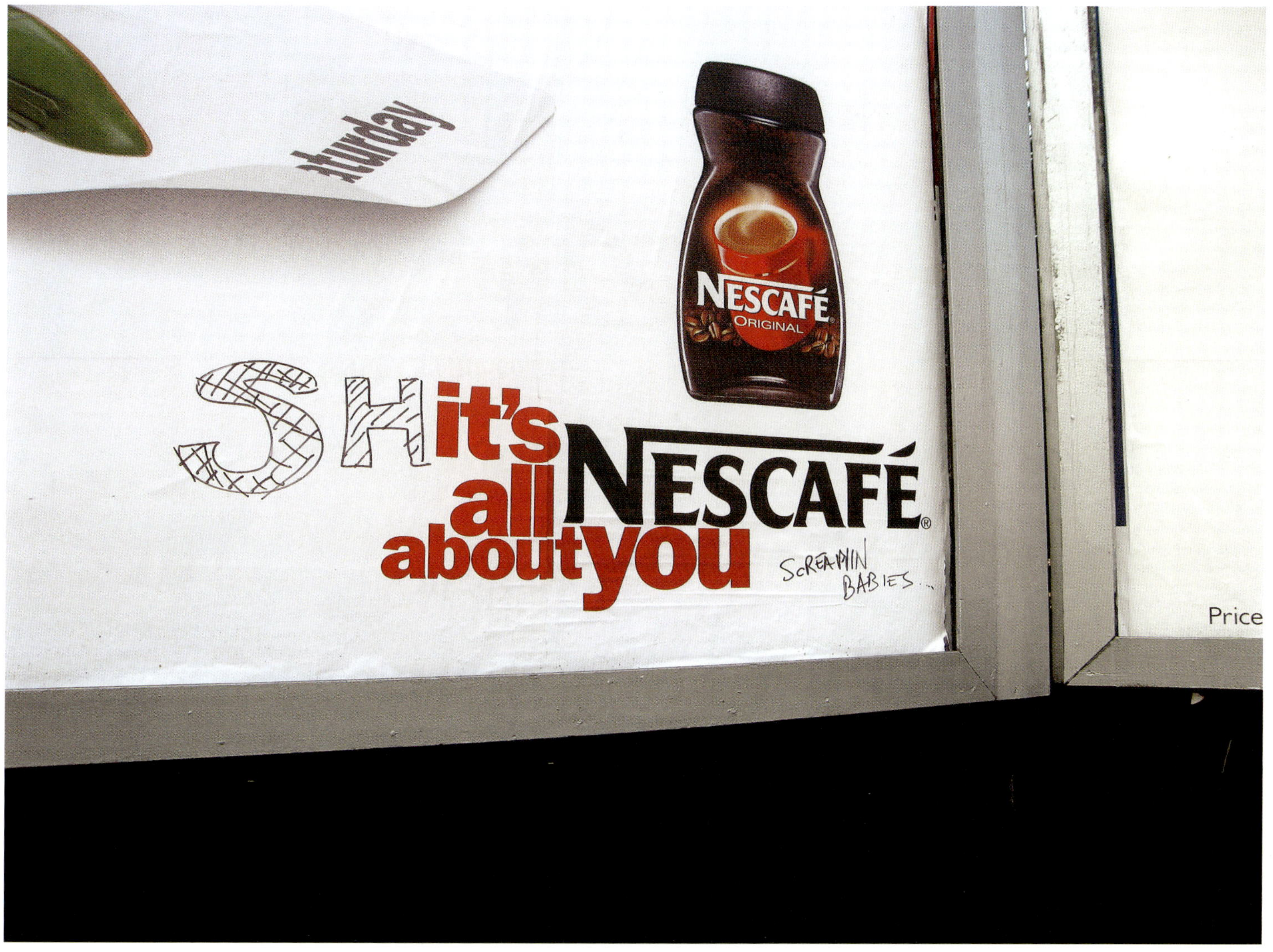

2006: Shit's all about you Nescafé. Screamin babies

[Nescafé's parent company Nestlé have been subject to boycotts since the 1970s, prompted by concern about the company's marketing of breast milk substitutes (infant formula), particularly in less economically developed countries (LEDCs), which campaigners claim contributes to the unnecessary death and suffering of babies, largely among the poor]

Source: Wikipedia

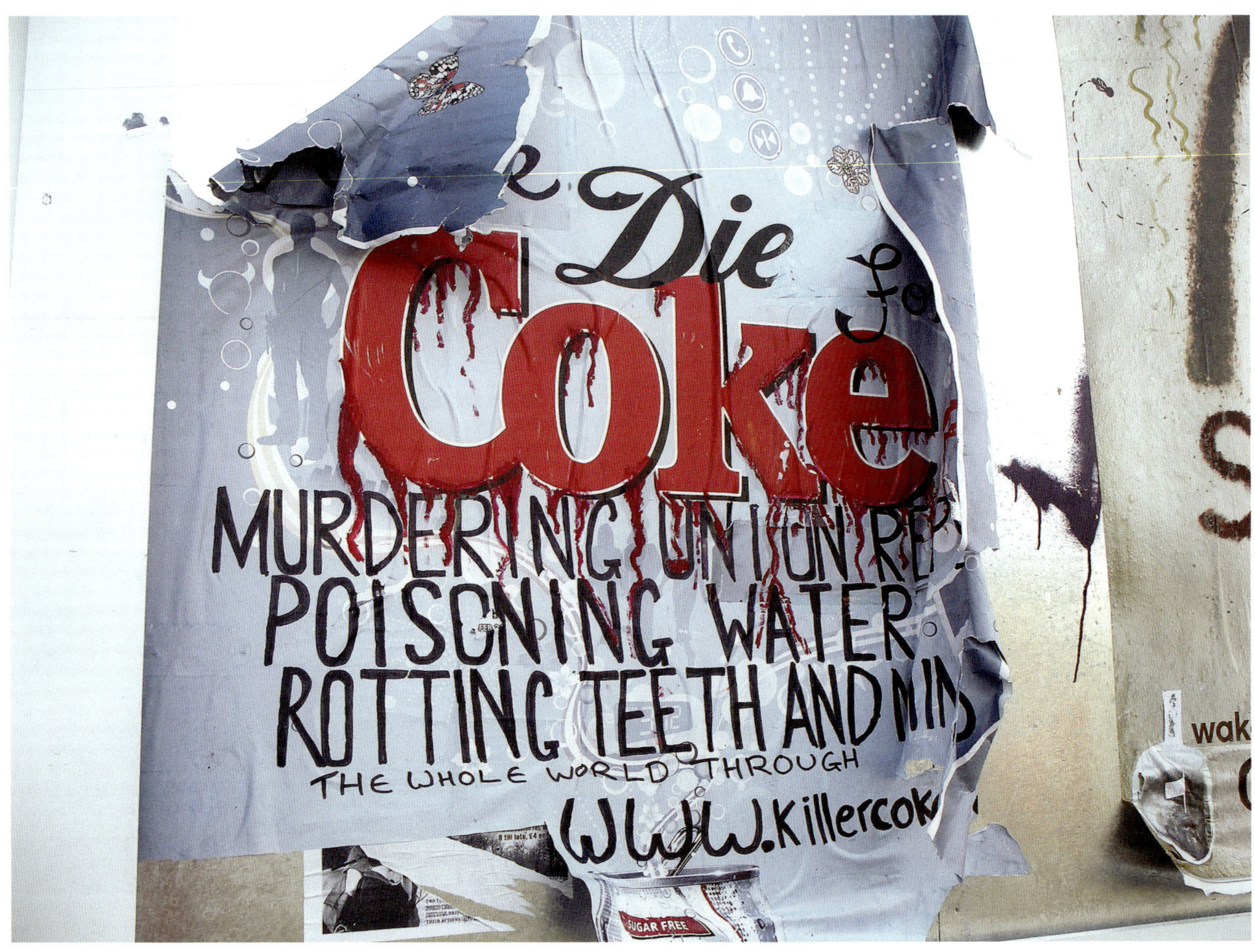

2007: Die Coke [www.killercoke.org]

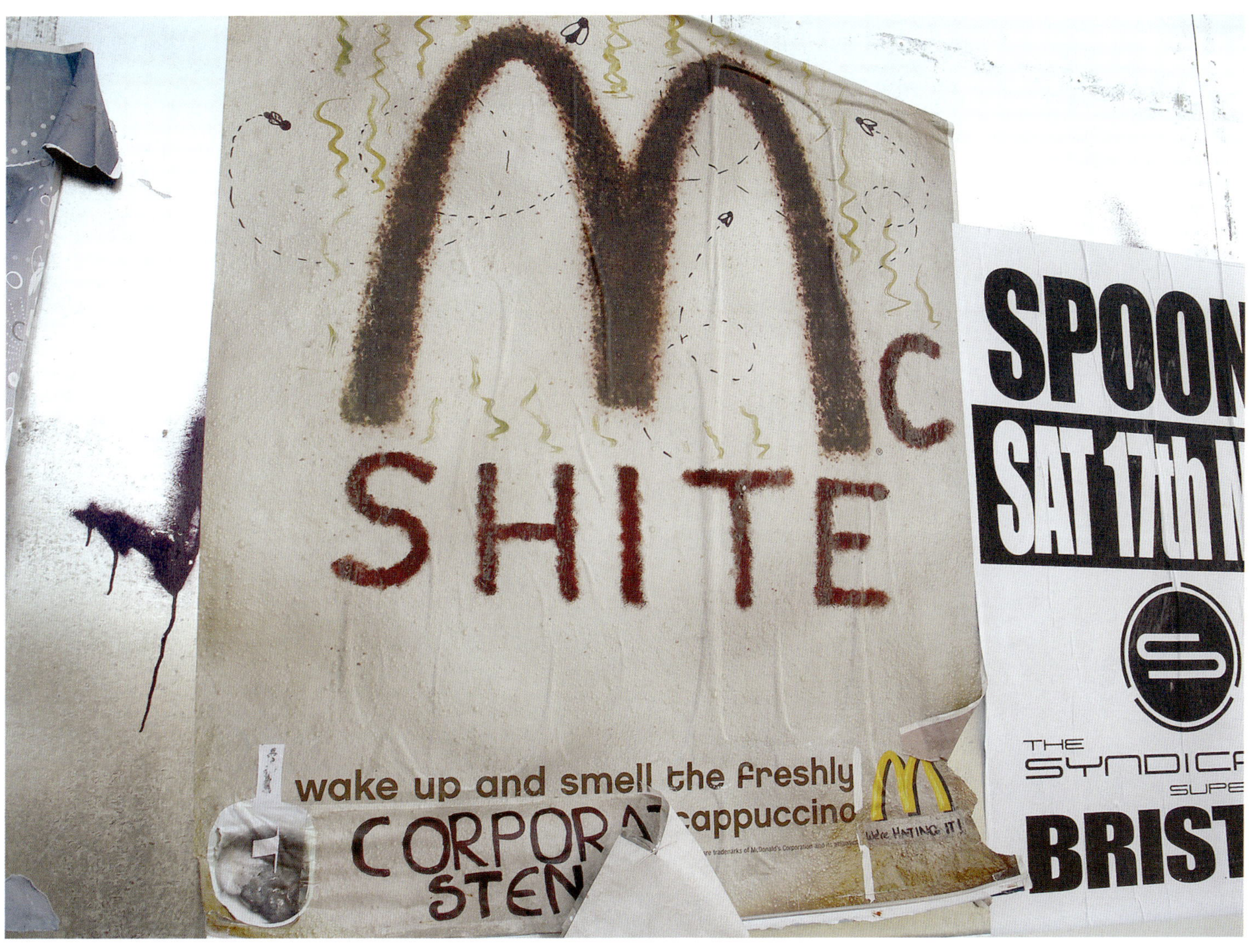

2007: McShite

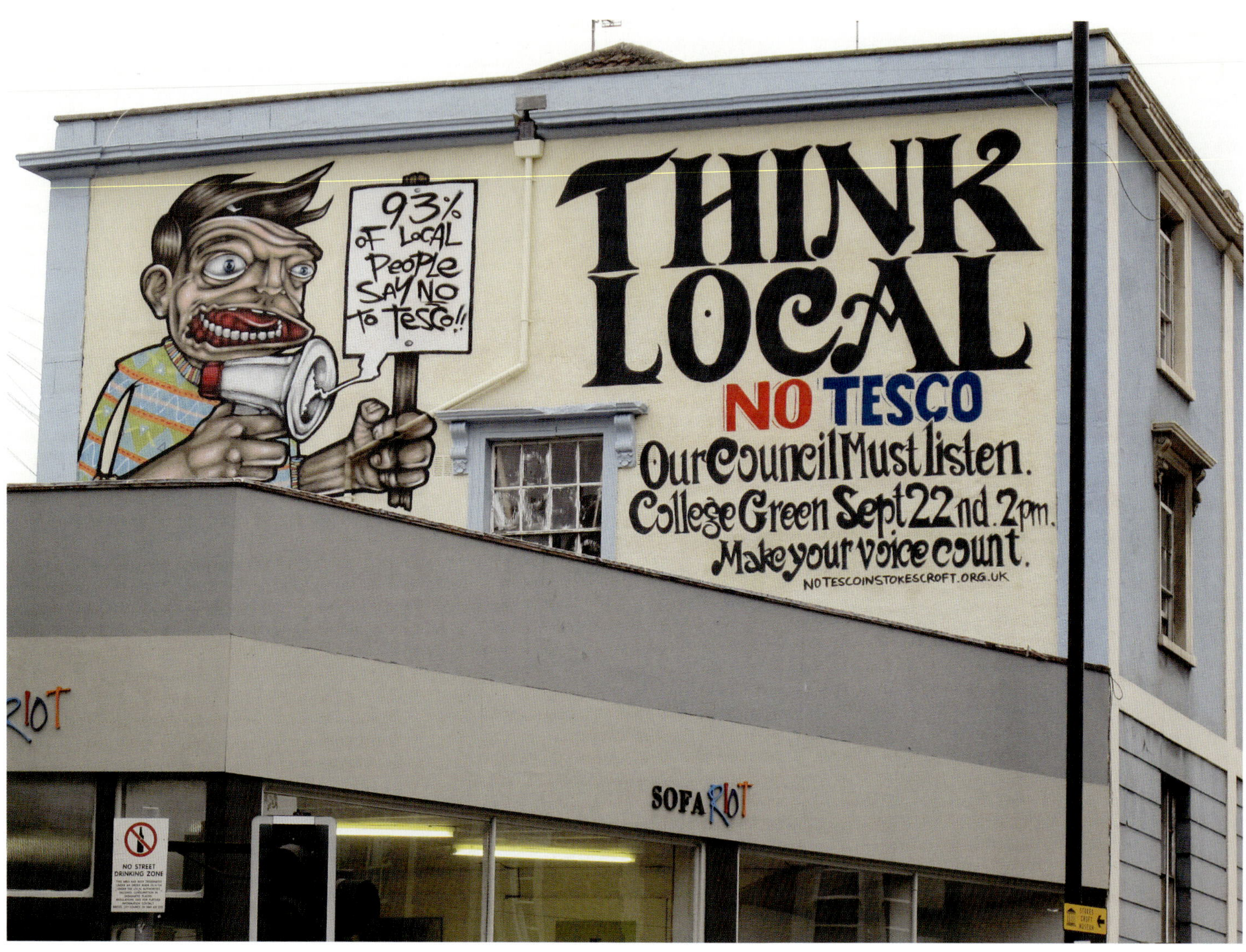

2010: Think local no Tesco [www.notescoinstokescroft.org.uk]

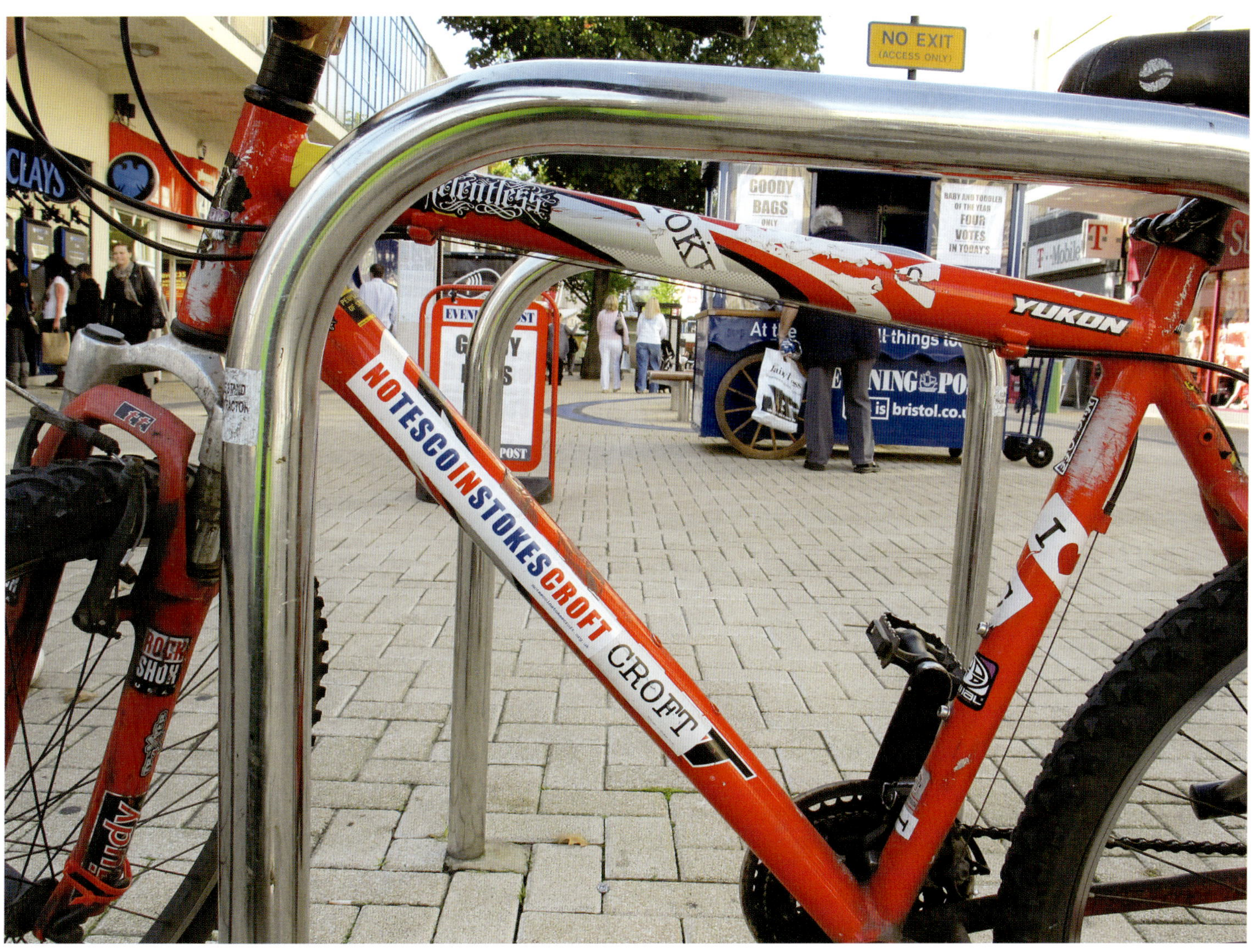

2010: No Tesco in Stokes Croft

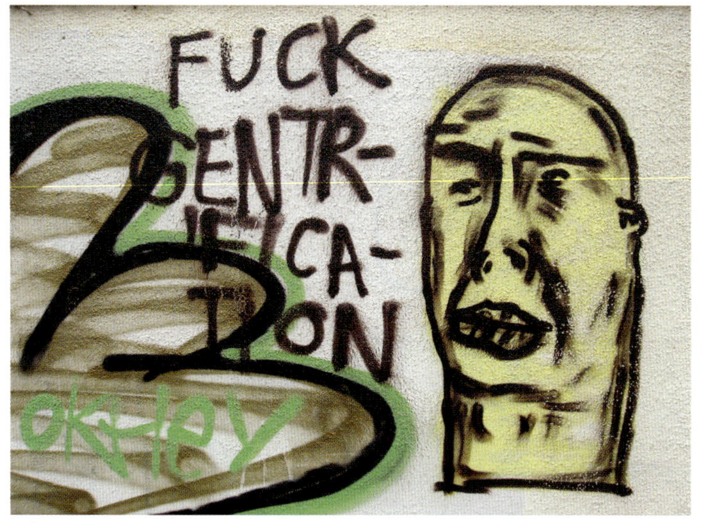

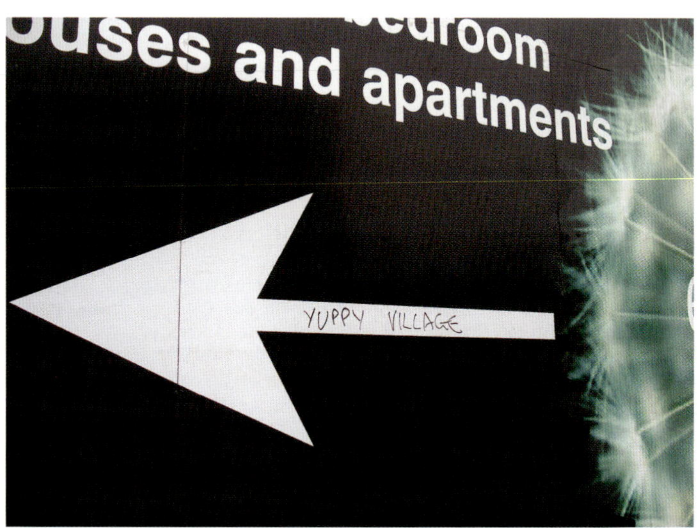

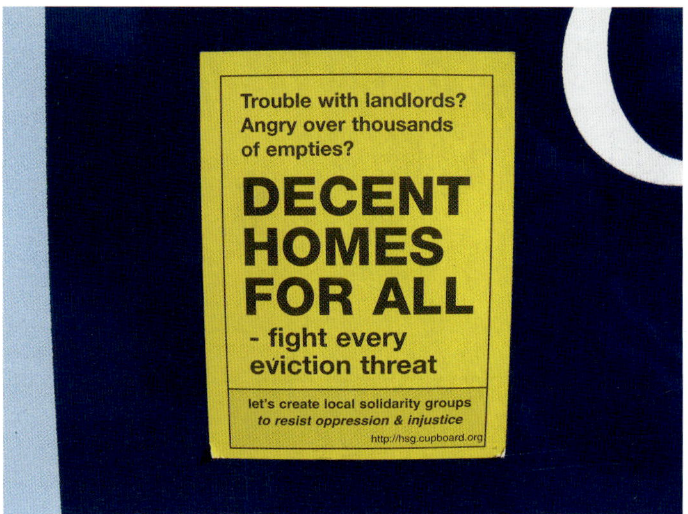

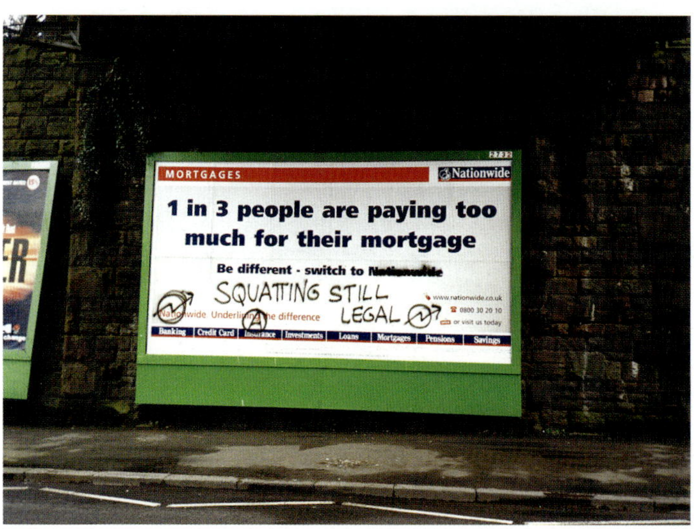

Clockwise from top left - 2008: Fuck gentrification | 2006: Yuppy village | 2001: Squatting still legal | 2009: Decent homes for all |

Housing...

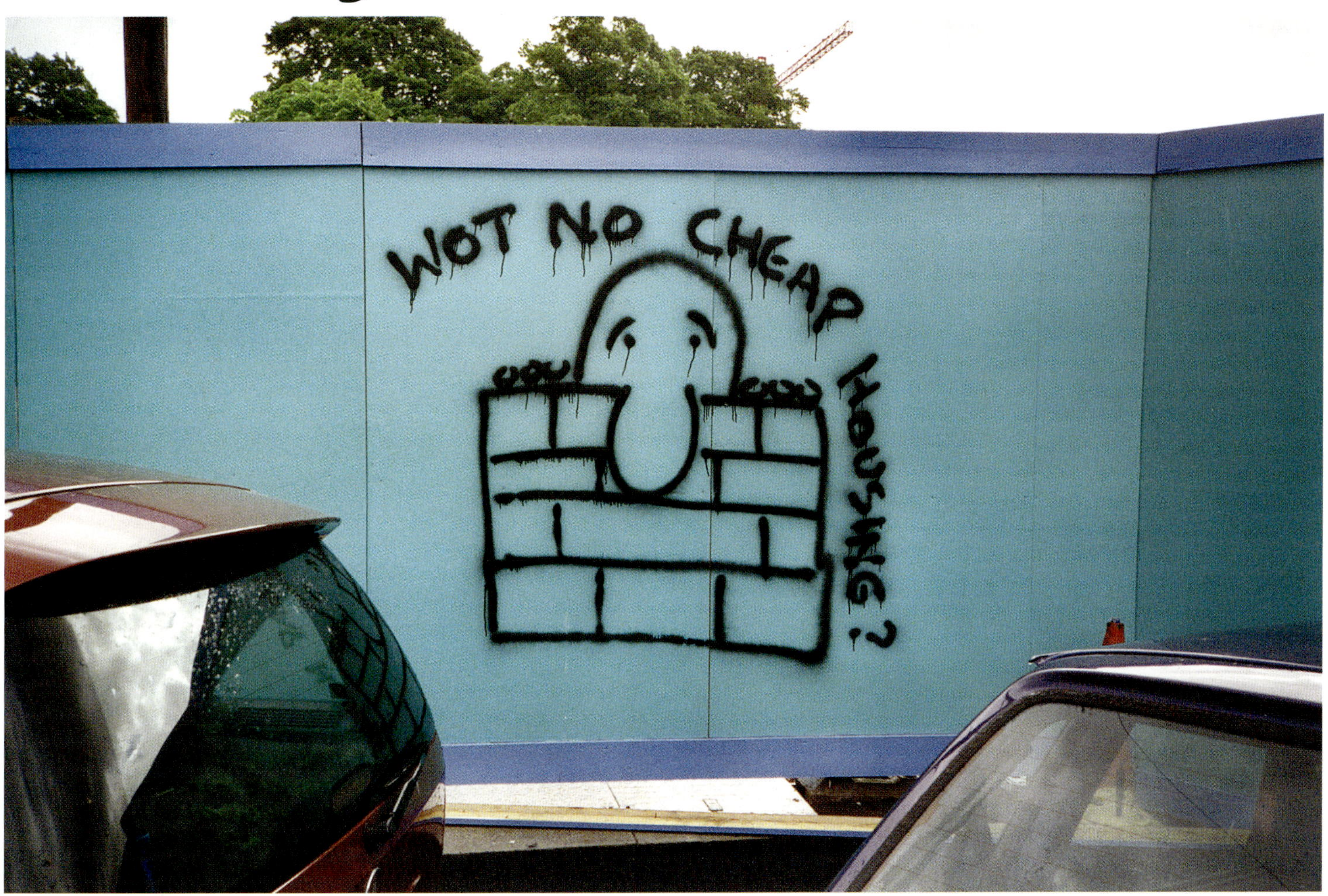

2005: Wot no cheap housing?

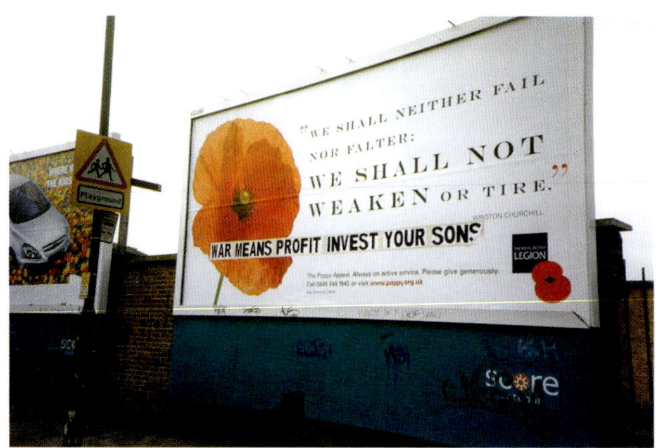
"WE SHALL NEITHER FAIL
NOR FALTER;
WE SHALL NOT
WEAKEN OR TIRE."
WINSTON CHURCHILL
WAR MEANS PROFIT INVEST YOUR SONS
THE ROYAL BRITISH LEGION
The Poppy Appeal. Always on active service. Please give generously.
Call 0845 845 1945 or visit www.poppy.org.uk

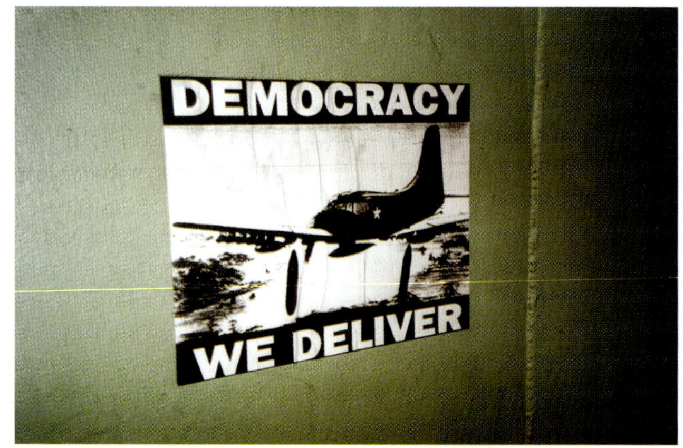
DEMOCRACY
WE DELIVER

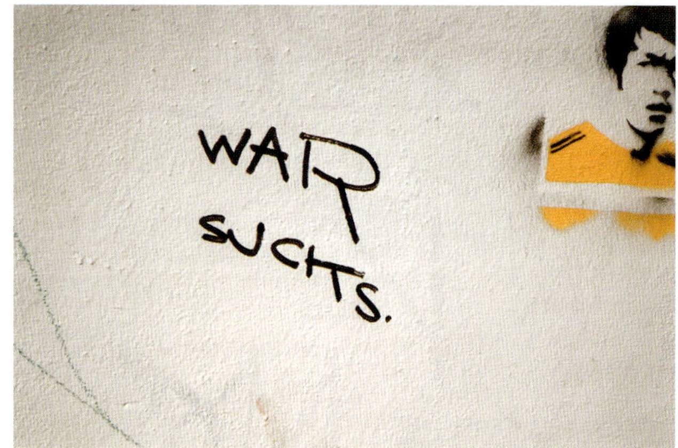
WAR
SUCHTS.

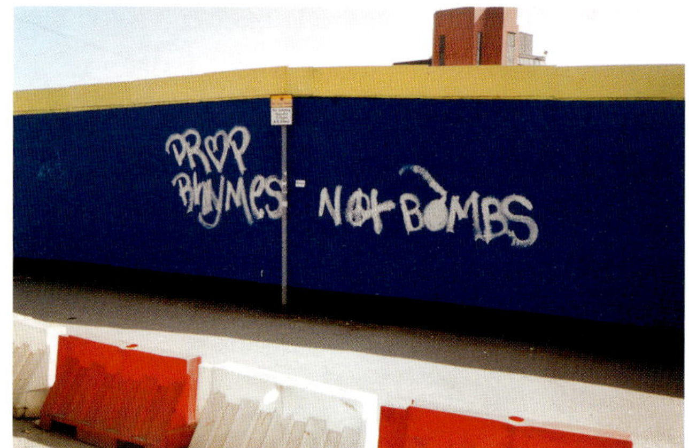
DROP
RHYMES - NOT BOMBS

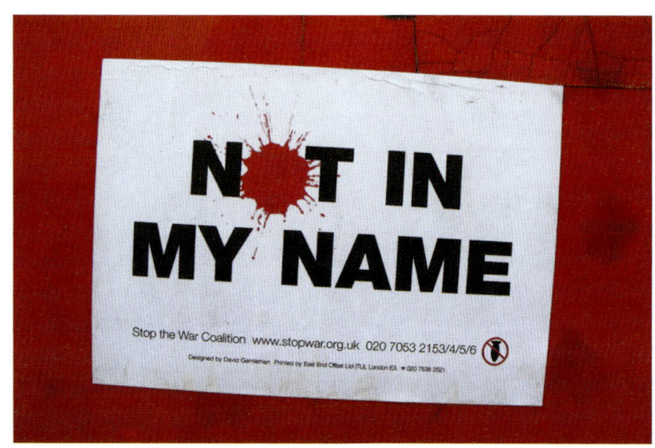
NOT IN
MY NAME
Stop the War Coalition   www.stopwar.org.uk   020 7053 2153/4/5/6
Designed by David Gentleman. Printed by East End Offset Ltd (TU), London E3. ☎ 020 7538 2521

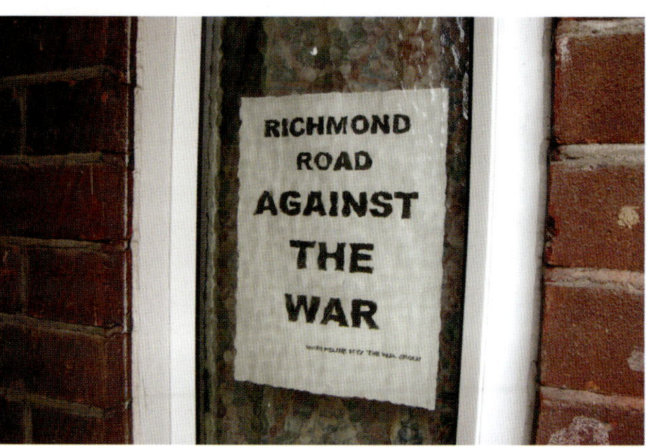
RICHMOND
ROAD
AGAINST
THE
WAR

War...

In the last decade the UK has been involved in:

* Sierra Leone Civil War (2000)
* The 'War on Terror' (2001—Present)
* The Afghanistan War (2001—Present)
* Iraq War and Iraqi insurgency (2003—present)

Earlier conflicts:

* Northern Ireland Troubles (1969-mid 1990s)
* Cod War Confrontation (1975—1976)
* Falklands War (1982)
* The First Gulf War (1990—1991)
* The Bosnian War (1995—1996)
* The Kosovo War (1999)

Source: Wikipedia

Clockwise from top left — 2002: War means profit invest your sons | 2003: Democracy we deliver | 2003: Drop rhymes not bombs | 2008: Richmond Road against the war | 2010: Not in my name (Stop the War Coalition) [www.stopwar.org.uk]) | 2003: War sucks |

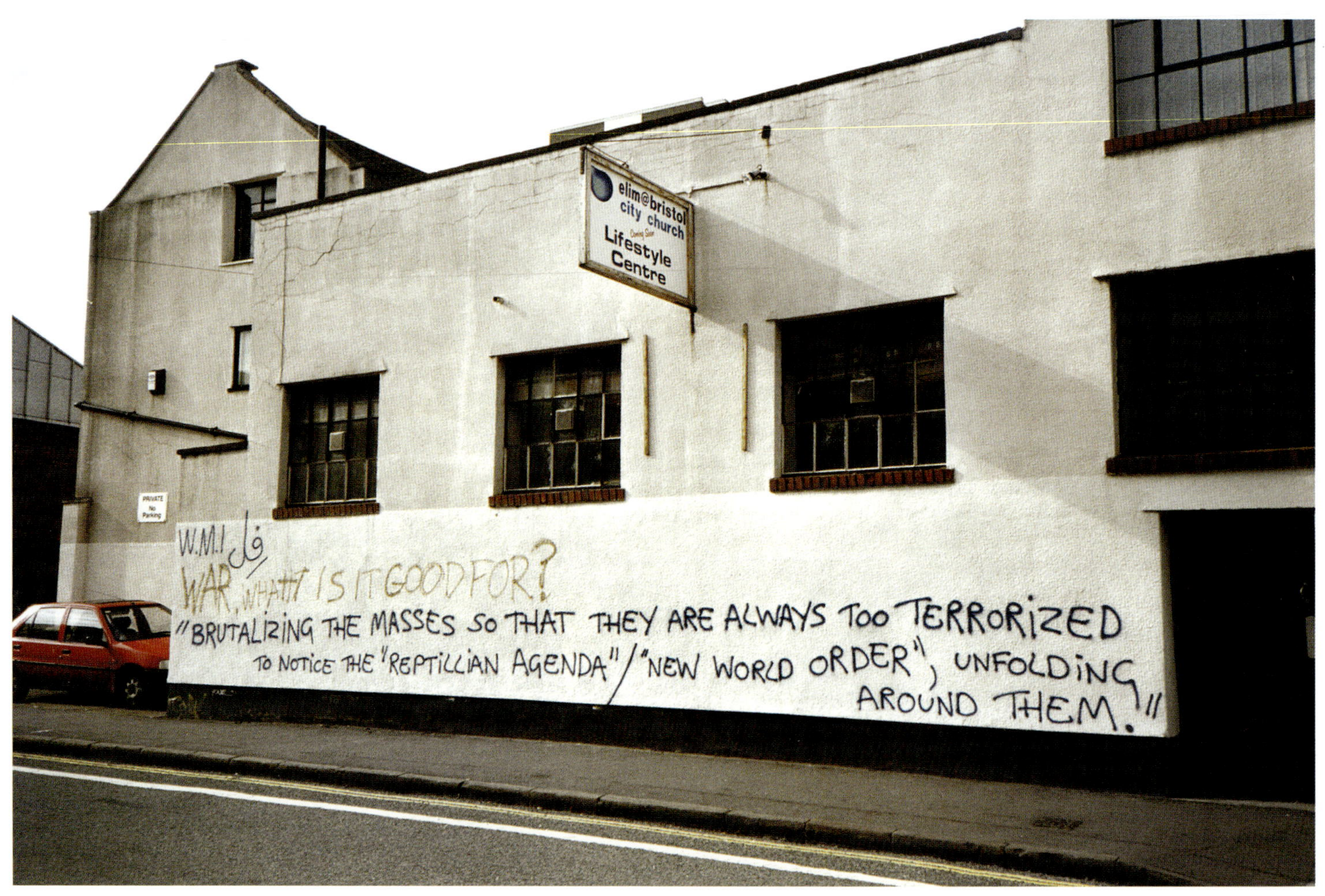

2002: War, what is it good for?

War...

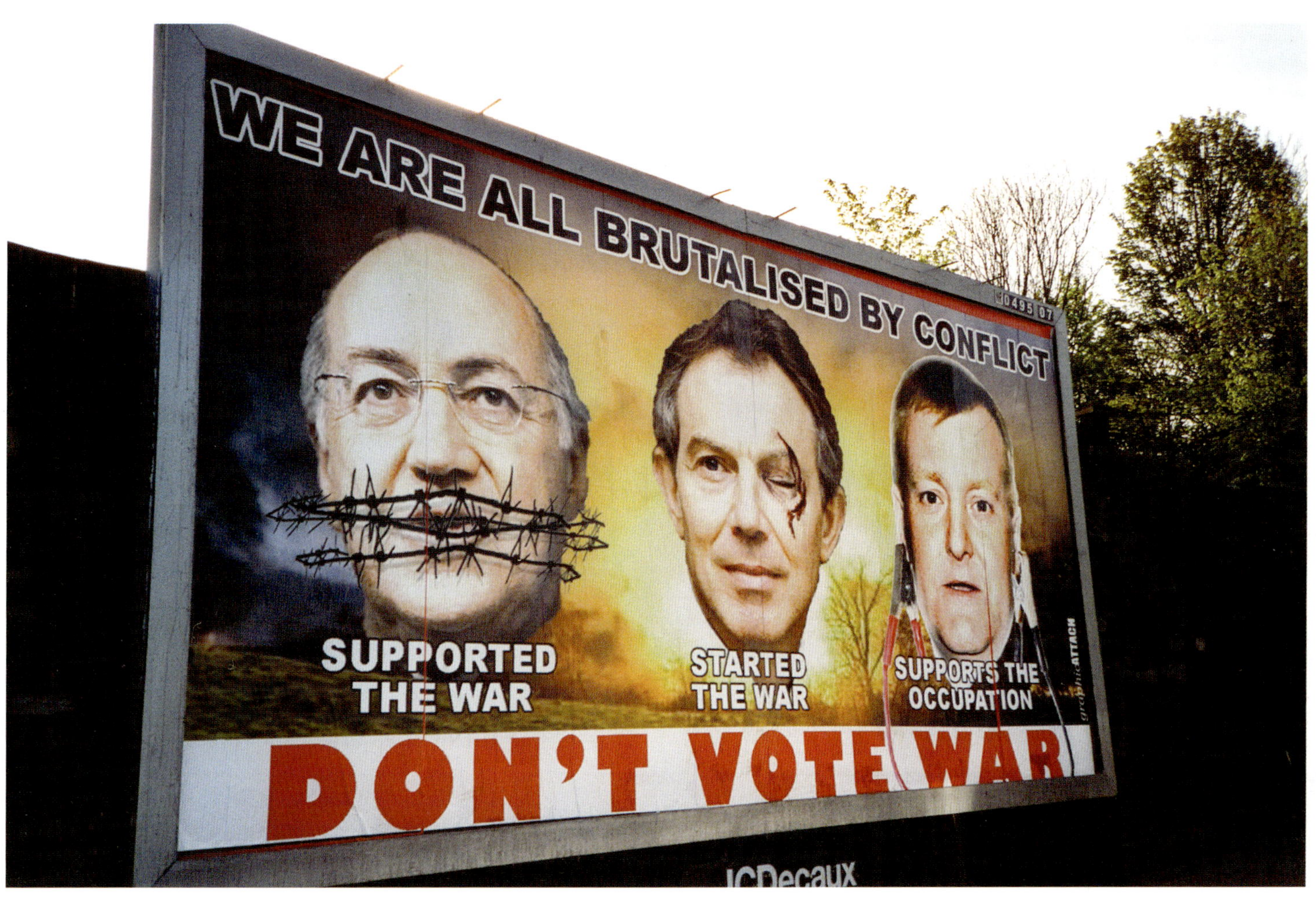

2005: We are all brutalised by conflict – Don't vote war

[This billboard by GraphicAttack shows then Conservative leader Michael Howard, Labour's Tony Blair, and Liberal Democrat Charles Kennedy, two years after the invasion of Iraq]

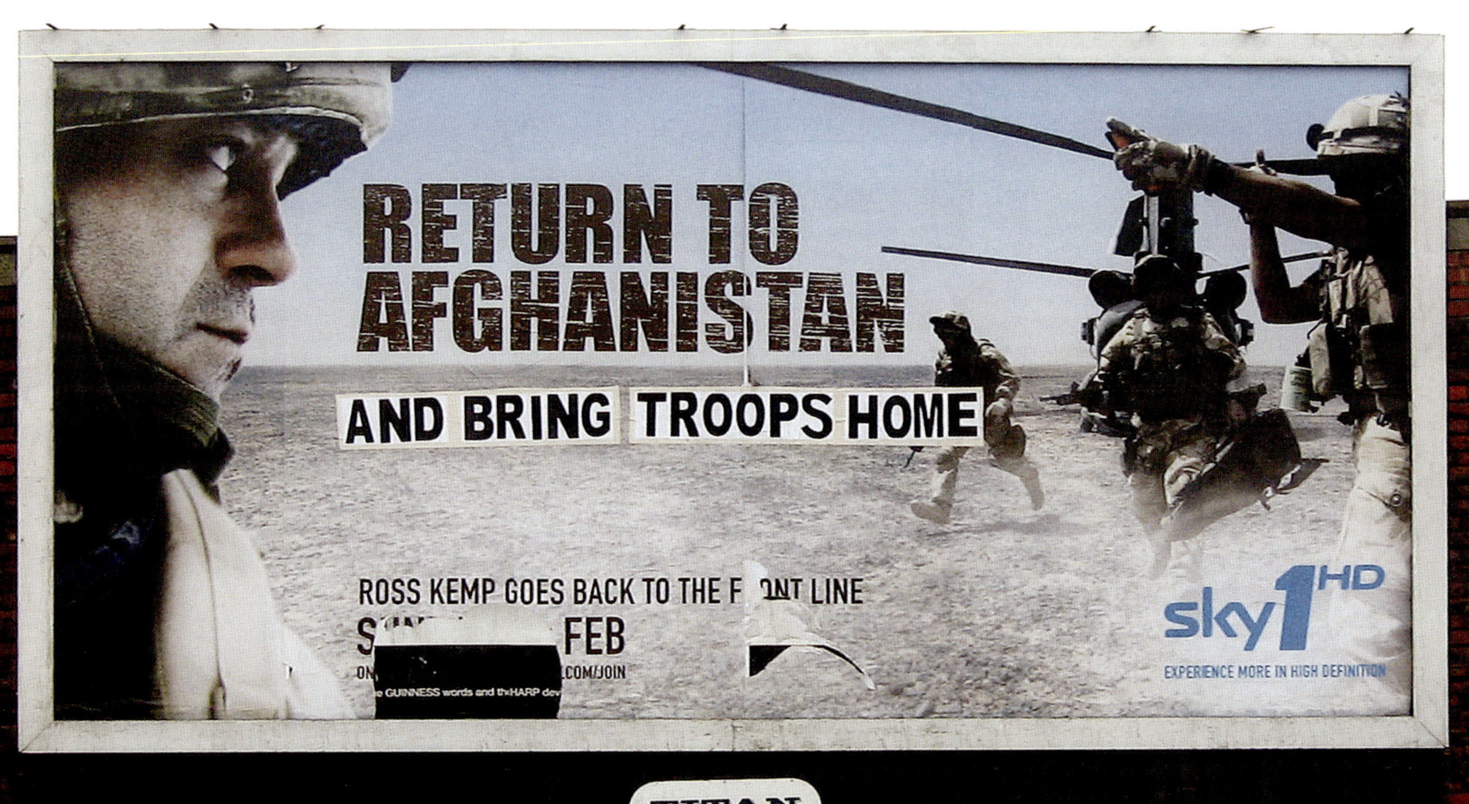

RETURN TO AFGHANISTAN
AND BRING TROOPS HOME
ROSS KEMP GOES BACK TO THE FRONT LINE
SUN FEB
sky1 HD
EXPERIENCE MORE IN HIGH DEFINITION
TITAN

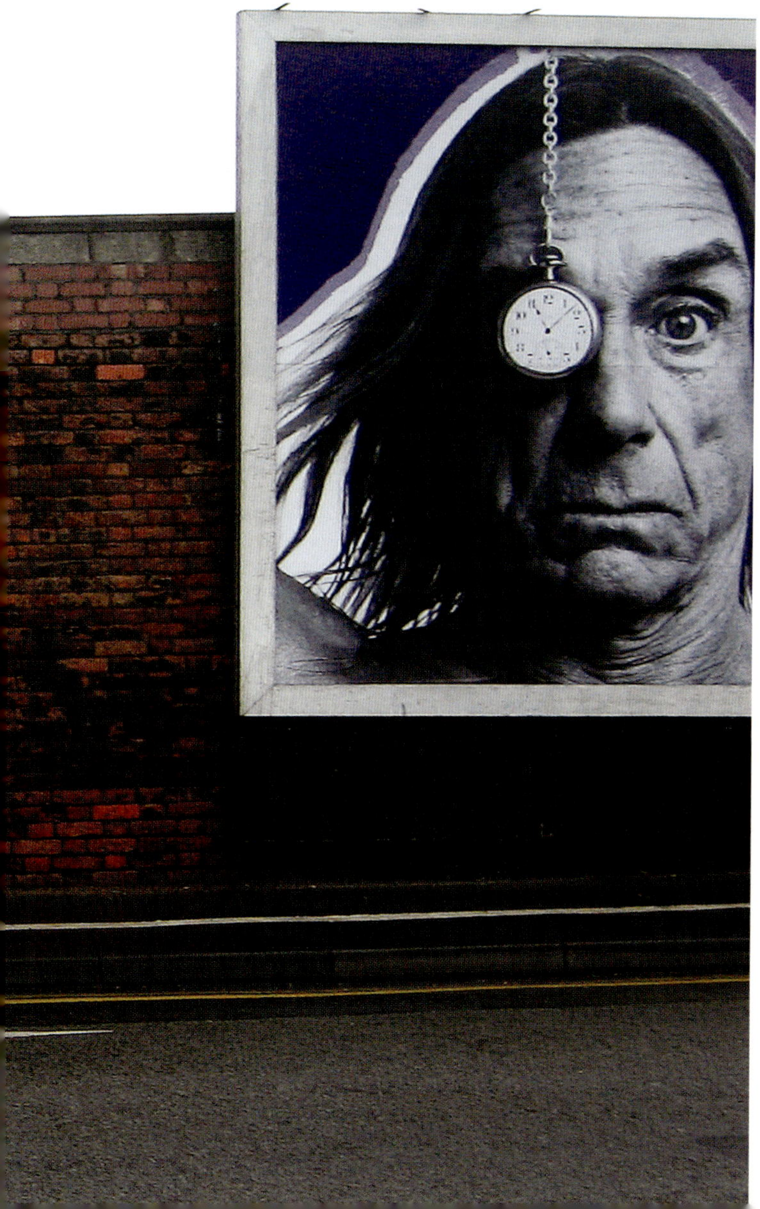

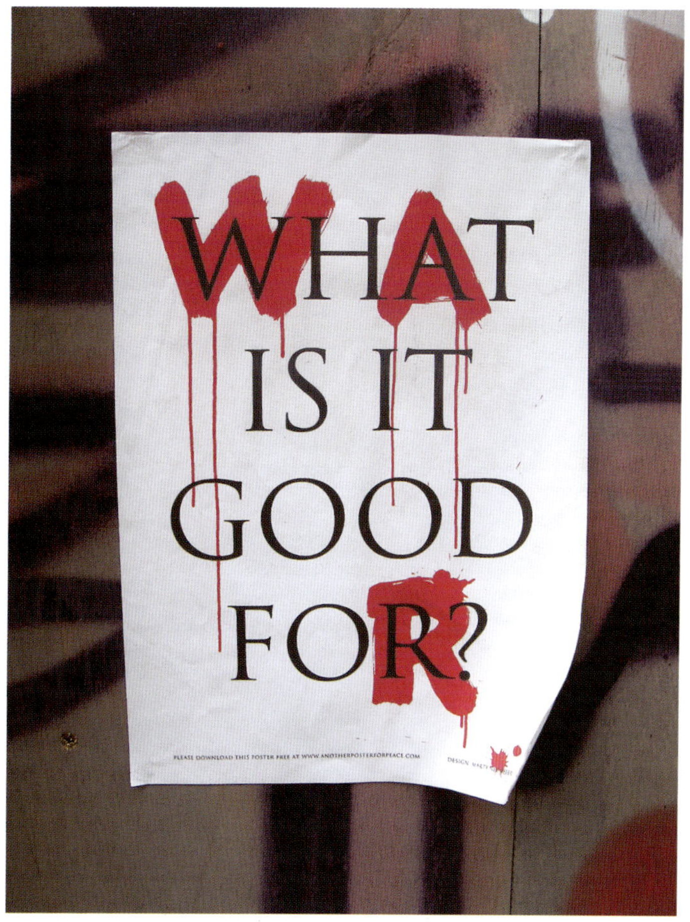

2009: Return to Afghanistan and bring troops home
[British troops have been part of an International
Security Assistance Force in Afghanistan since 2001]

2010: What is it good for?
[www.anotherposterforpeace.com]

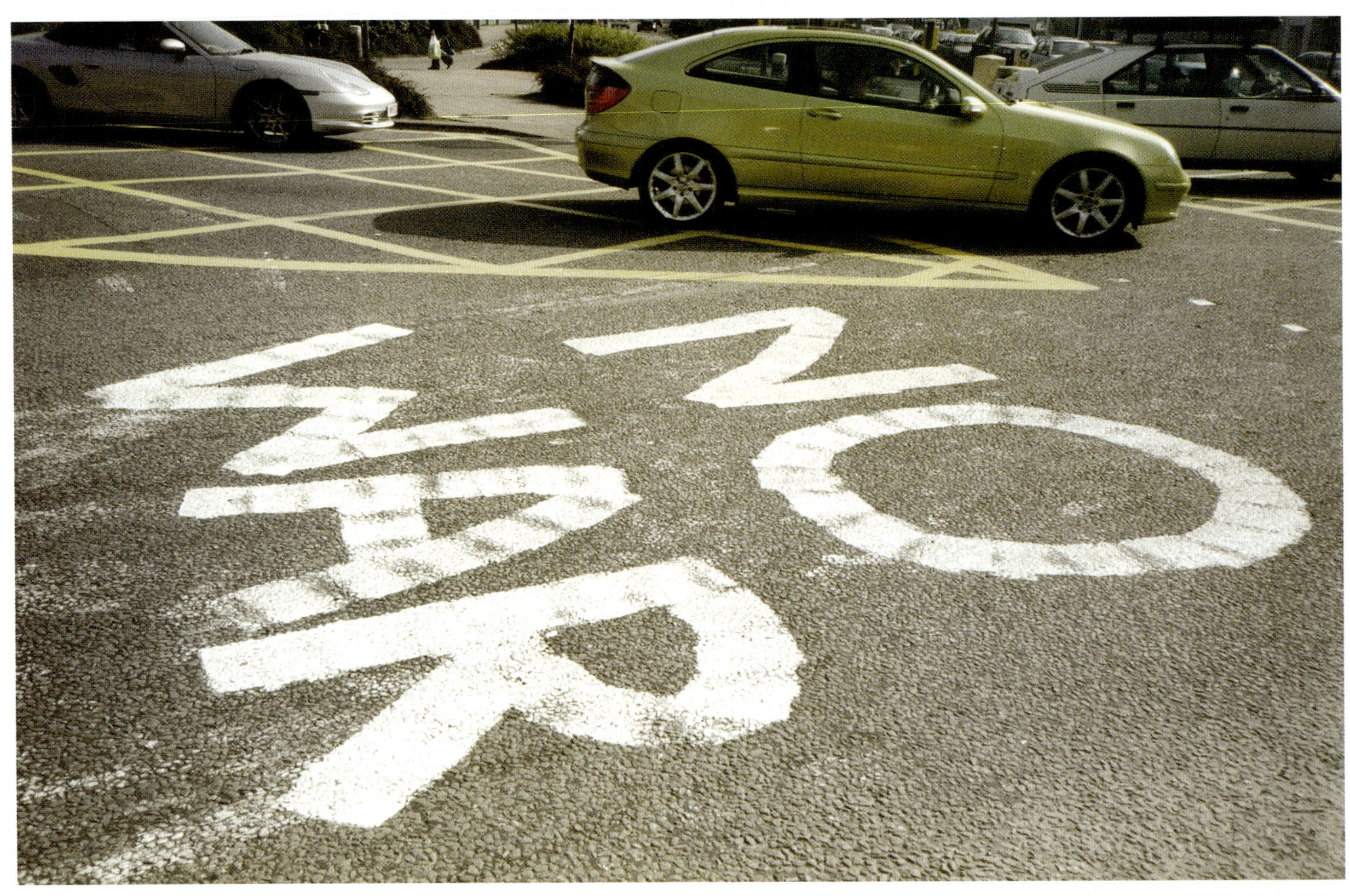

2003: No War

War...

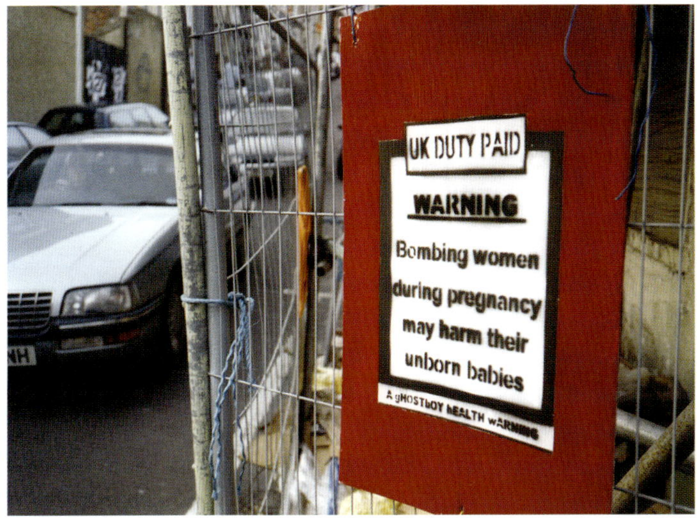

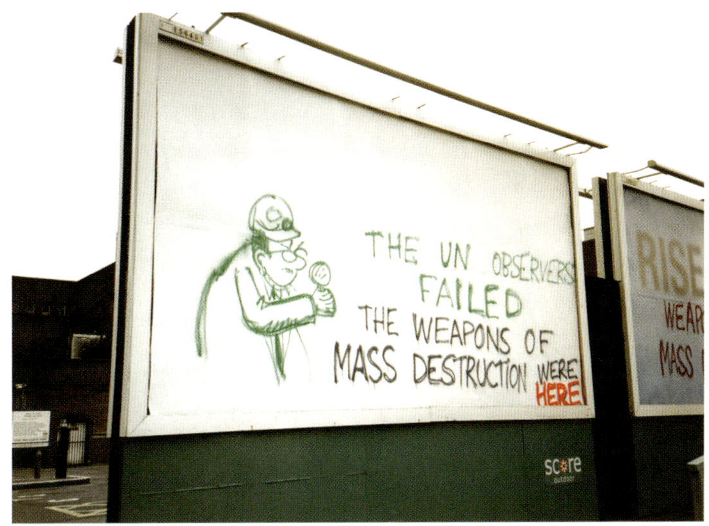

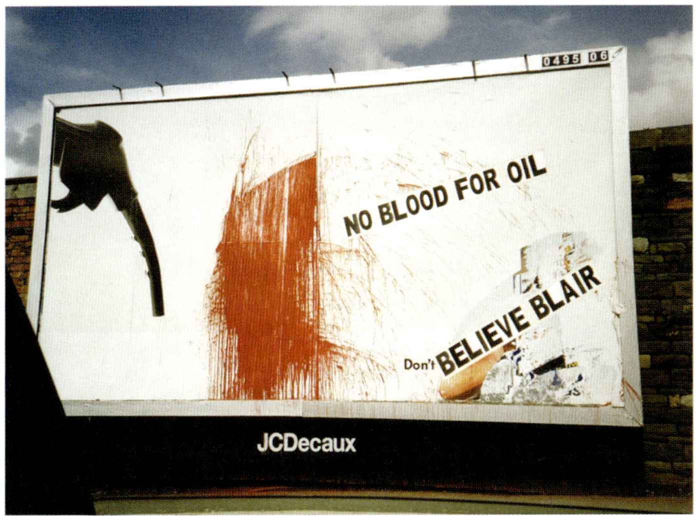

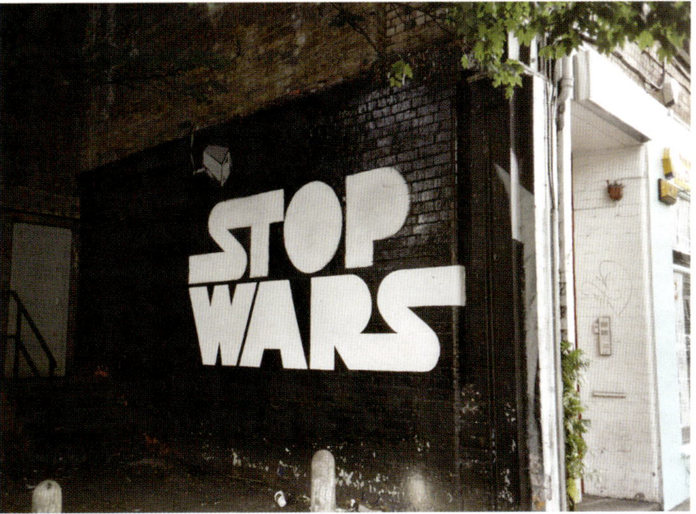

All 2003: Clockwise from top left – Bombing women during pregnancy may harm their unborn babies (a gHOSTbOY health warning) | UN observers failed – the weapons of mass destruction were here | Stop Wars | No blood for oil – don't believe Blair |

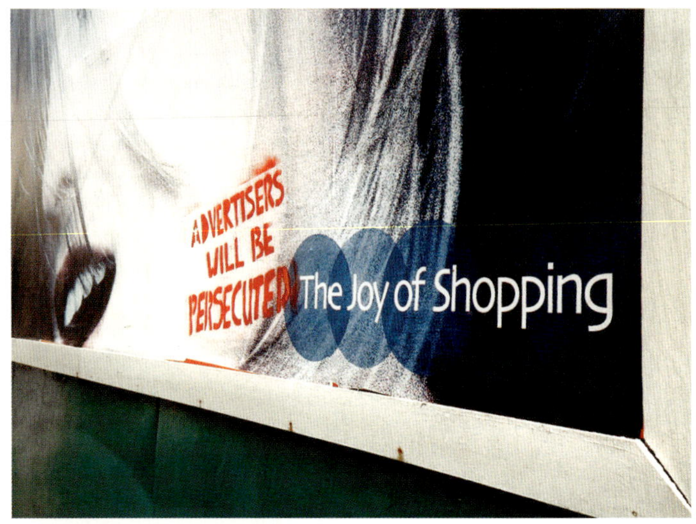

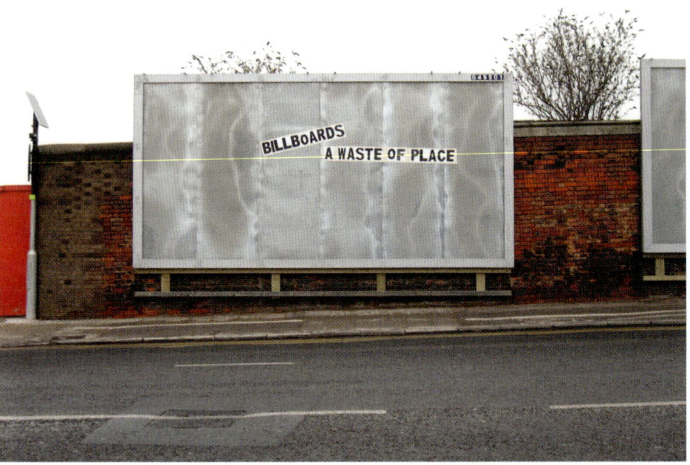

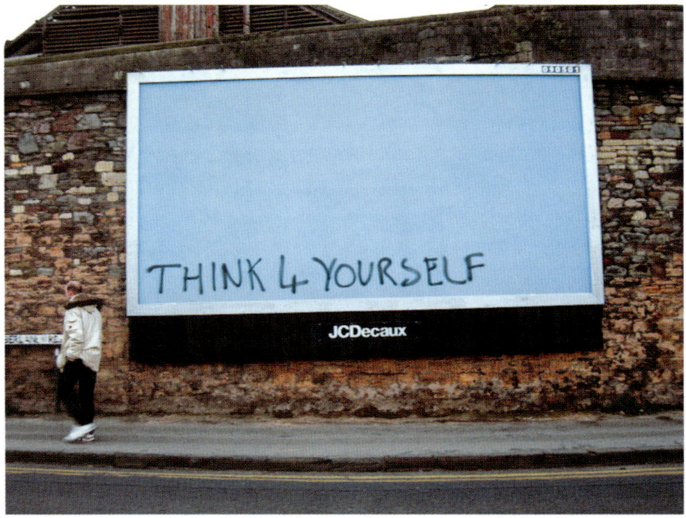

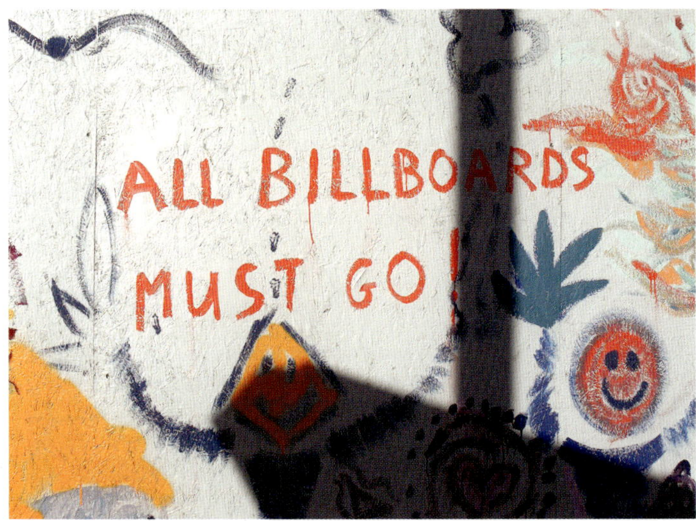

Clockwise from top left – 2002: Advertisers will be persecuted | 2007: Billboards a waste of place | 2005: All billboards must go | 2008: Think 4 yourself |

Billboards and advertising...

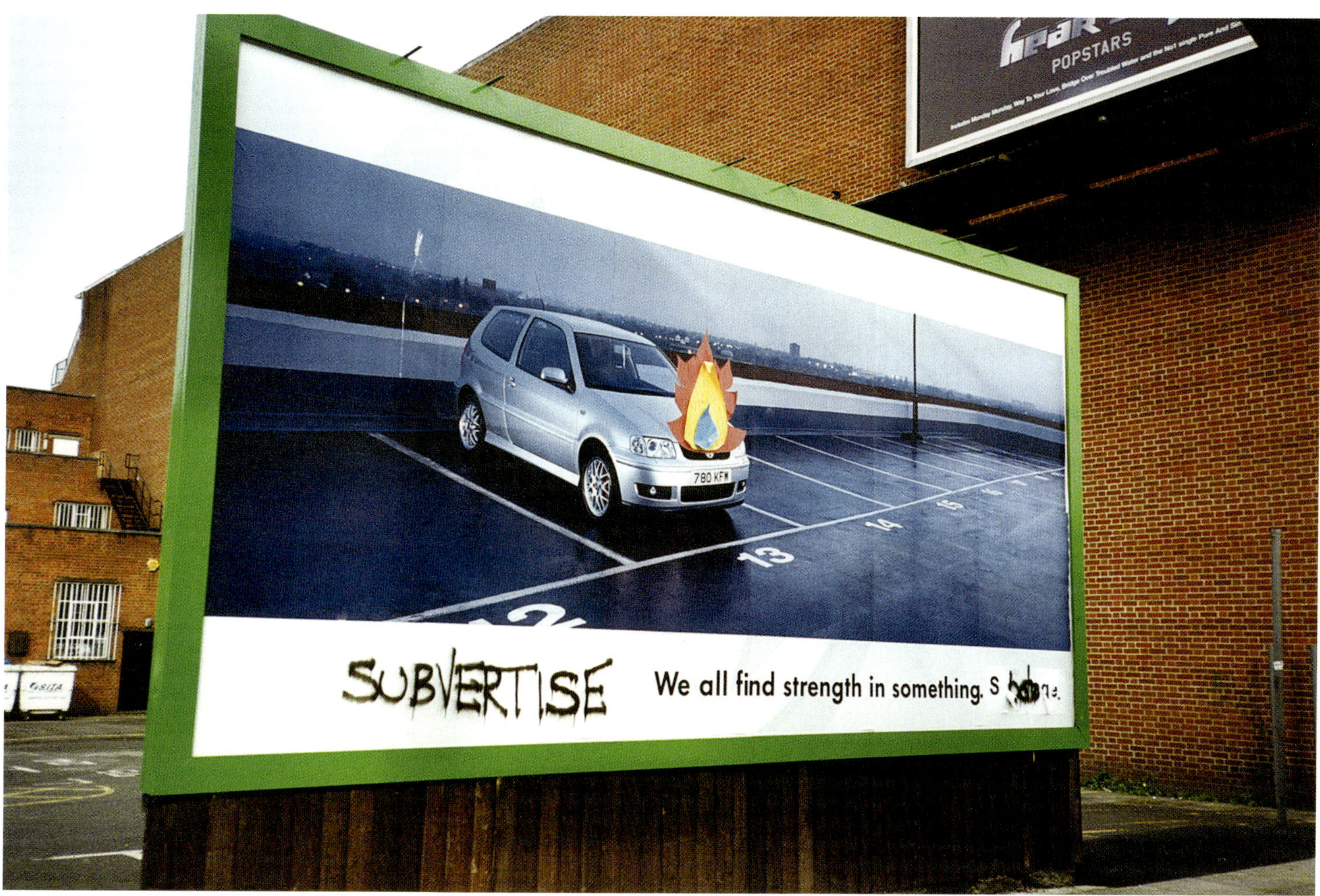

2001: Subvertise

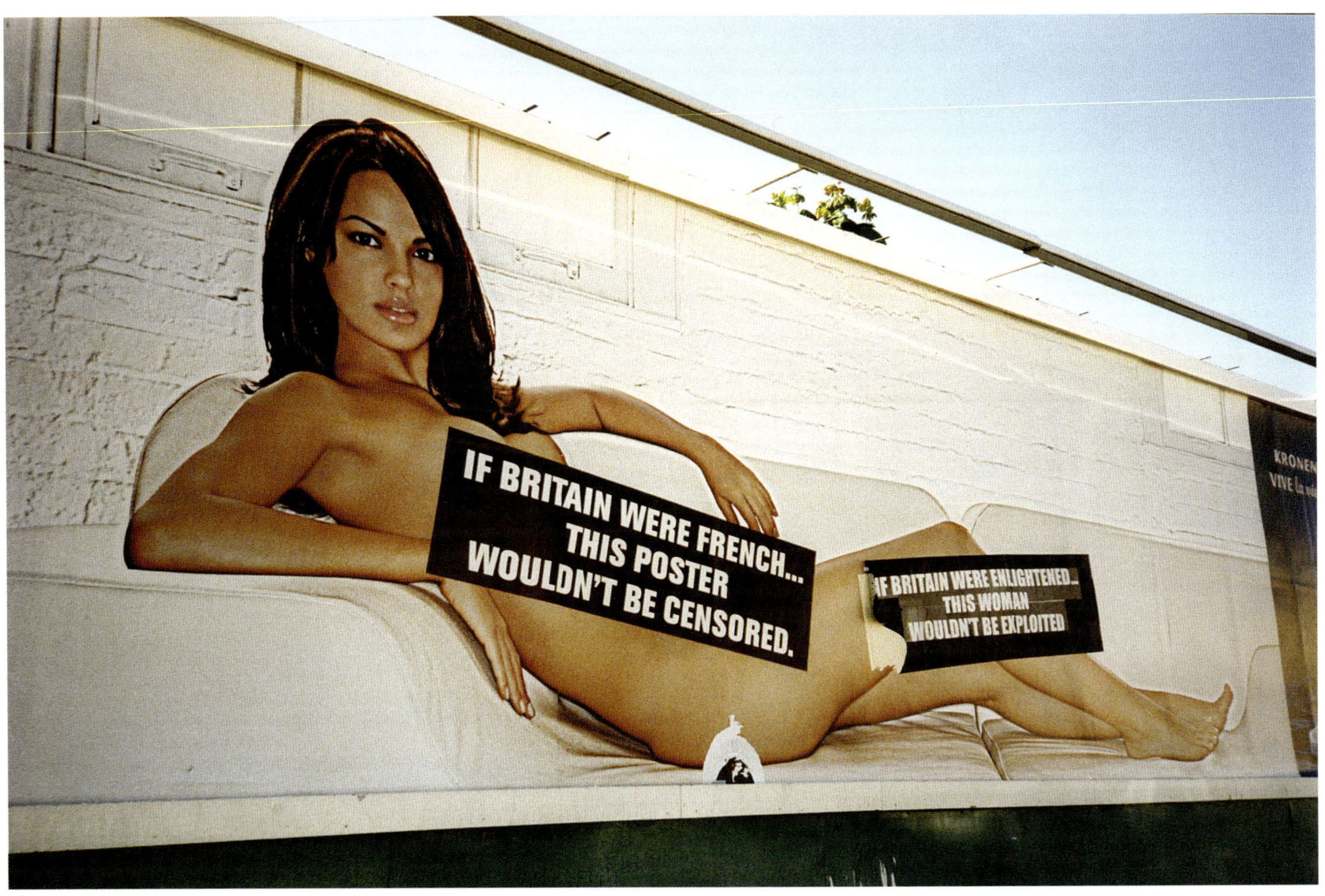

2002: If Britain were enlightened... this woman wouldn't be exploited

Billboards and advertising...

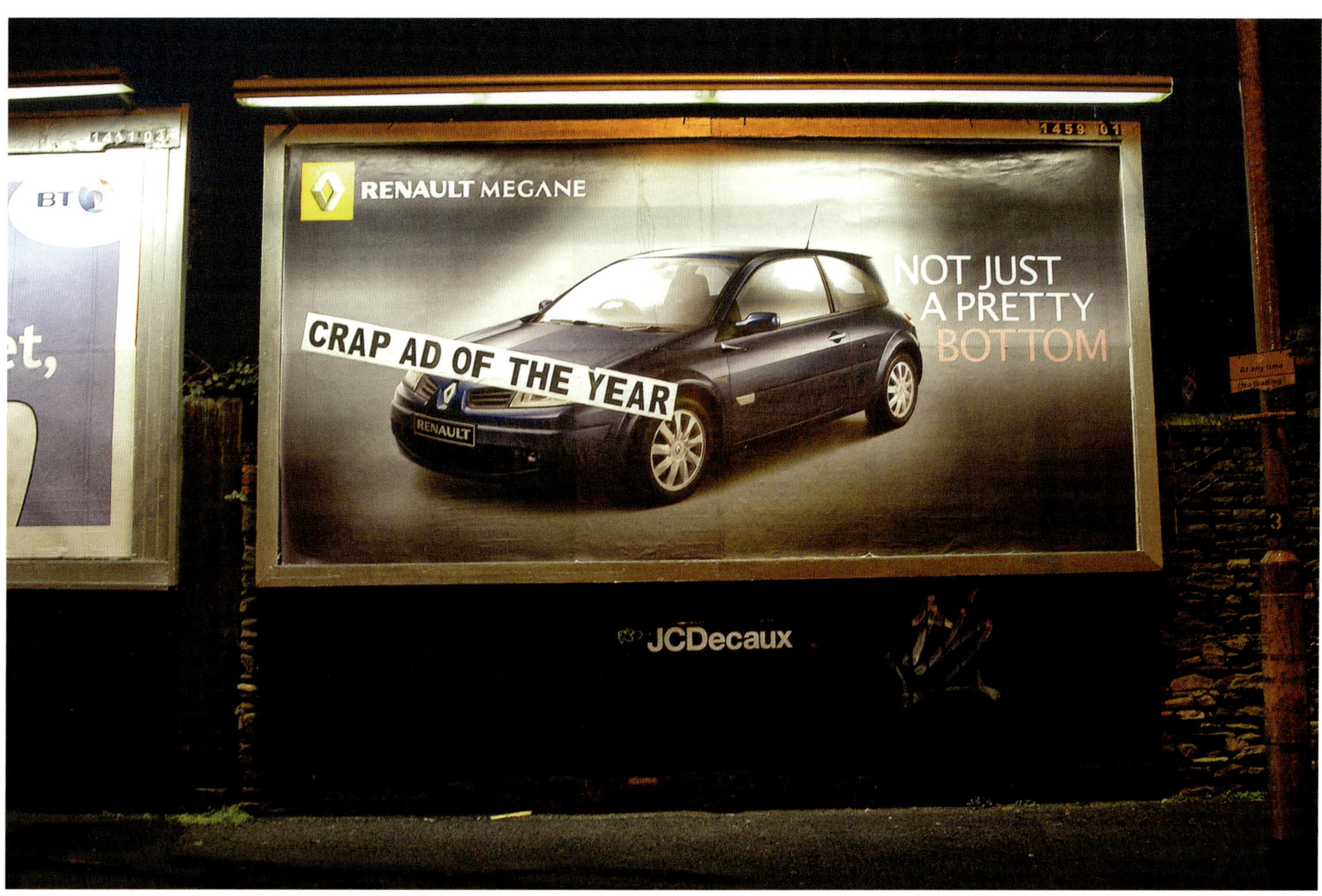

2006: Crap ad of the year

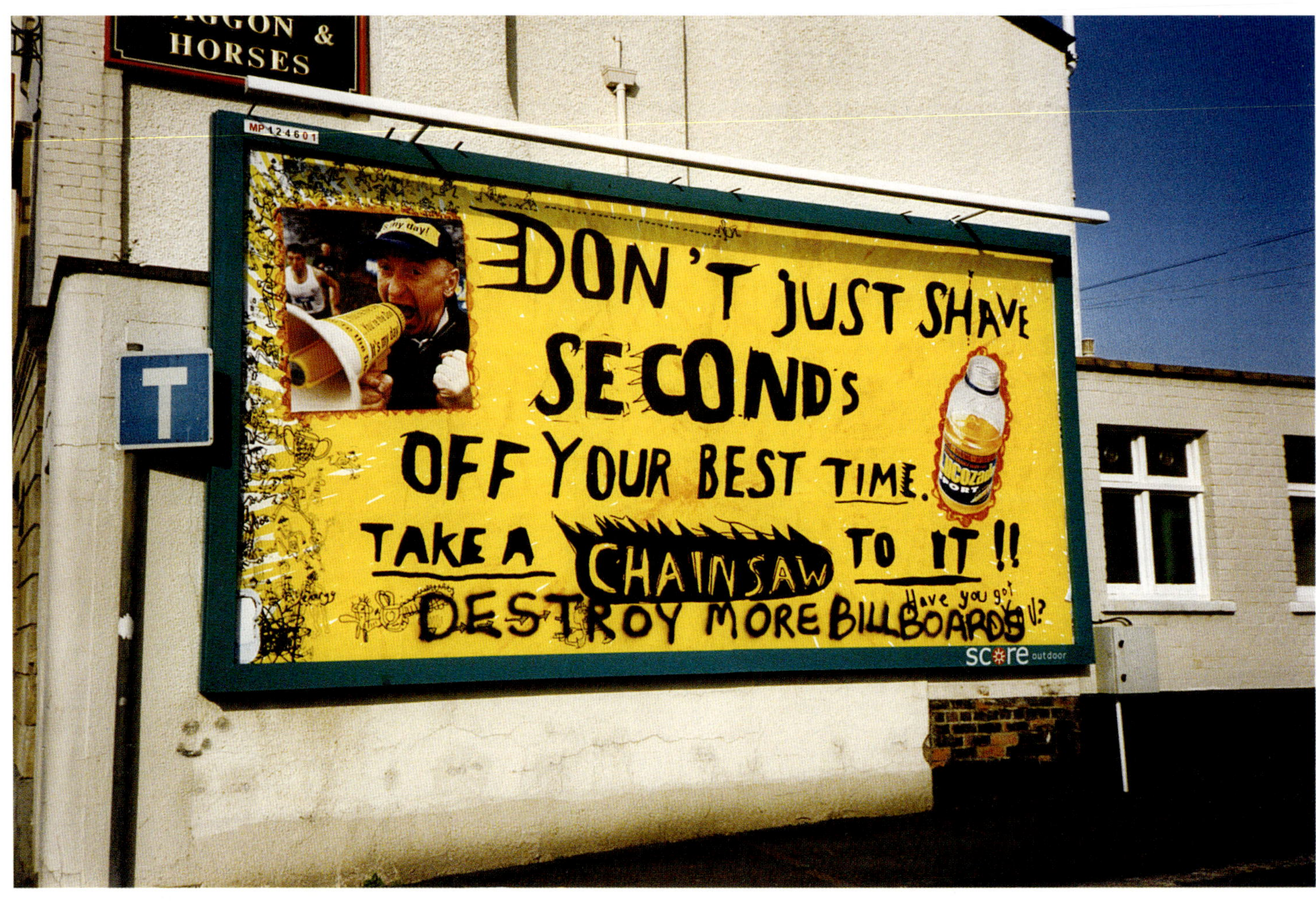

2001: Destroy more billboards

Billboards and advertising...

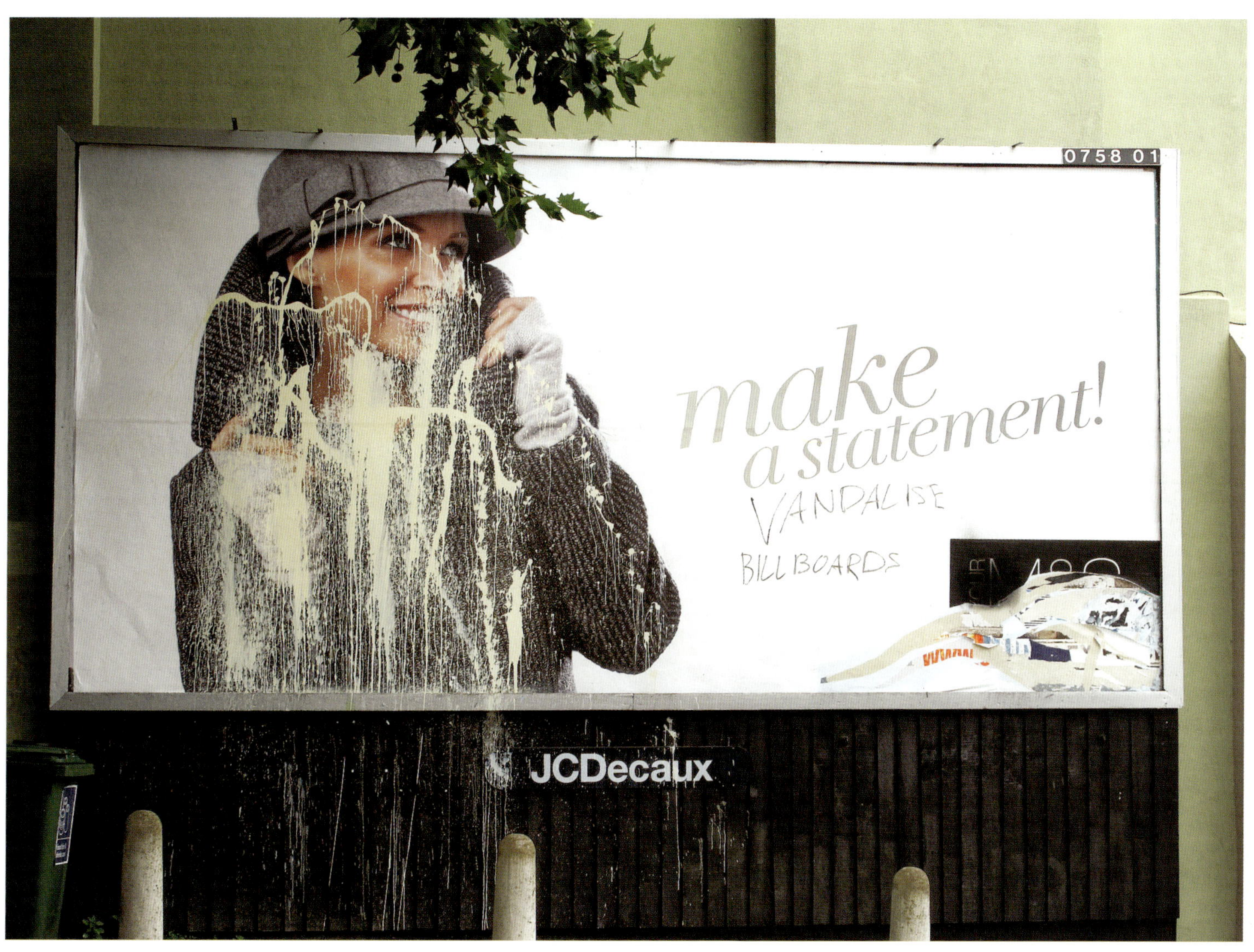

2010: Make a statement! Vandalise billboards

Next page – 2008: Imagine a world without billboards

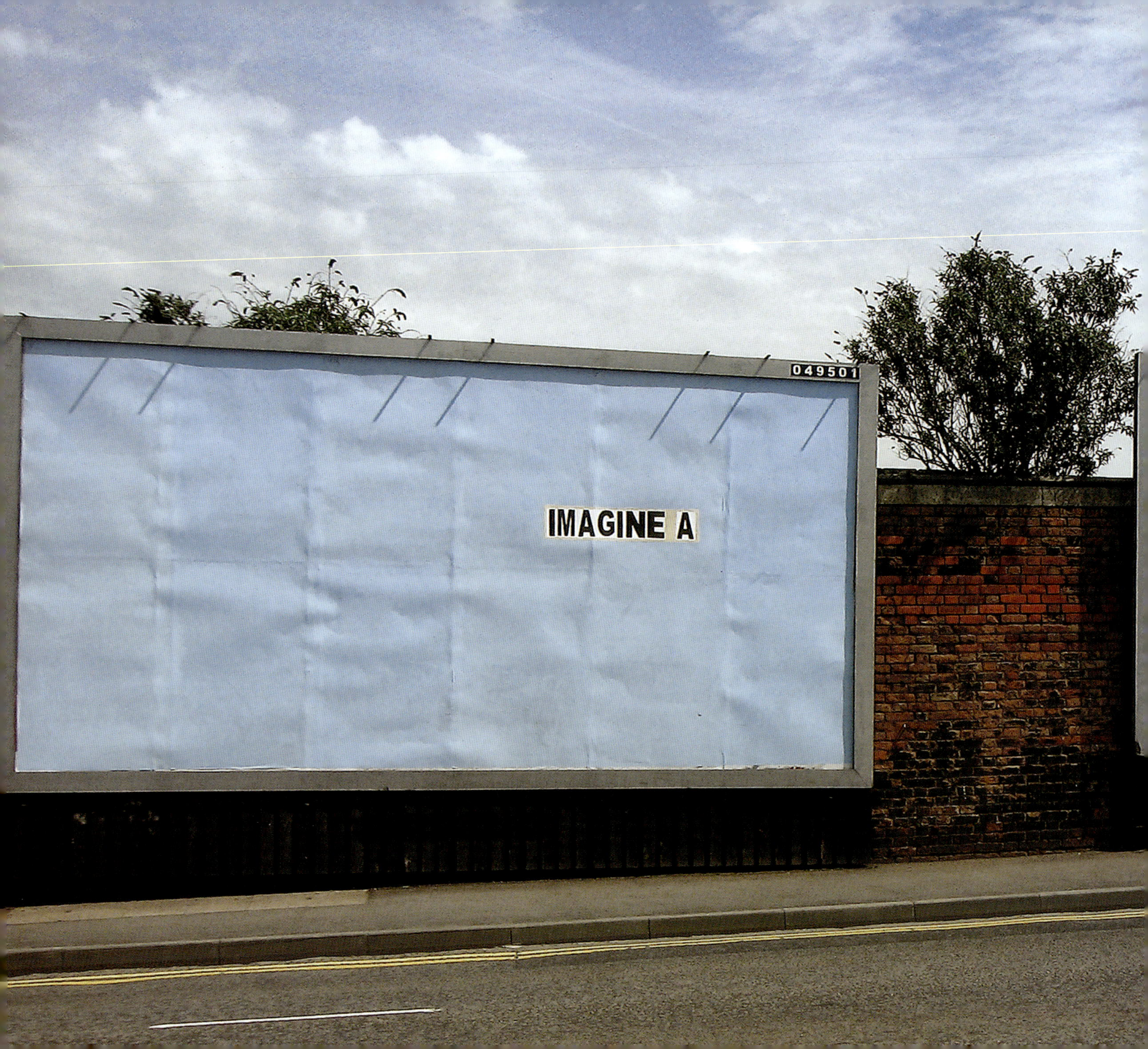

049501
IMAGINE A

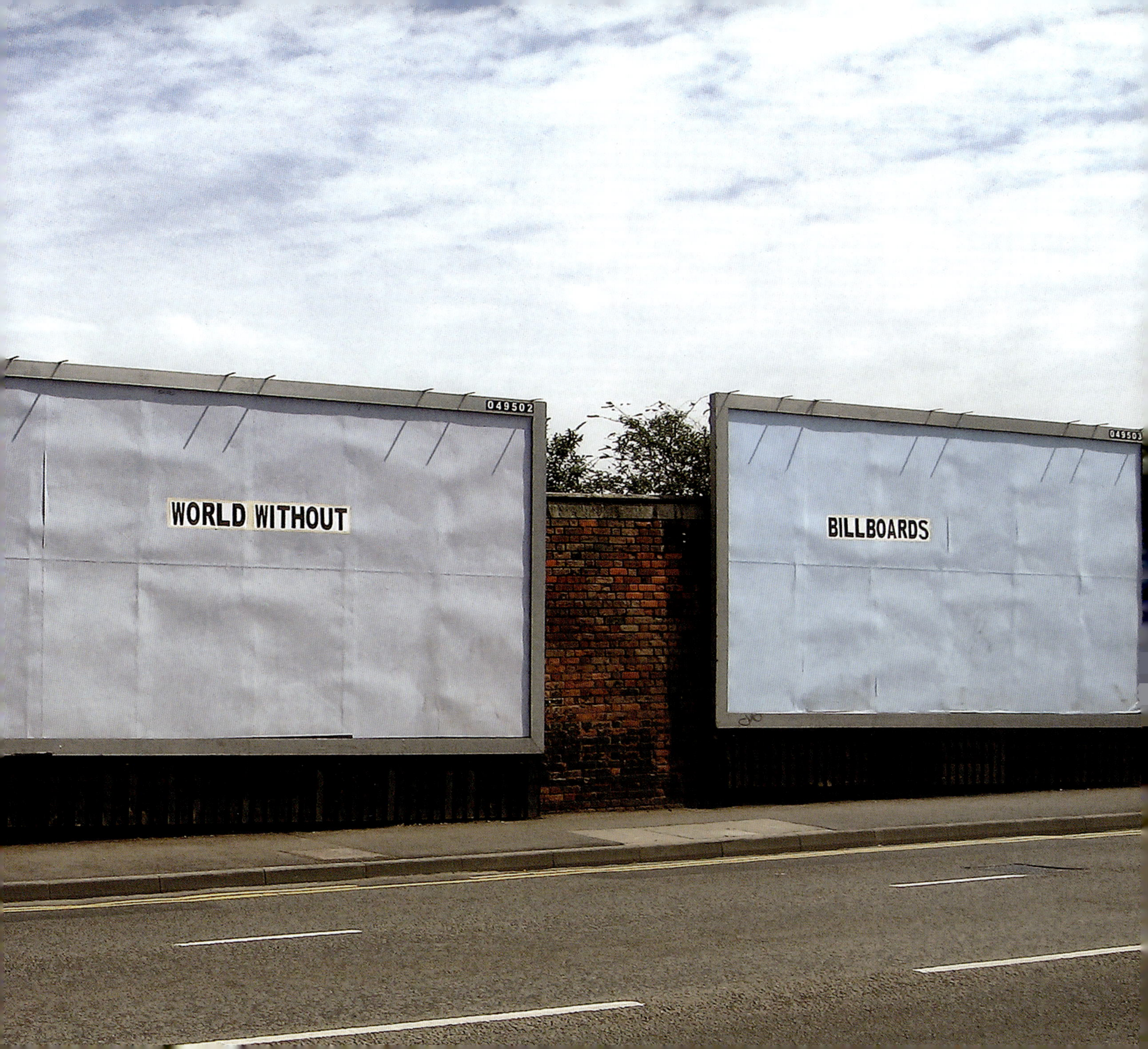
WORLD WITHOUT
BILLBOARDS
049502
049503

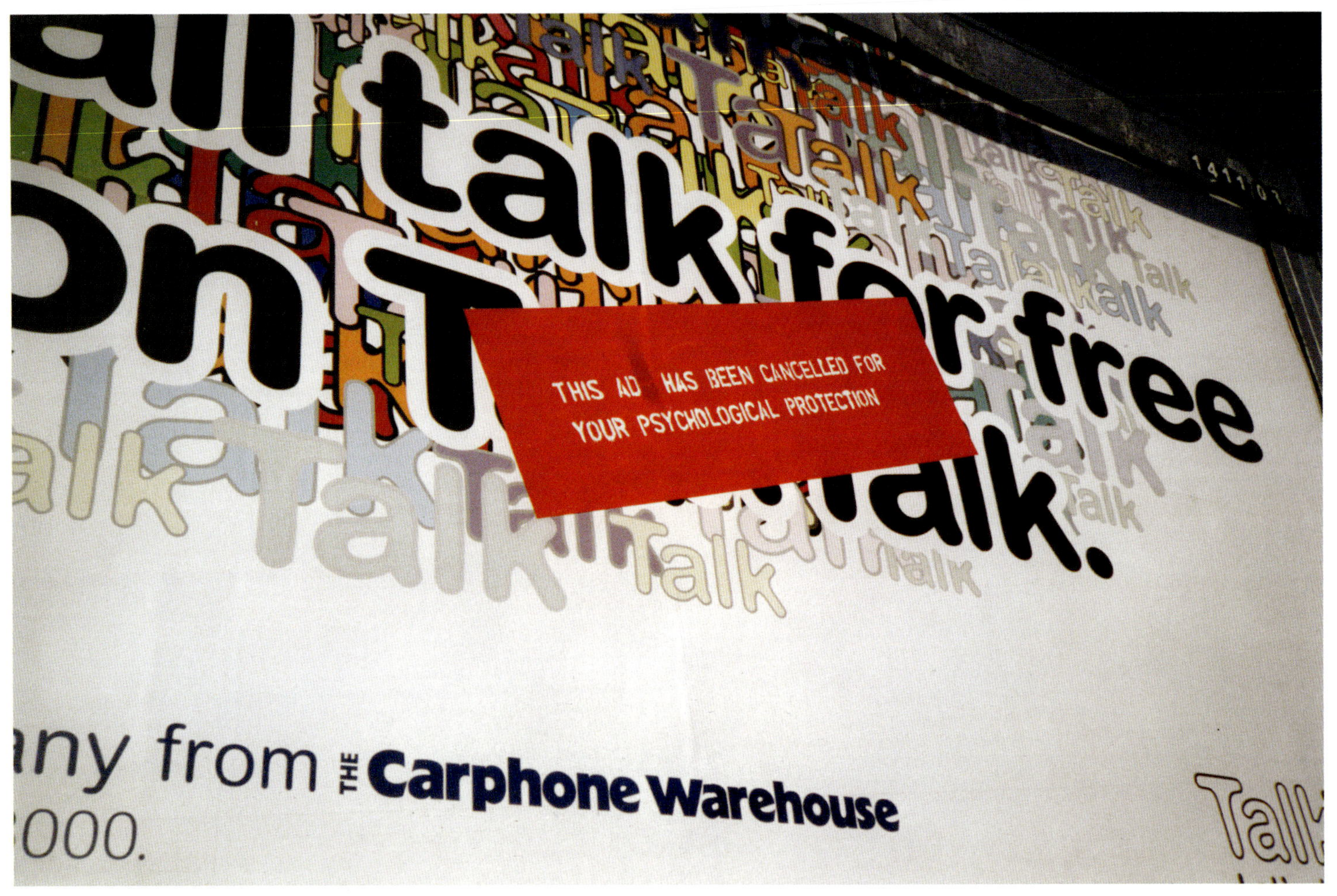

2004: This ad has been cancelled for your psychological protection

Billboards and advertising...

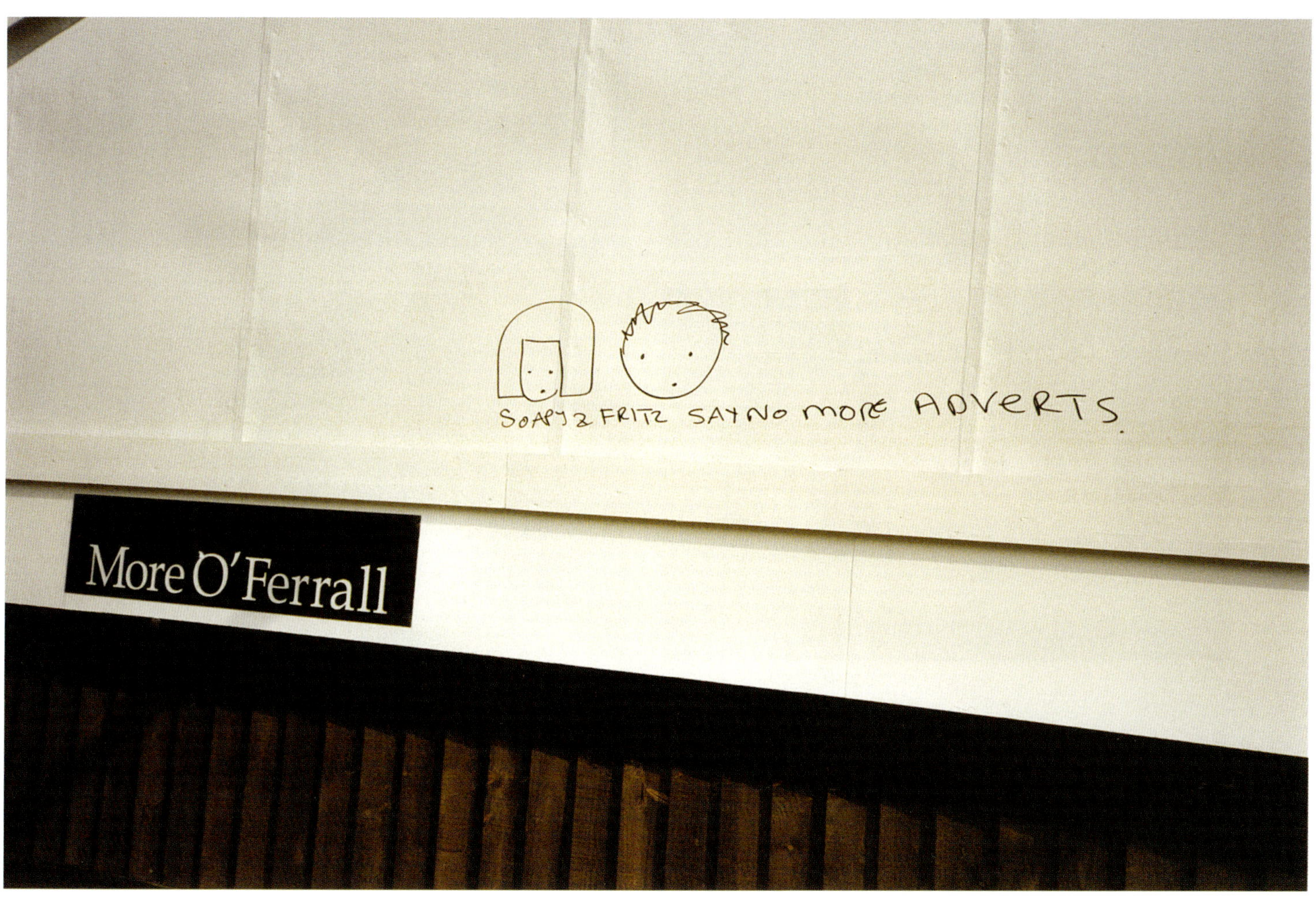

2001: Soapy & Fritz say no more adverts

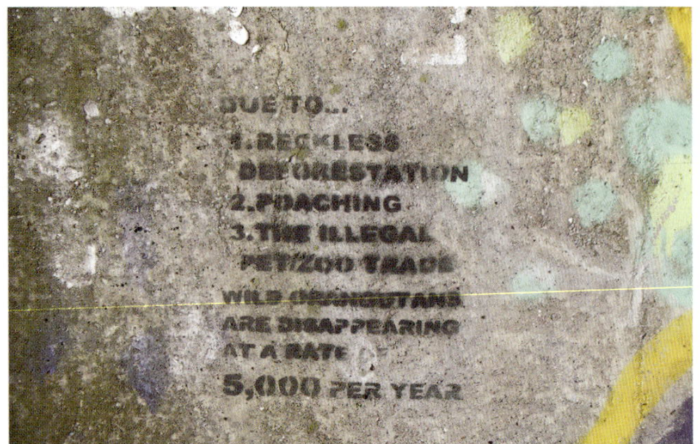
DUE TO...
1. RECKLESS
   DEFORESTATION
2. POACHING
3. THE ILLEGAL
   PET/ZOO TRADE
WILD ORANGUTANS
ARE DISAPPEARING
AT A RATE
5,000 PER YEAR

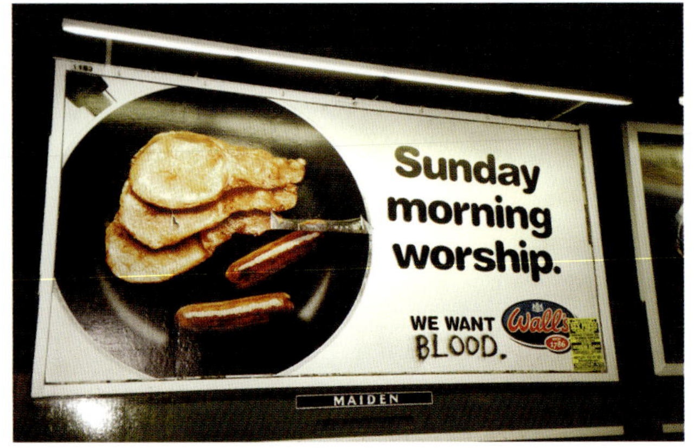
Sunday
morning
worship.
WE WANT
BLOOD.
Wall's
MAIDEN

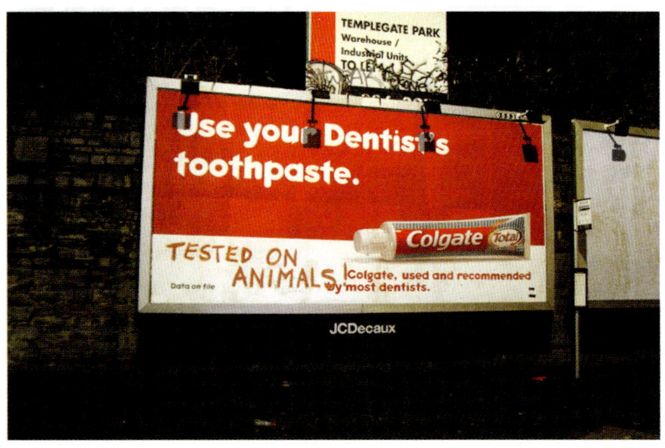
TEMPLEGATE PARK
Warehouse /
Industrial Units
TO LET
Use your Dentist's
toothpaste.
TESTED ON
ANIMALS!
Colgate Total
Data on file
Colgate, used and recommended
by most dentists.
JCDecaux

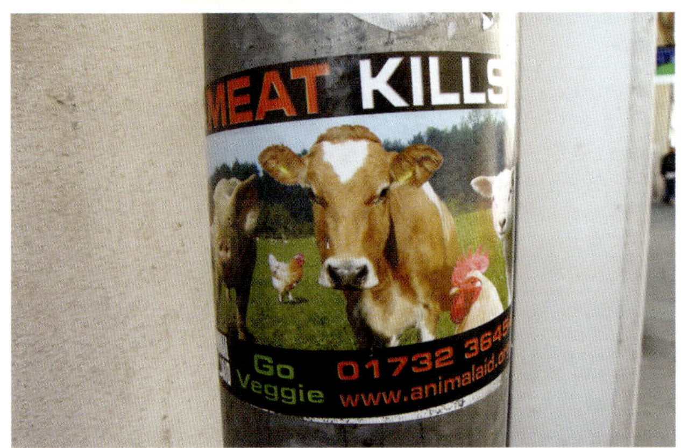
MEAT KILLS
Go
Veggie
01732 3645
www.animalaid.or

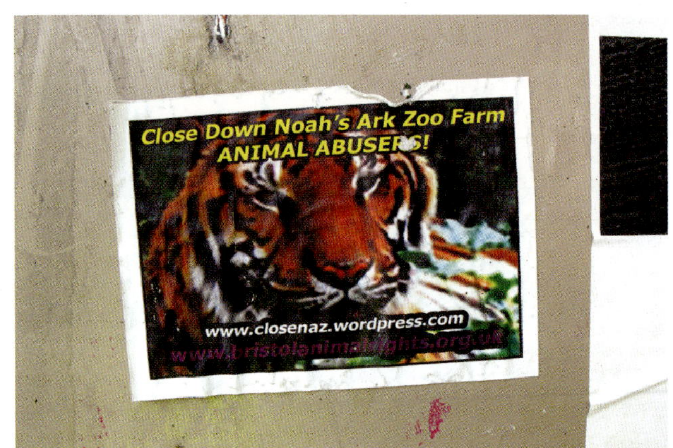
Close Down Noah's Ark Zoo Farm
ANIMAL ABUSERS!
www.closenaz.wordpress.com
www.bristolanimalrights.org.uk

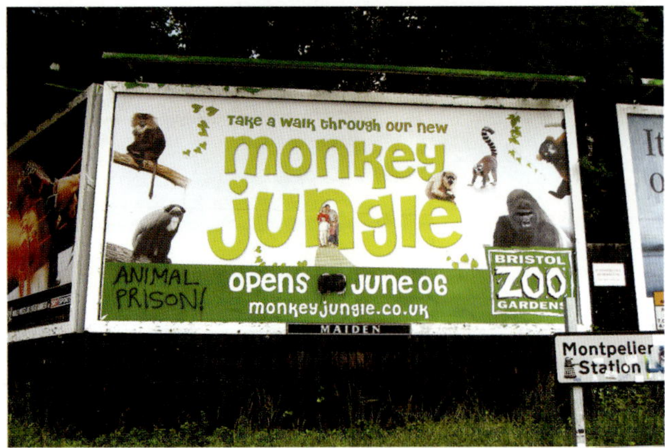
take a walk through our new
monkey
jungle
ANIMAL
PRISON!
opens   JUNE 06
monkeyjungle.co.uk
BRISTOL
ZOO
GARDENS
MAIDEN
Montpelier
Station

Animals...

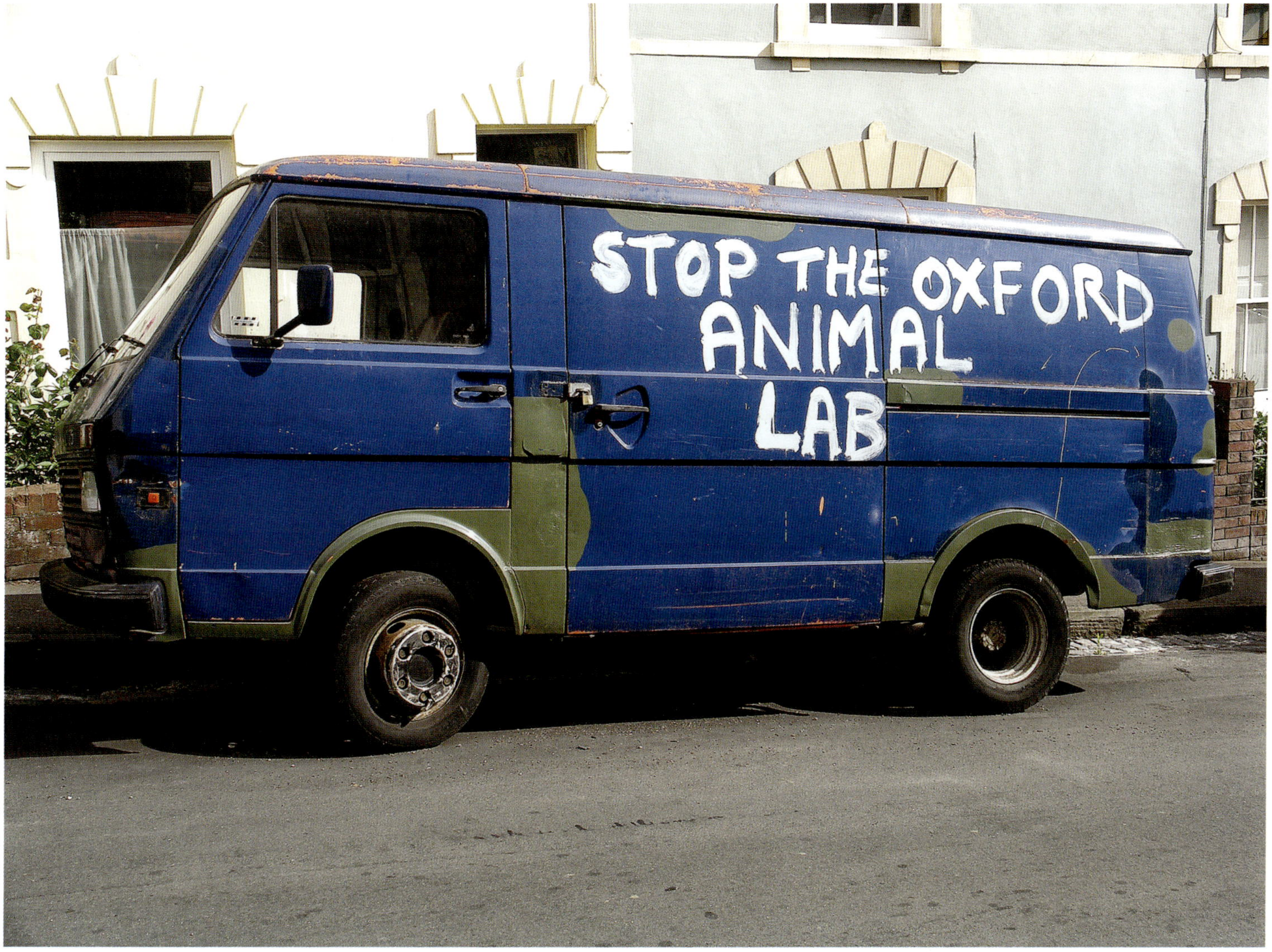

2006: Stop the Oxford animal lab

Previous page. Clockwise from top left – 2007: Due to reckless deforestation | 2002: Sunday morning worship we want blood | 2009: Meat kills. Go veggie [www.animalaid.org.uk] | 2006: Monkey jungle animal prison | 2010: Close down Noah's Ark Zoo Farm [www.closenaz.wordpress.com, www.bristolanimalrights.org.uk. This zoo teaches a creationist version of history] | 2006: Colgate. Tested on animals |

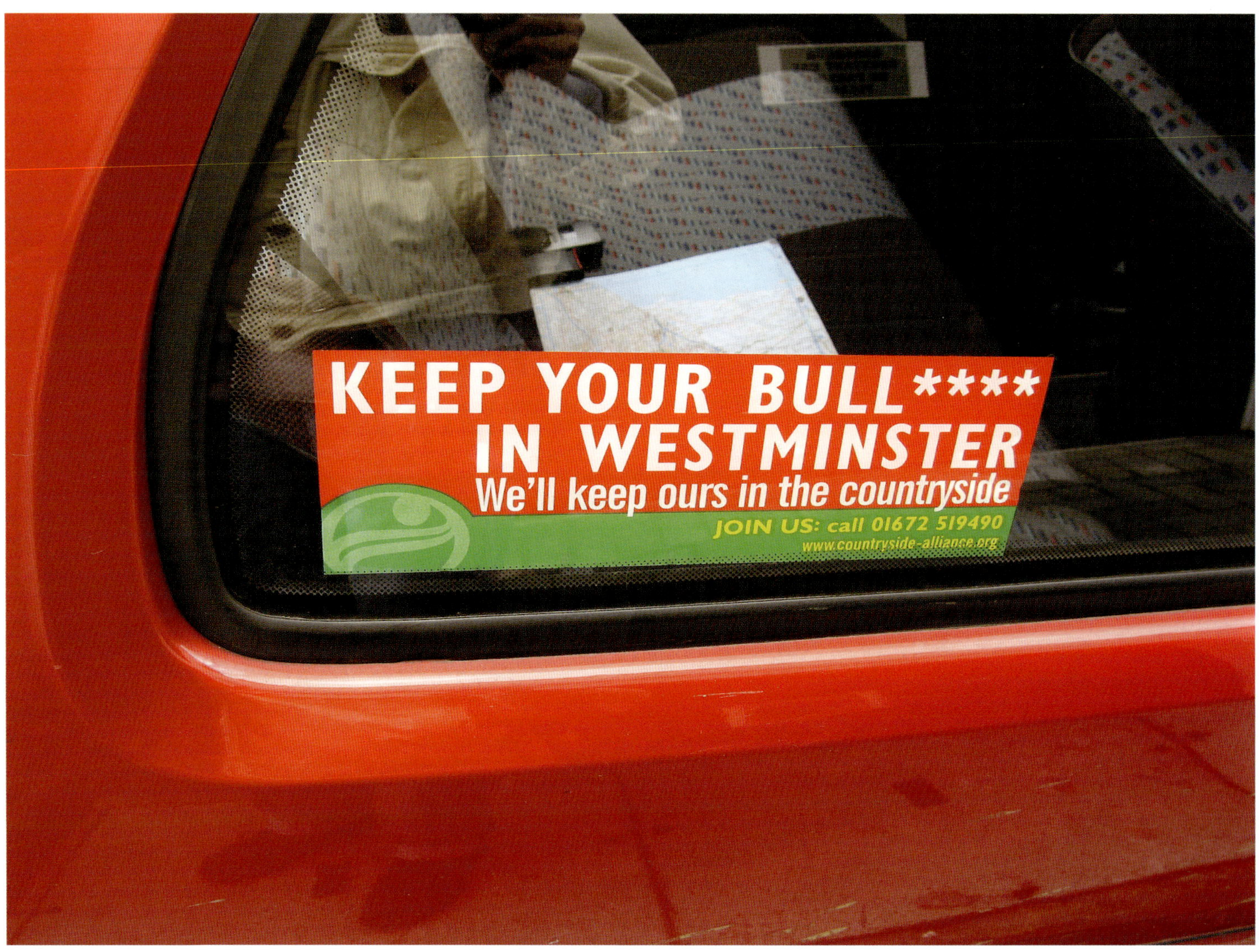

2006: Keep your bull**** in Westminster [www.countryside-alliance.org]

Animals...

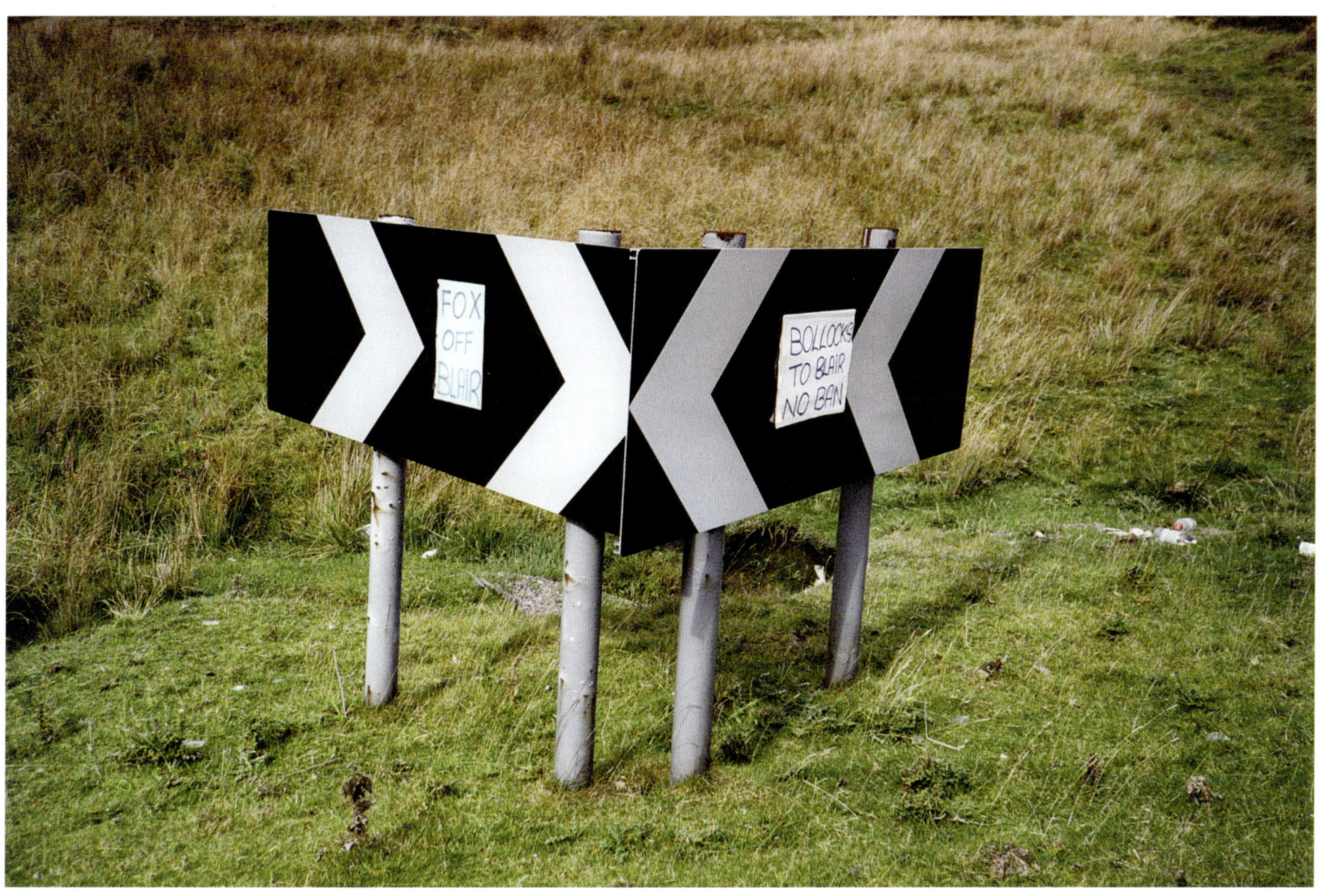

2004: Fox off Blair. Bollocks to Blair, No ban

[Location: South Wales valleys at the height of the debate on banning fox-hunting. Later in 2004 the ban became law]

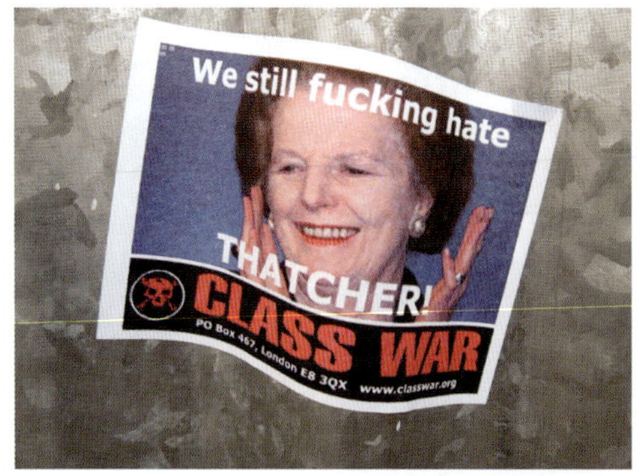

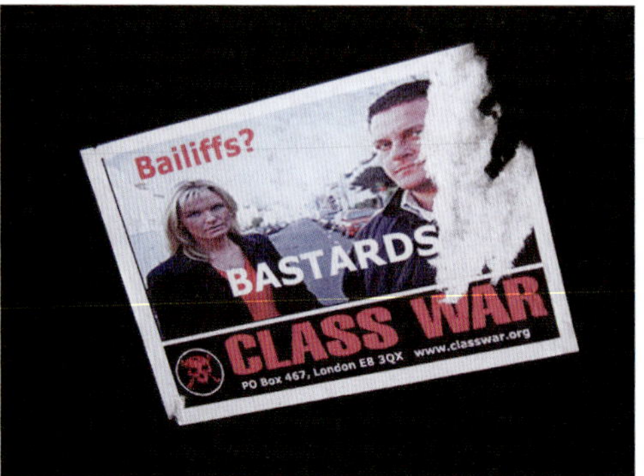

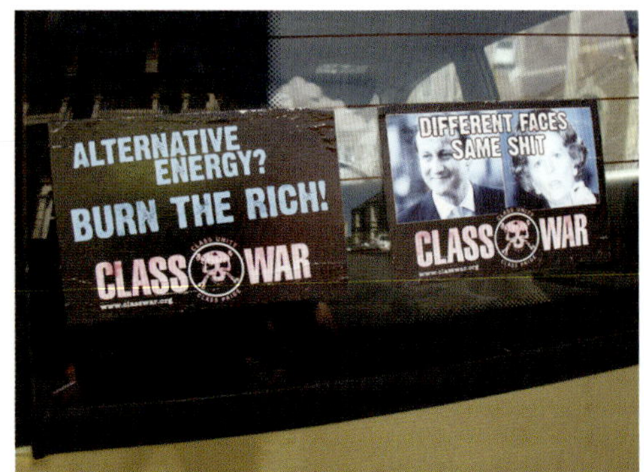

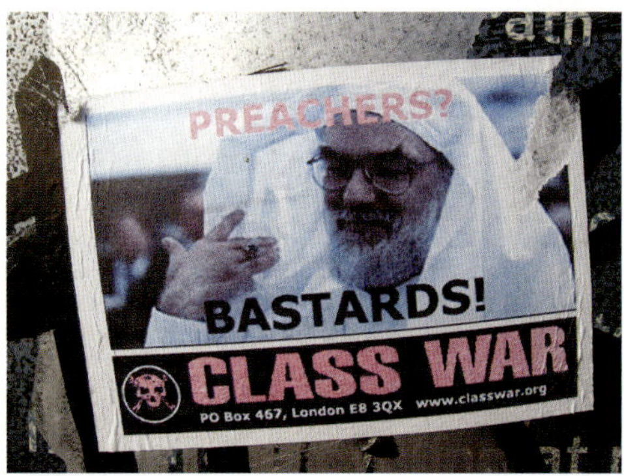

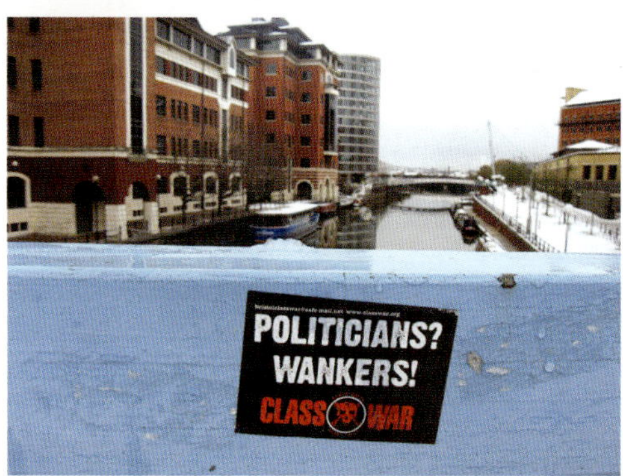

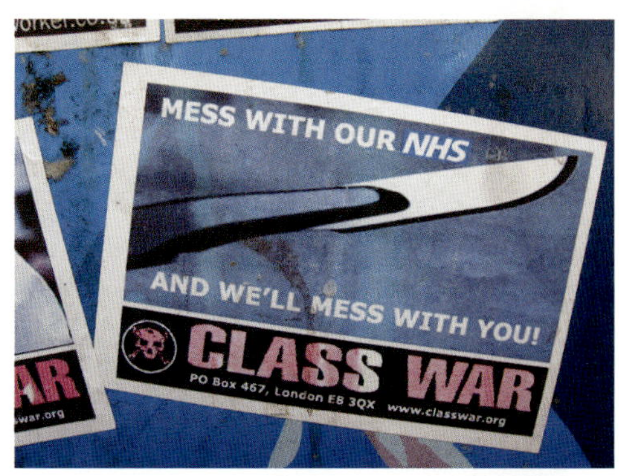

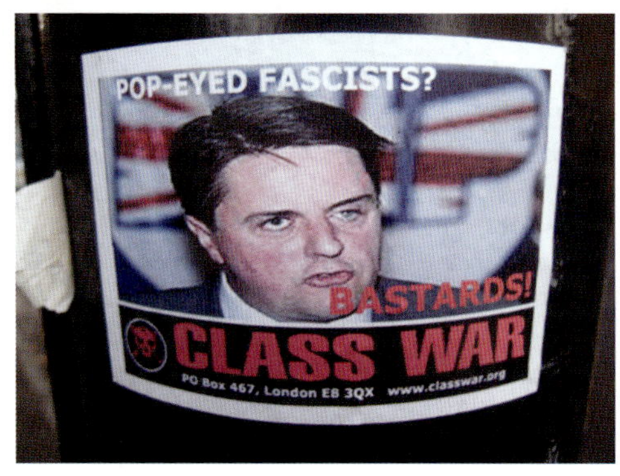

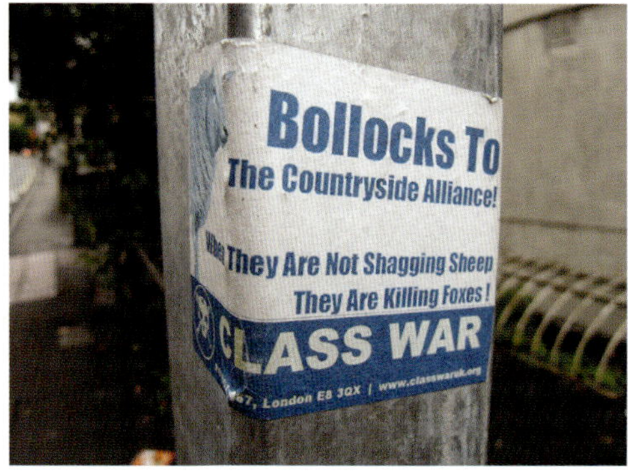

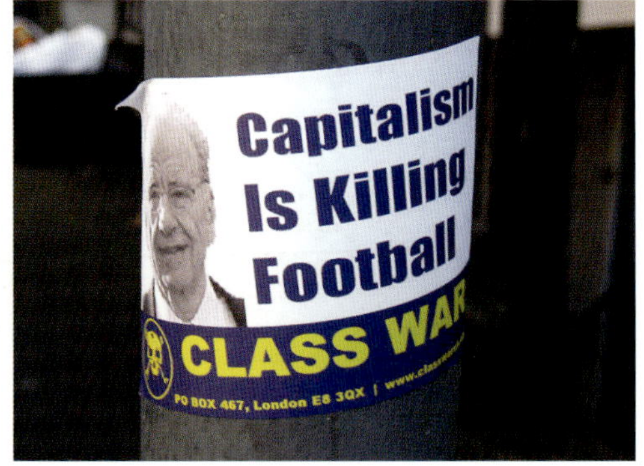

Top row from left — 2008: We still fucking hate Thatcher! | 2007: Bailiffs? Bastards | 2010: Alternative energy? Burn the rich + Same faces different shit [Cameron and Thatcher] | Middle row from left - 2008: Preachers? Bastards! | 2009: Politicians? Wankers! | 2008: Mess with our NHS and we'll mess with you! | Bottom row from left - 2009: Pop-eyed fascists? Bastards [Nick Griffin, BNP] | 2007: Bollocks to the Countryside Alliance! When they are not shagging sheep they are killing foxes | 2006: Capitalism is killing football [Rupert Murdoch, owner of Sky TV] |

Class War...

Class War is a UK class struggle based group and newspaper originally set up in 1983, subsequently mutating, disappearing and reviving by turns. Their uncompromisingly simple and insulting stickers make me smile.

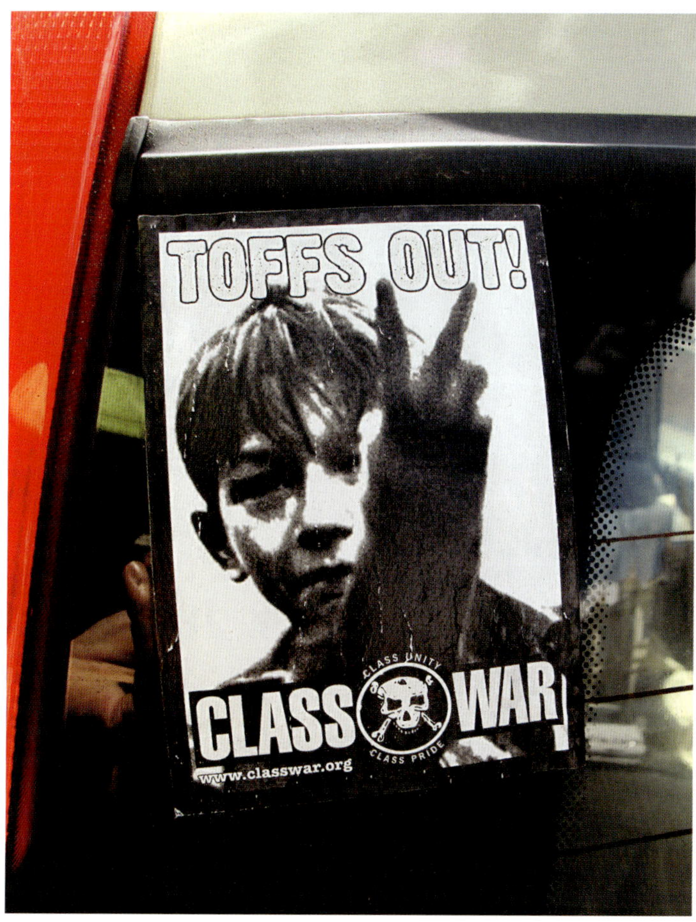

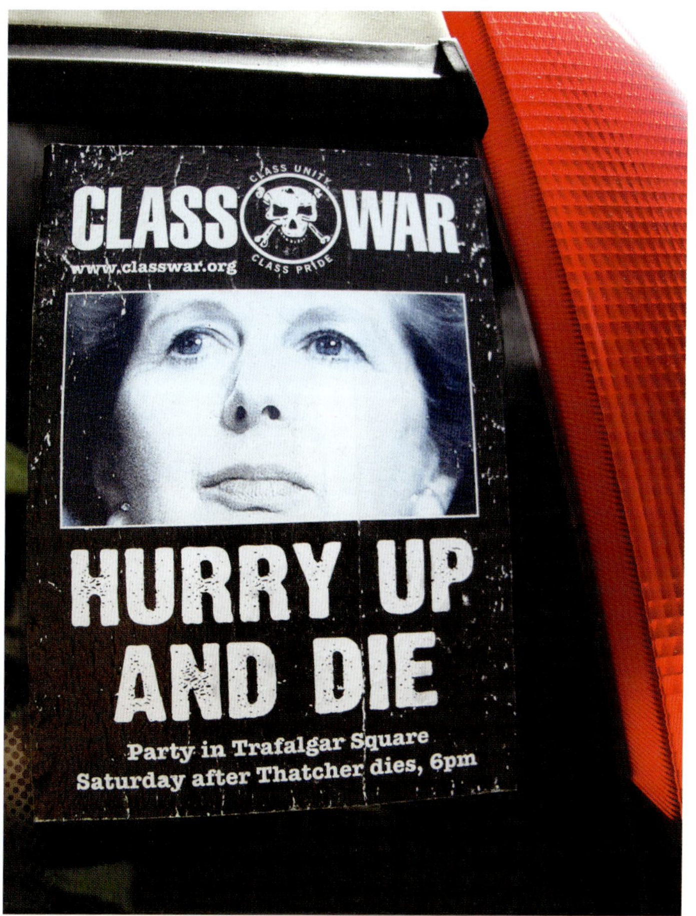

2010: Toffs out! [The image is from Ken Loach's 1969 film 'Kes']

2010: Hurry up and die. Party in Trafalgar Square Saturday after [Margaret] Thatcher dies, 6pm

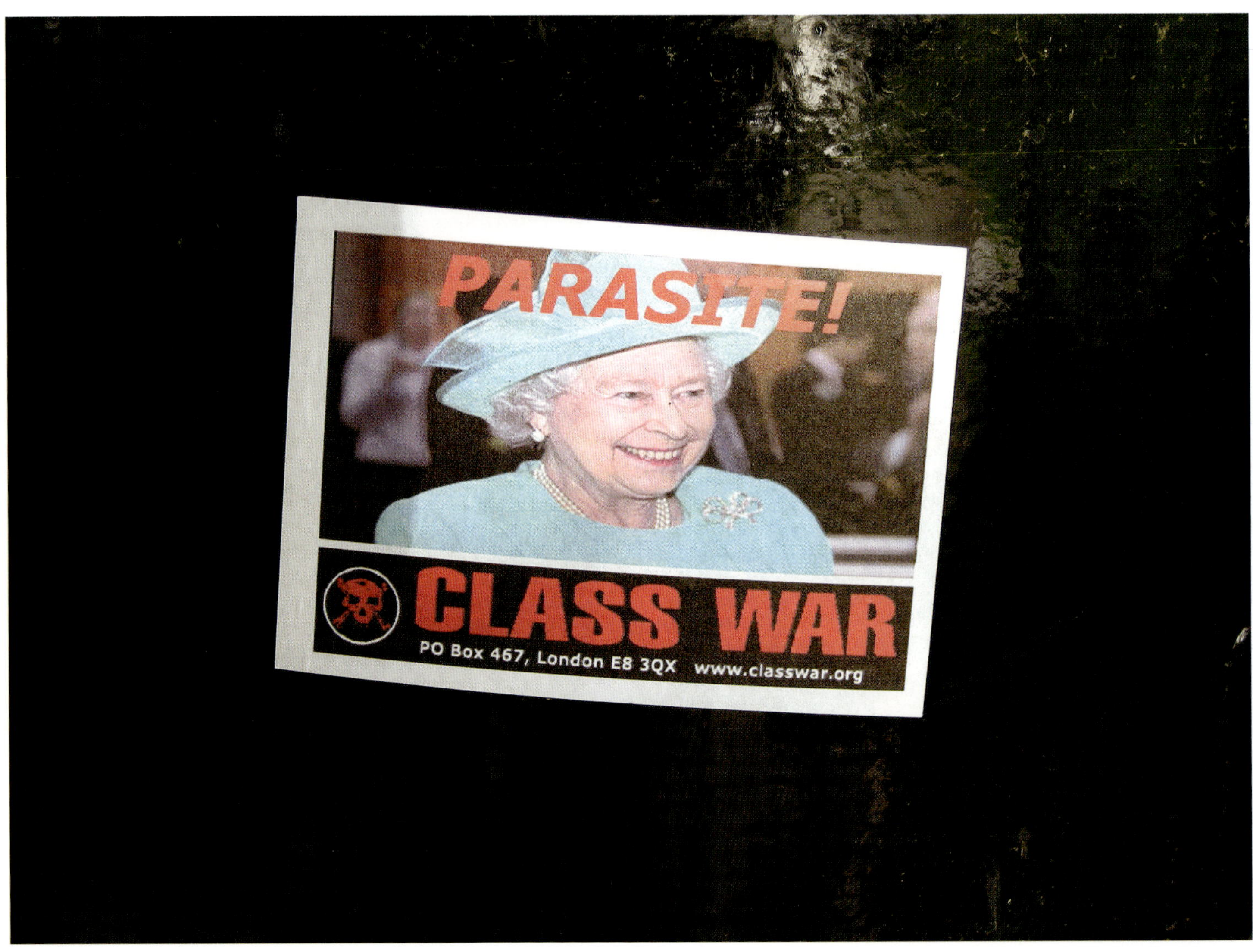

2007: Parasite! Class War [location: my local park]

Class War...

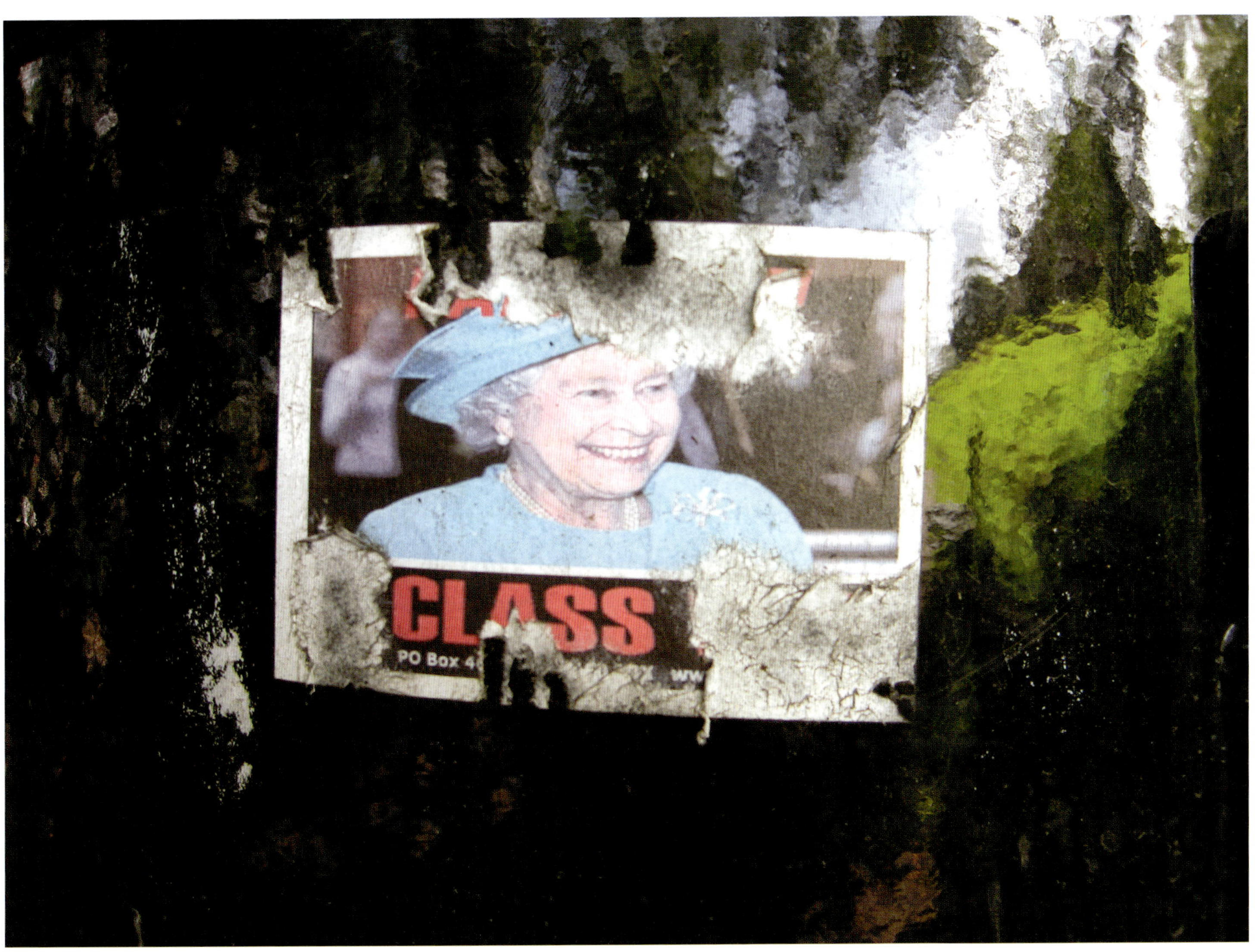

2007: Class [same sticker 2 months later]

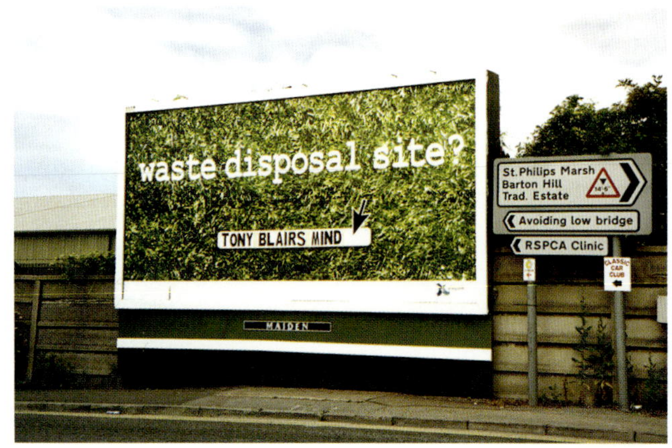
waste disposal site?
TONY BLAIRS MIND
St. Philips Marsh
Barton Hill
Trad. Estate
Avoiding low bridge
RSPCA Clinic
CLASSIC CAR CLUB
MAIDEN

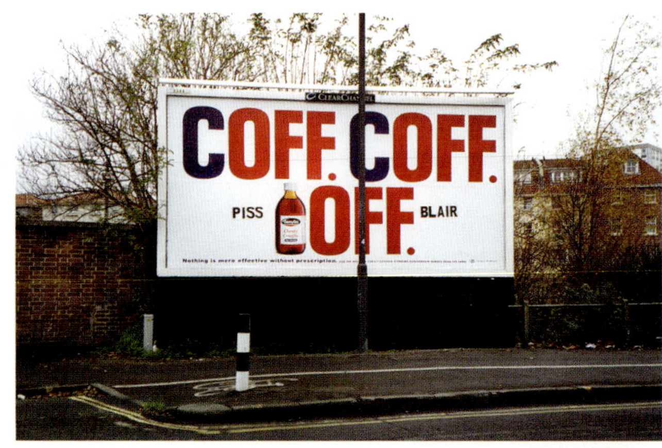
ClearChannel
COFF. COFF.
OFF.
PISS   BLAIR
Nothing is more effective without prescription.

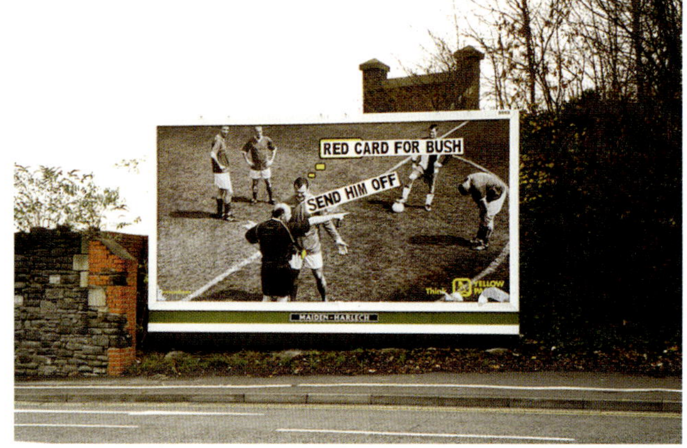
RED CARD FOR BUSH
SEND HIM OFF
Think
YELLOW
MAIDEN-HARLECH

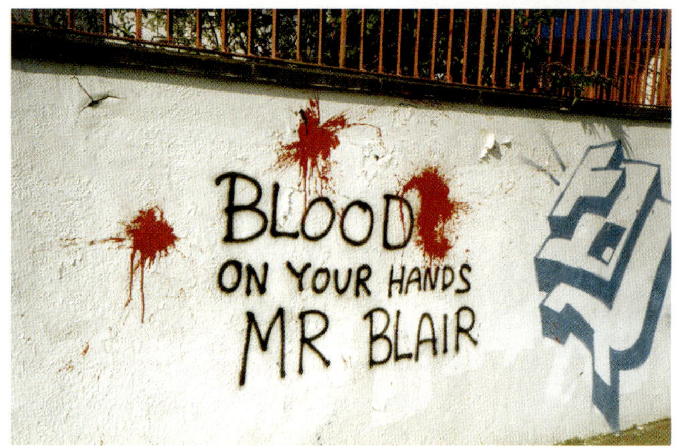
BLOOD
ON YOUR HANDS
MR BLAIR

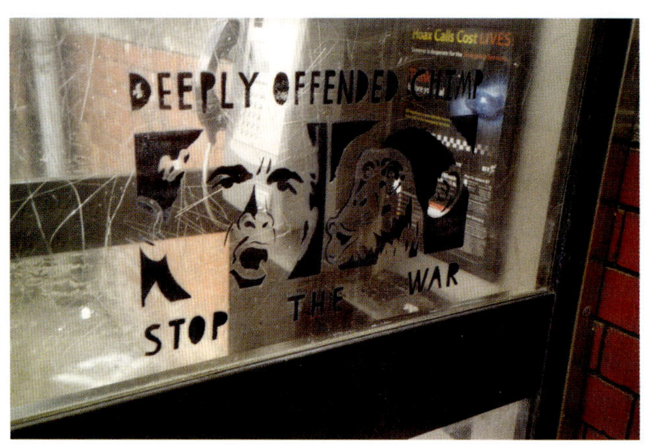
Hoax Calls Cost LIVES
DEEPLY OFFENDED CHIMP
STOP   THE   WAR

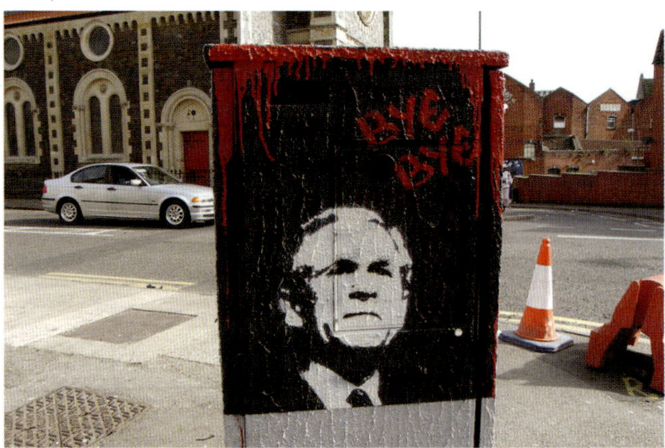
BYE BYE

Bush and Blair...

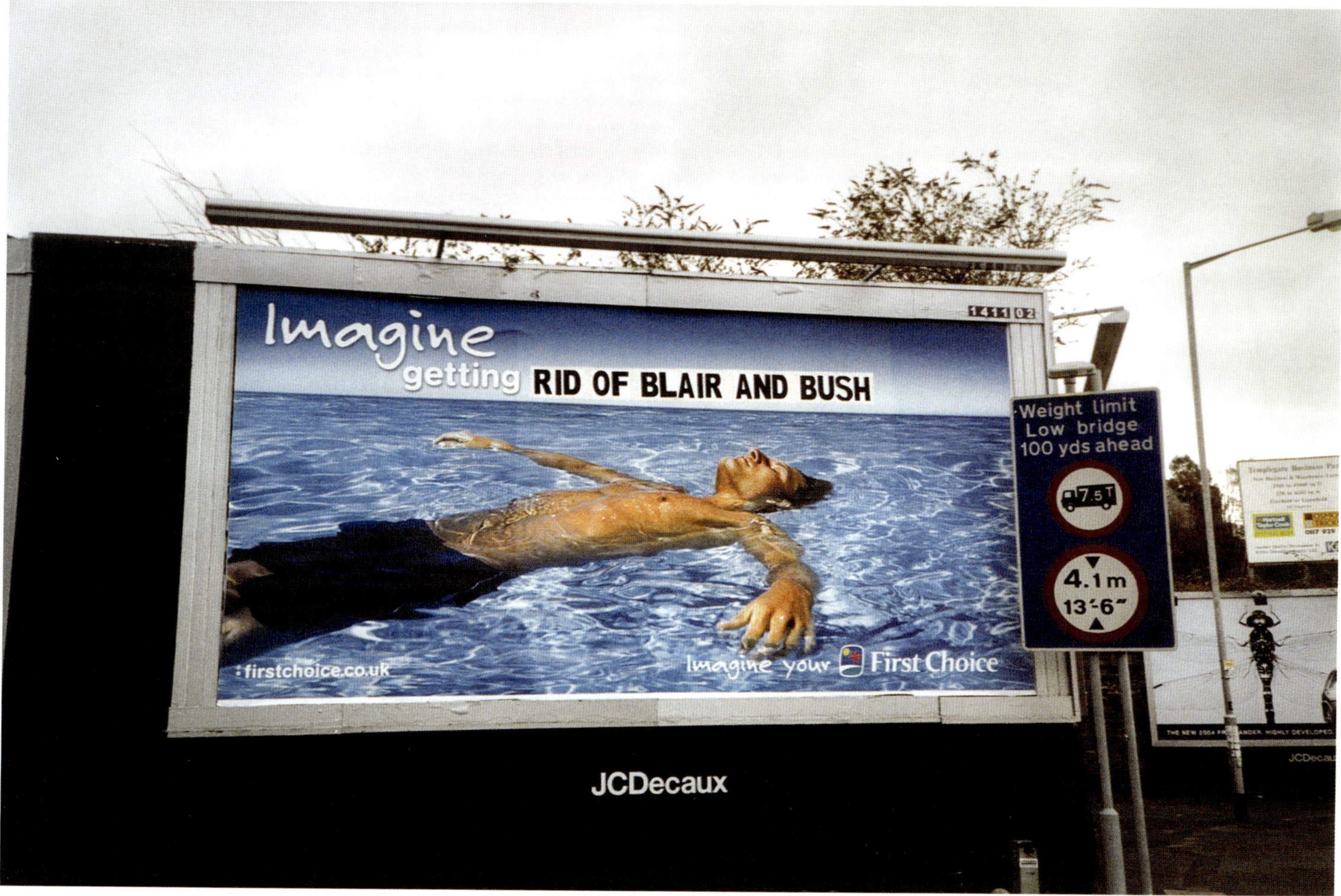

2004: Imagine getting rid of Blair and Bush

Left. Clockwise from top left – 2002: Tony Blairs mind | 2004: Piss off Blair | 2003: Blood on your hands Mr Blair | 2009: Bye bye [George Bush left the White House in January 2009] | 2004: Deeply offended chimp | 2003: Red card for Bush. Send him off |

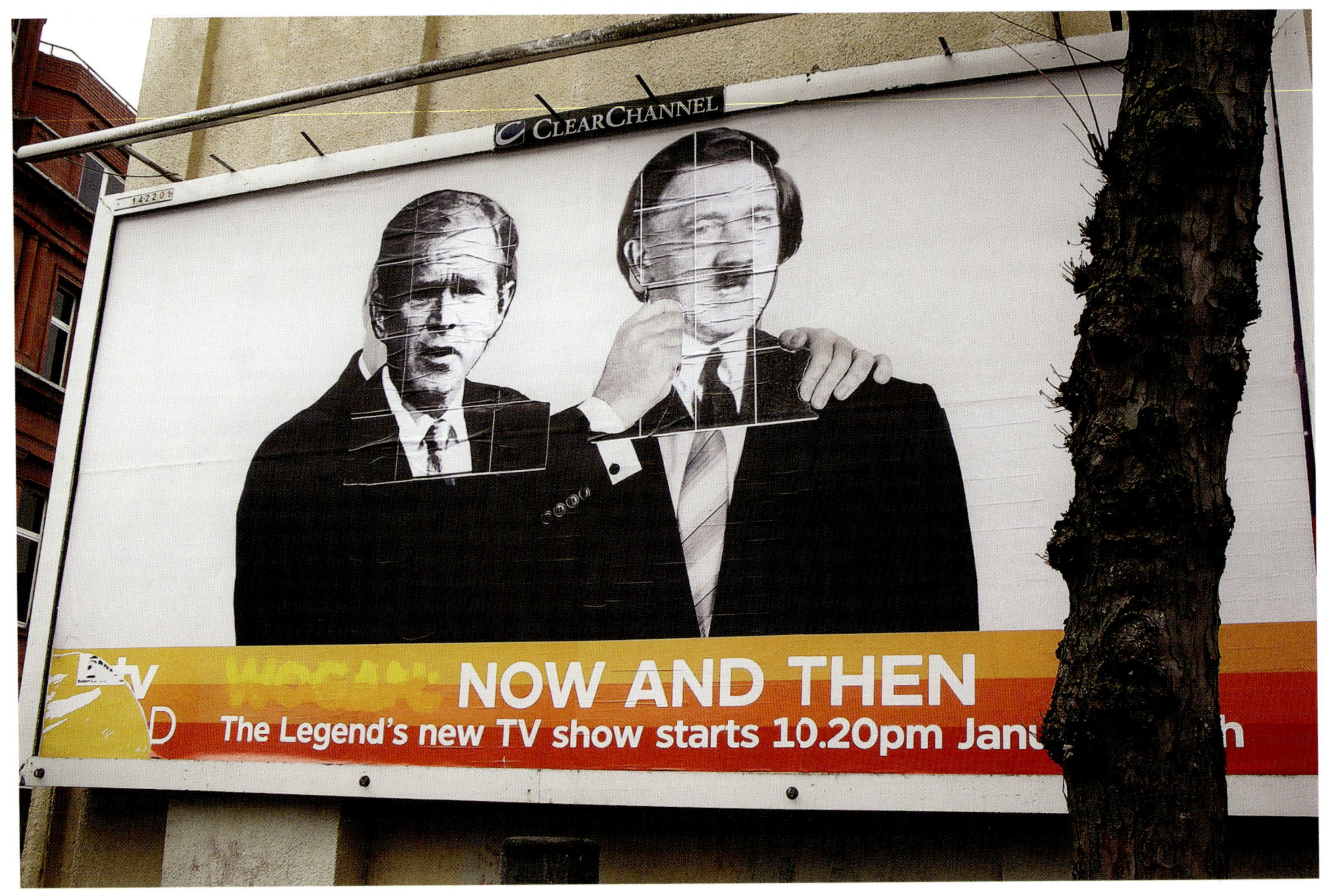

2006: Now and then [Bush and Hitler replacing Terry Wogan in ad for the 'Wogan Now and Then' TV series]

Bush and Blair...

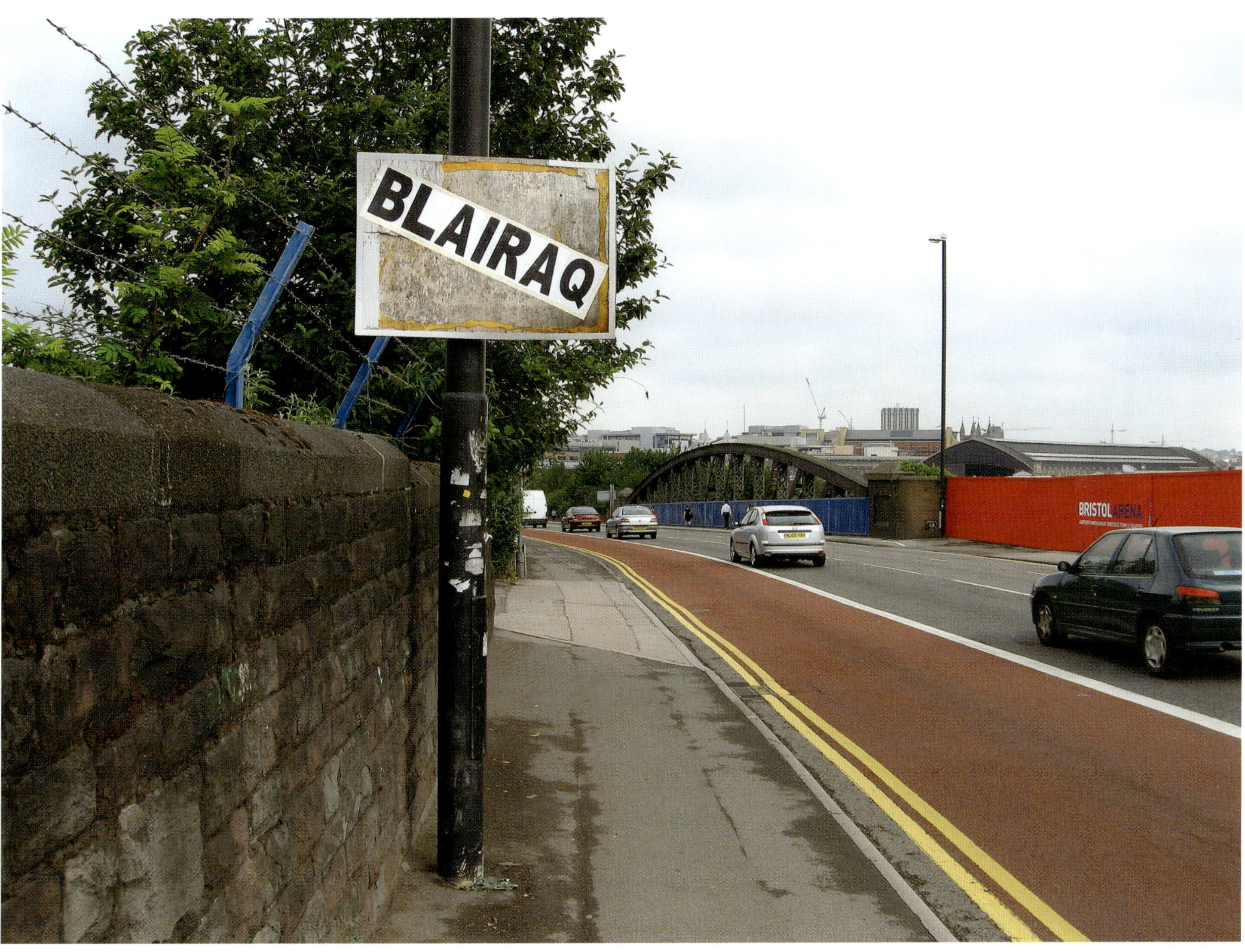

2007: Blairaq

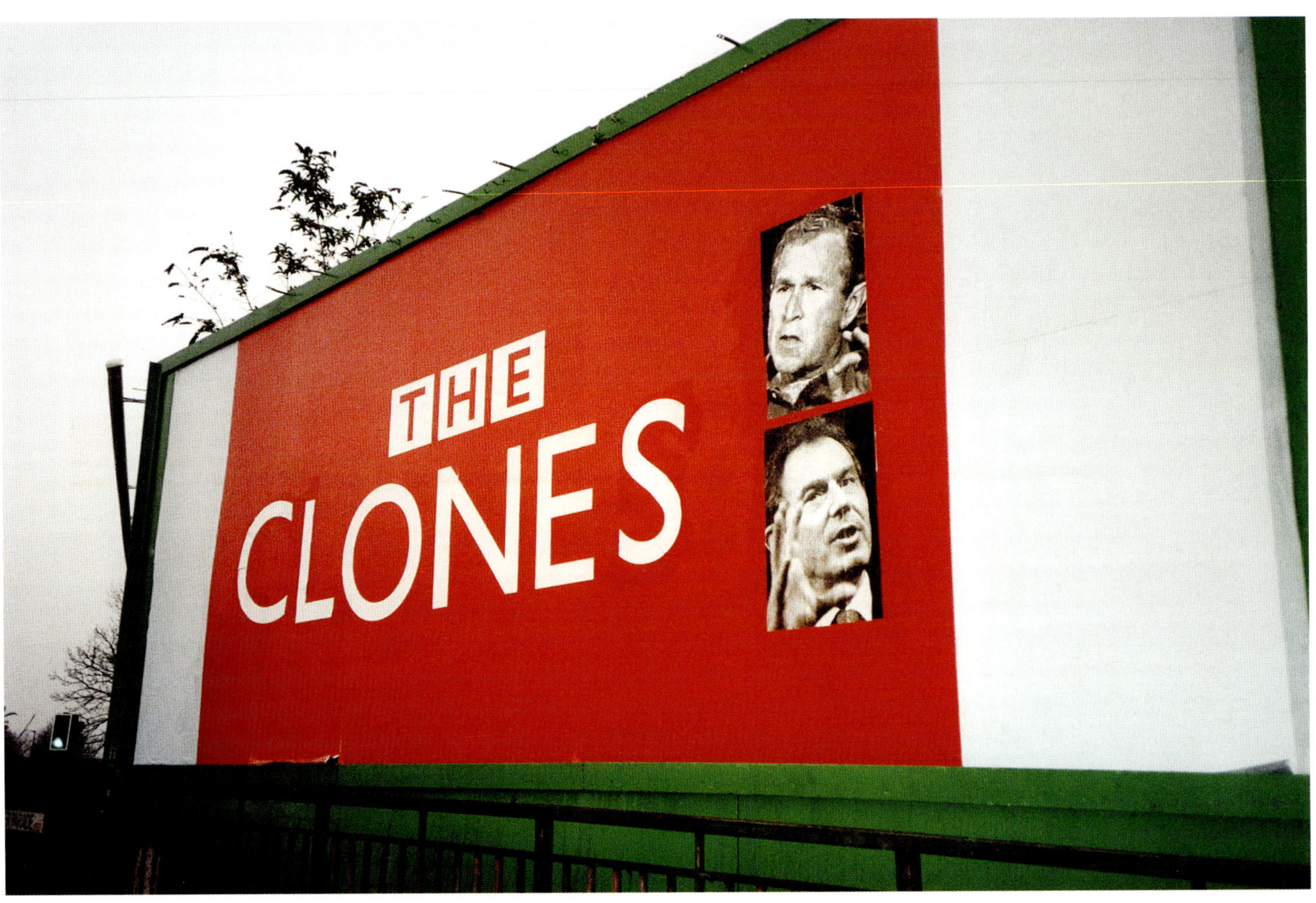

Above – 2002: The Clones

Right. Clockwise from top left – 2006: Liar liar knickers on fire | 2006: George Bush and Son. Family Butchers | 2001: Go Green smoke Bush [green and bush both refer to cannabis, smoke also refers to a gun just fired] | 2004: Blair + Bush = 2 x 2 = 5 | 2007: Last time in Chequers [Chequers is the country residence of the Prime Minister. Tony Blair was succeeded as PM by Gordon Brown in June 2007. He's wearing comic strip character Rupert the Bear's check trousers and scarf] | 2002: Who controls who? Bush controls Blair |

Bush and Blair...

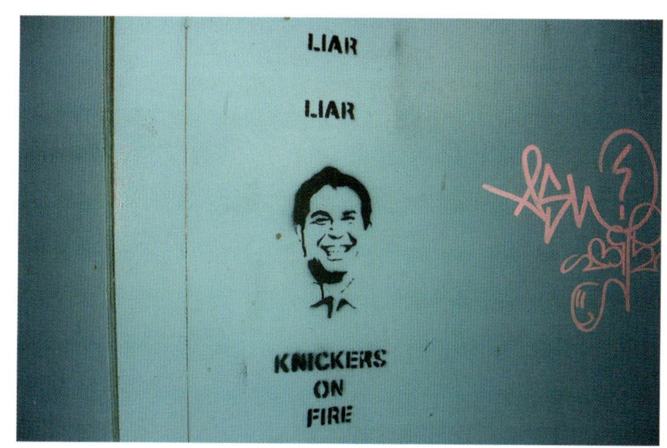

LIAR
LIAR
KNICKERS
ON
FIRE

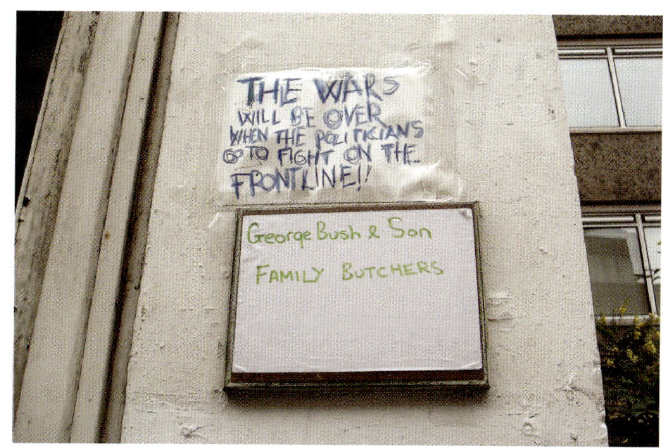

THE WARS
WILL BE OVER
WHEN THE POLITICIANS
GO TO FIGHT ON THE
FRONTLINE!!
George Bush & Son
FAMILY BUTCHERS

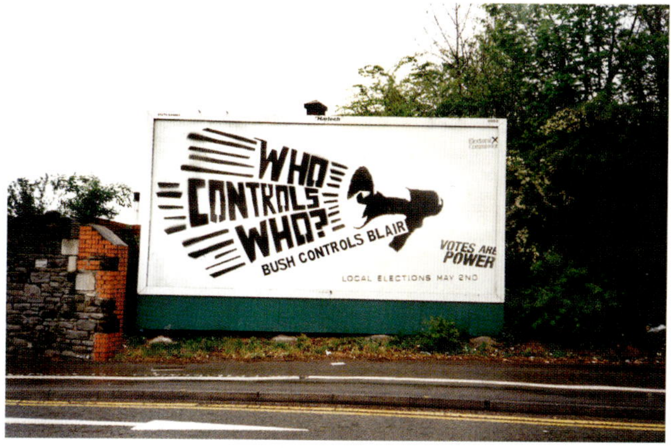

WHO
CONTROLS
WHO?
BUSH CONTROLS BLAIR
VOTES ARE
POWER
LOCAL ELECTIONS MAY 2ND

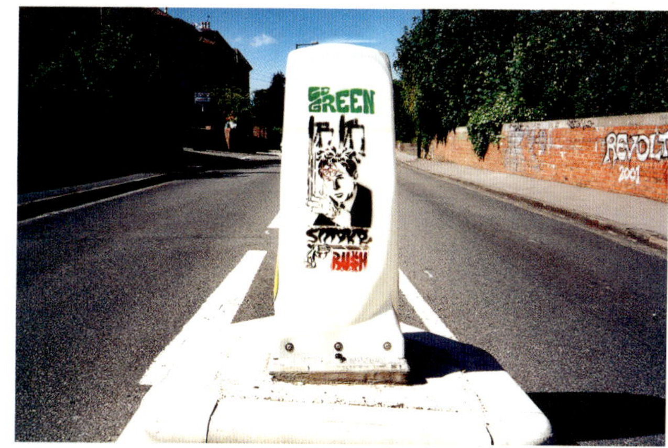

GO GREEN
REVOLT
2001

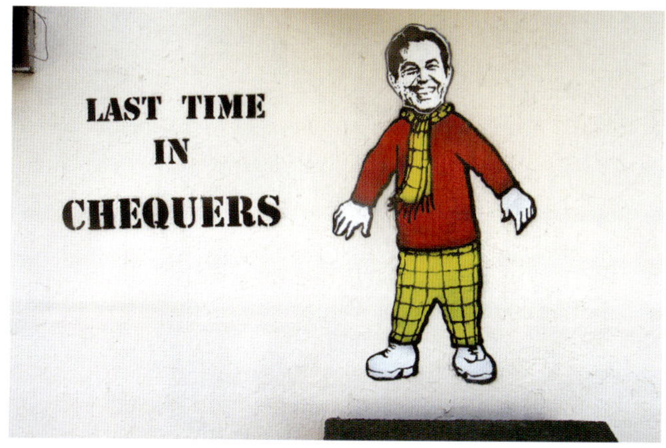

LAST TIME
IN
CHEQUERS

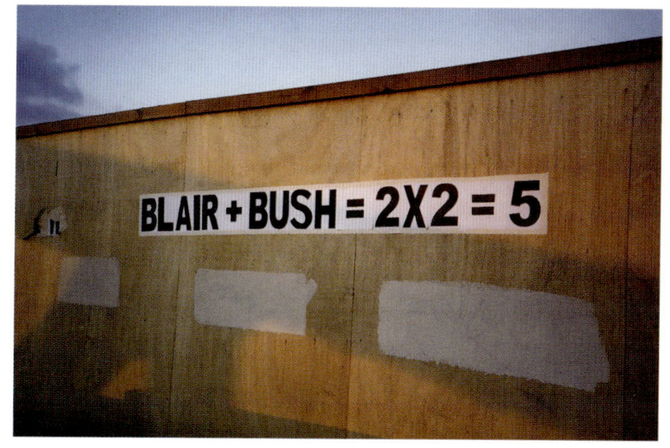

BLAIR + BUSH = 2X2 = 5

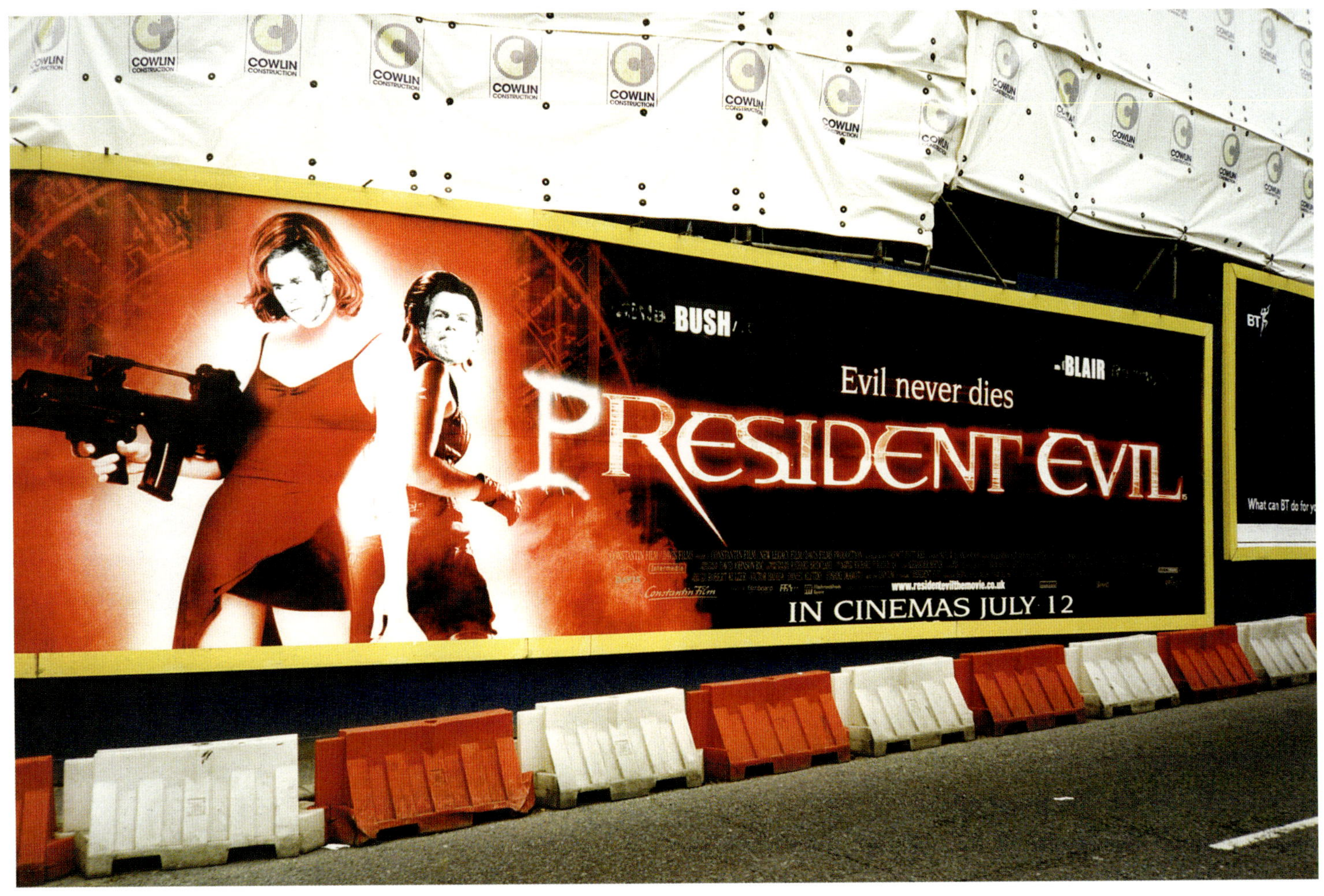

2002: President Evil

Bush and Blair...

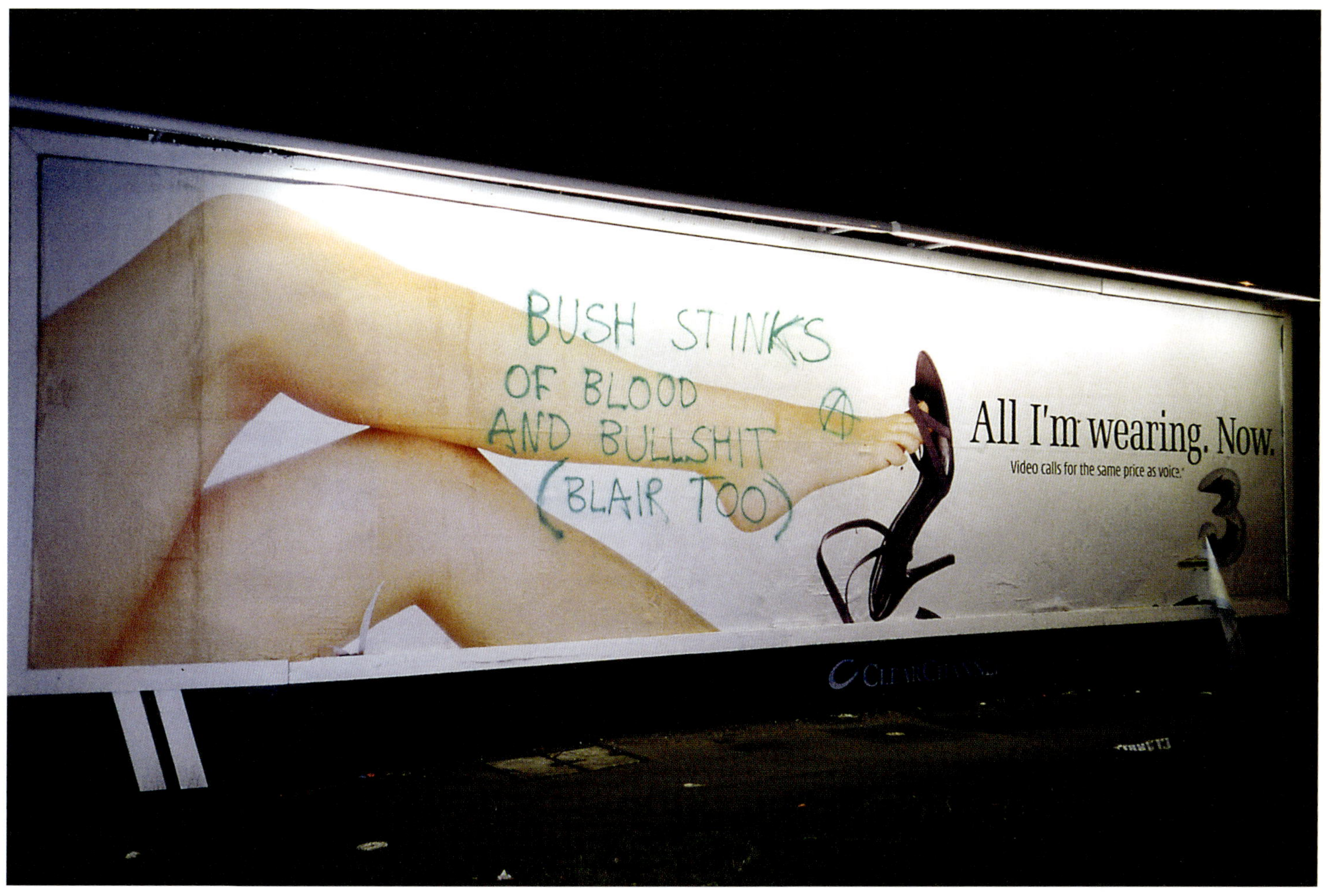

2003: Bush stinks of blood and bullshit (Blair too)

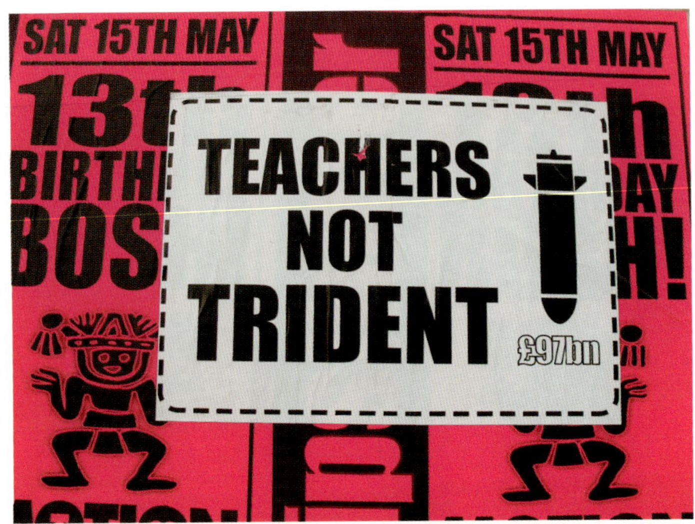

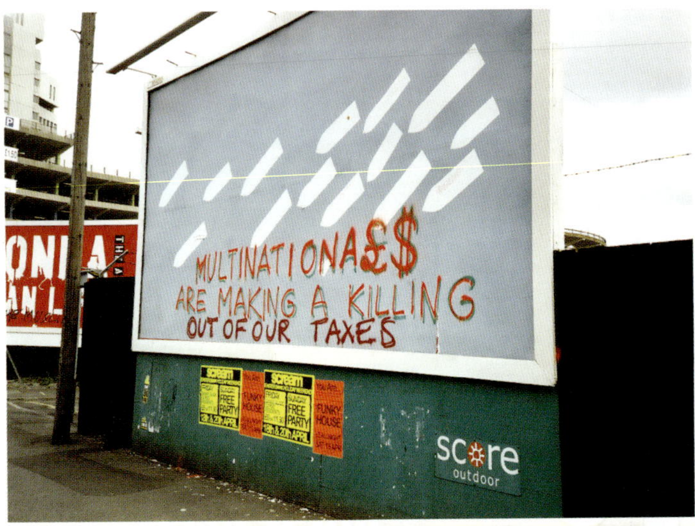

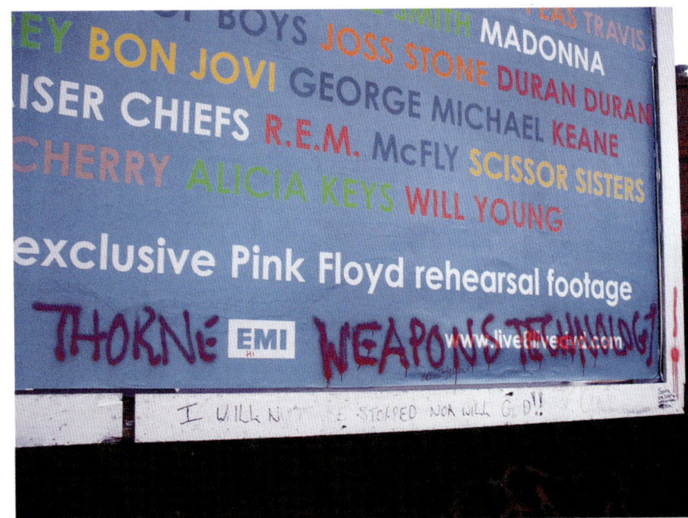

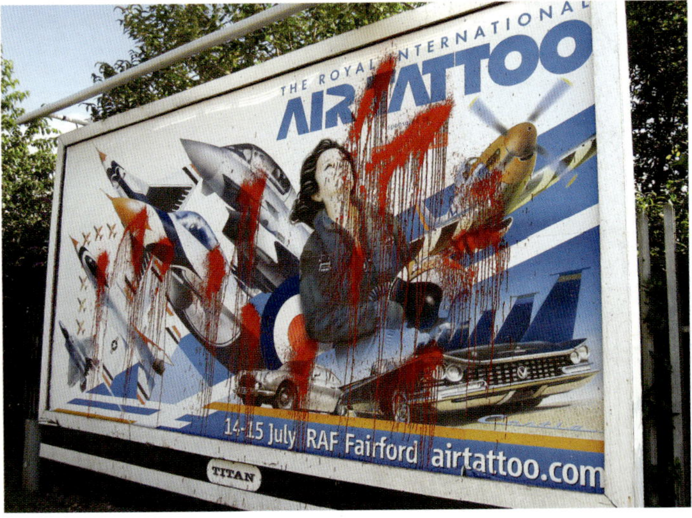

Clockwise from top left – 2010: Teachers not Trident | 2003: Multinationa£$ are making a killing out of our taxes | 2007: Royal International Air Tattoo, RAF Fairford [www.airtattoo.com] | 2005: Thorne EMI weapons technology [The EMI record label's association with weapons actually ended 10 years previously in 1995, when owners Thorn EMI sold its defence businesses] |

Arms Trade...

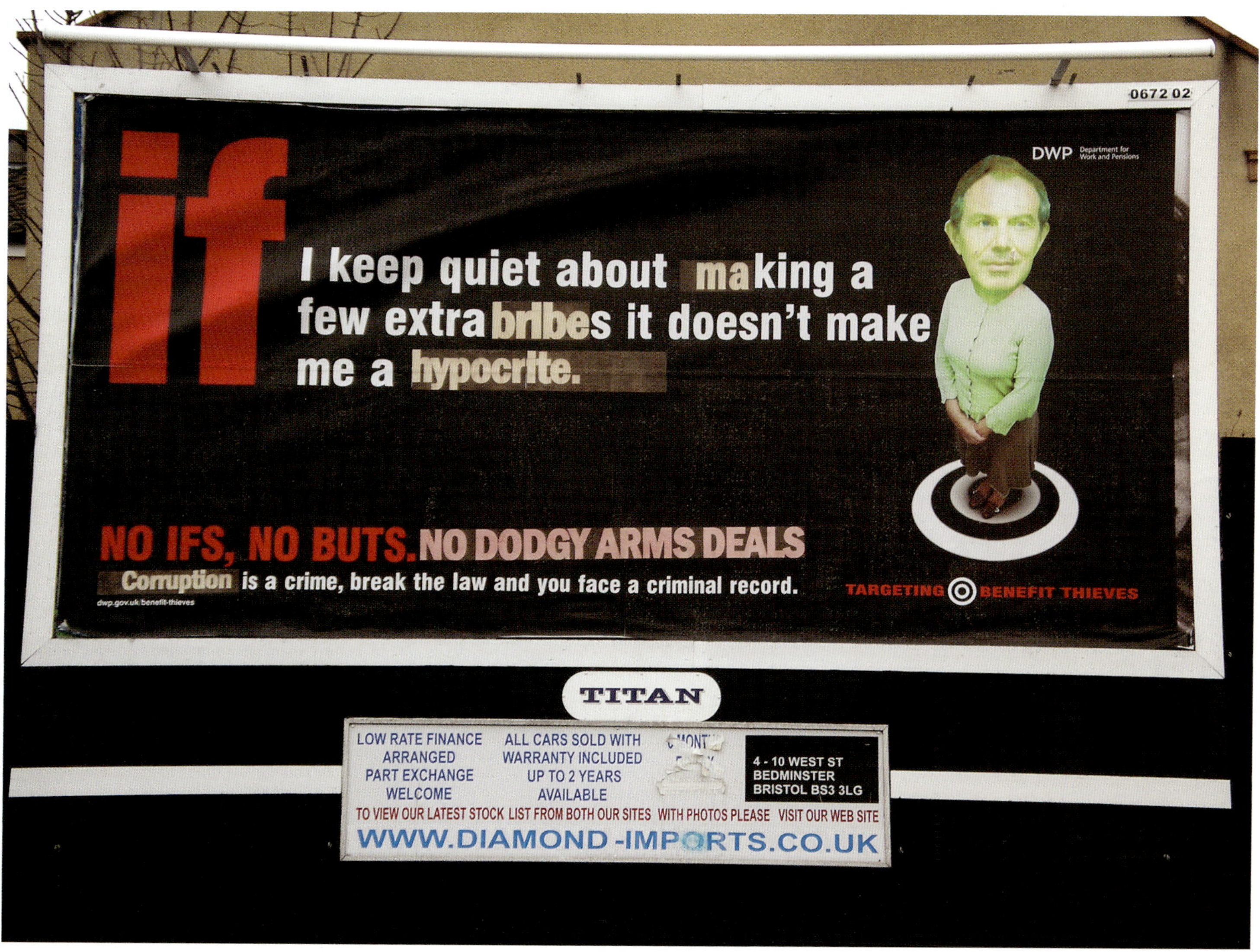

2006: If I keep quiet about making a few extra bribes

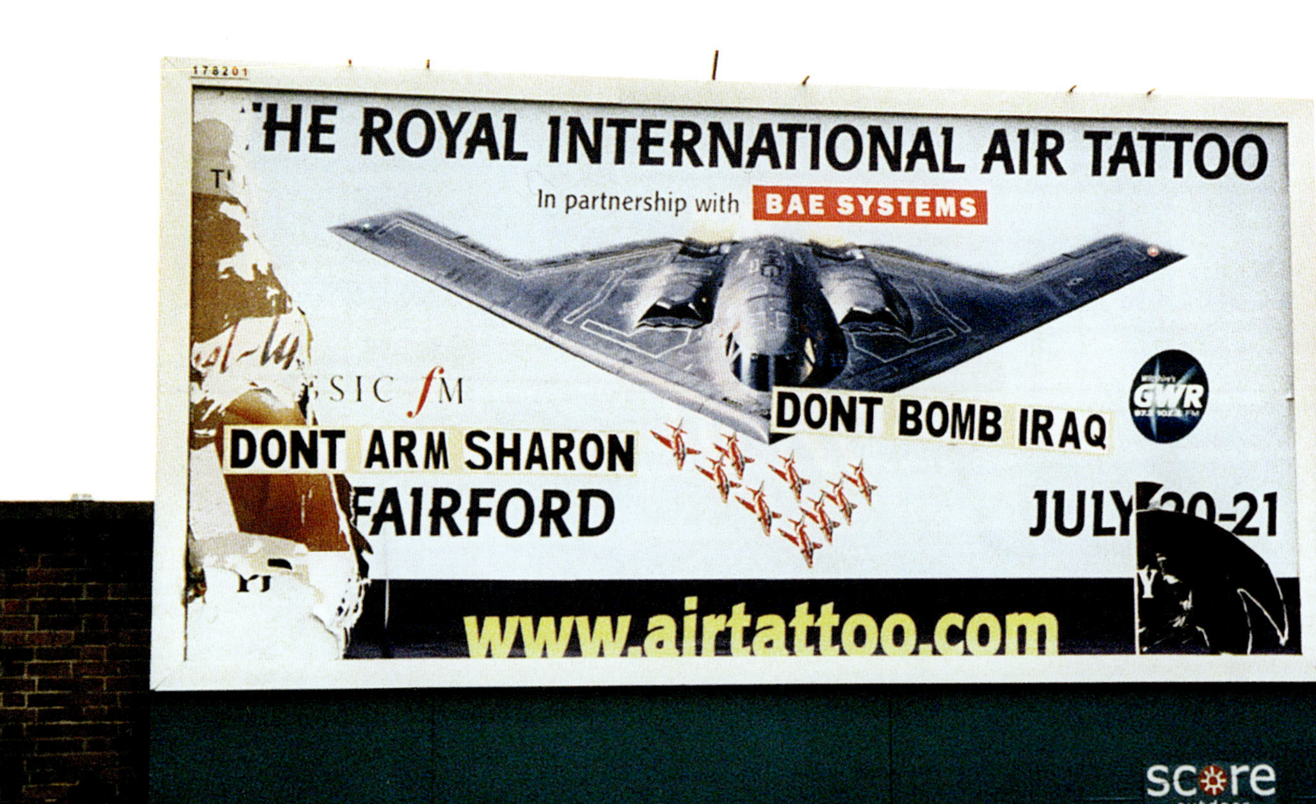178201
'HE ROYAL INTERNATIONAL AIR TATTOO
In partnership with BAE SYSTEMS
SIC fM
DONT ARM SHARON
FAIRFORD
DONT BOMB IRAQ
GWR
JULY 20-21
www.airtattoo.com
score
outdoor

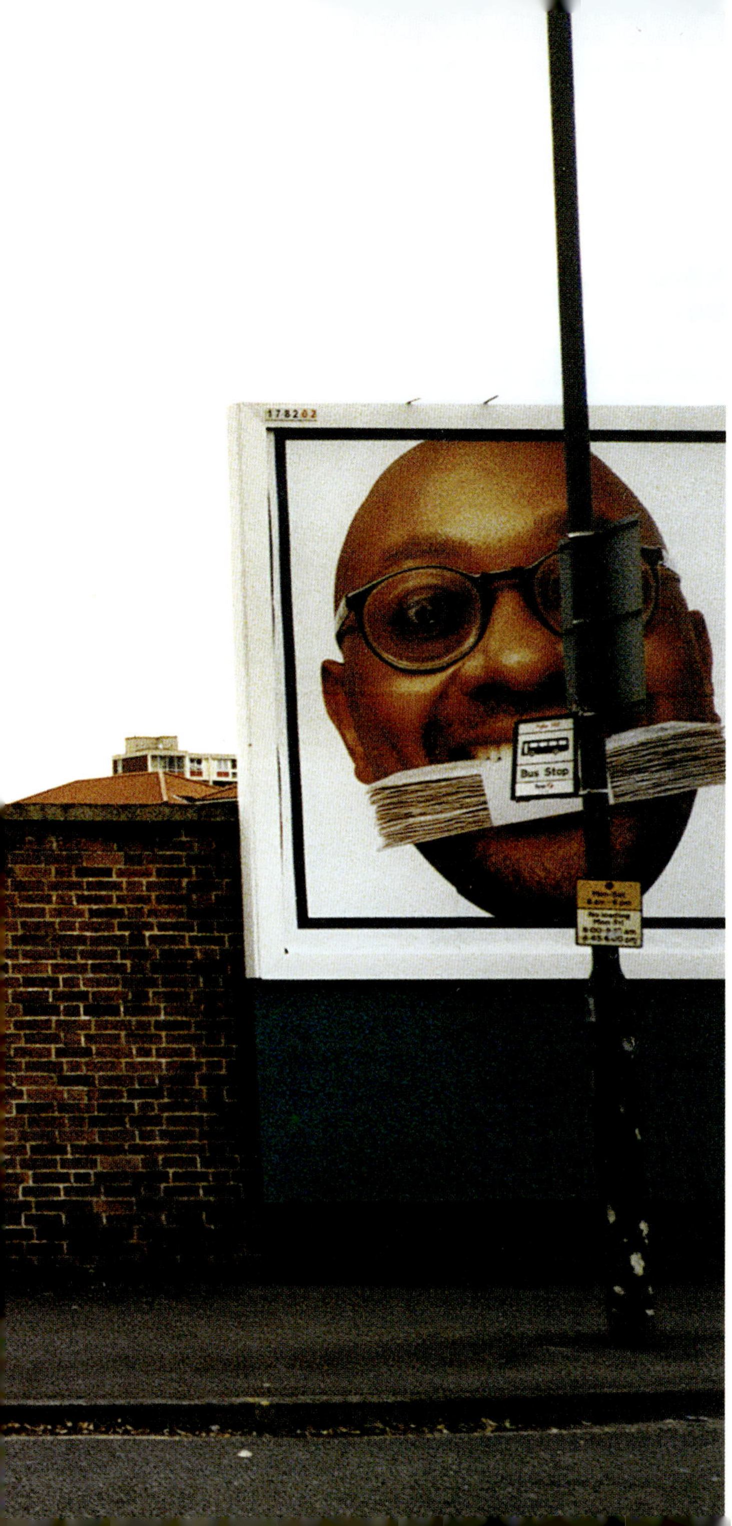

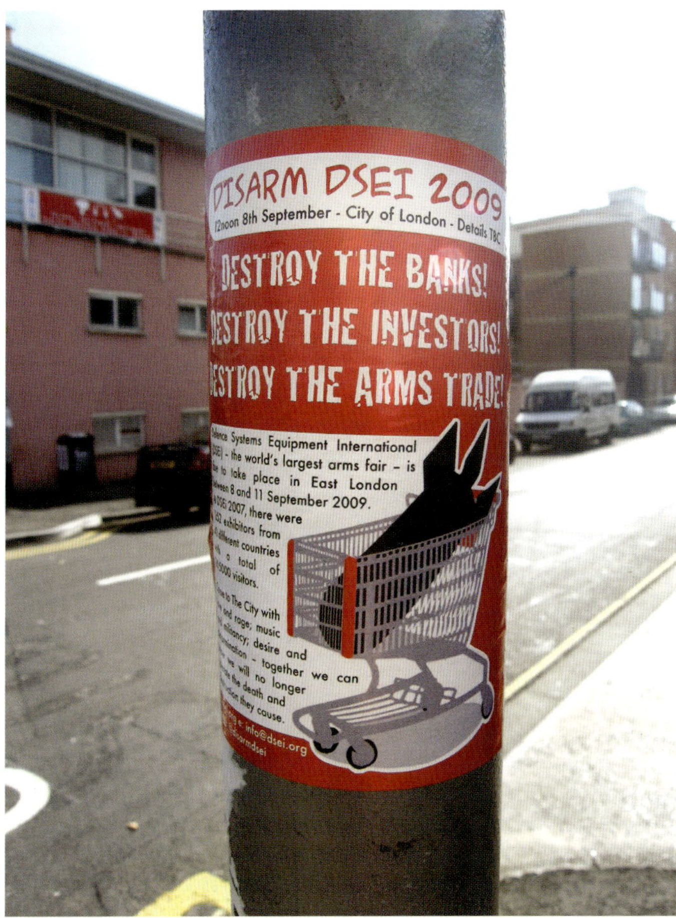

2009: Disarm DSEI. [A call to disrupt the Defence Systems Equipment International – the world's largest arms fair. www.desei.org]

Left — 2002: Dont arm Sharon. [Ariel Sharon was Israel's Prime Minister from 2001 to 2006]

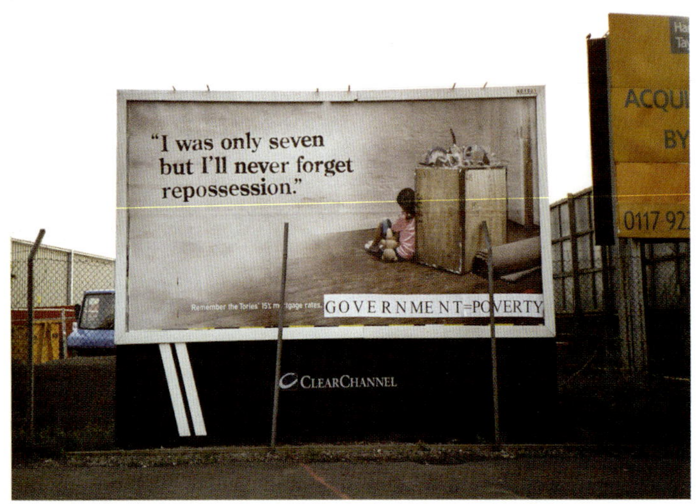

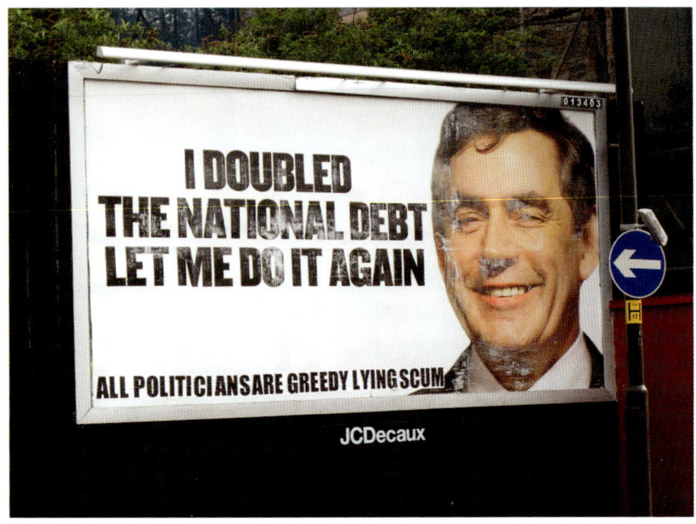

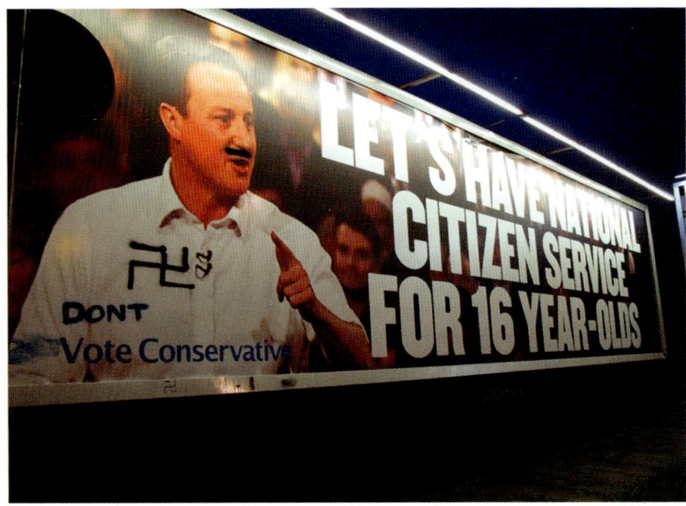

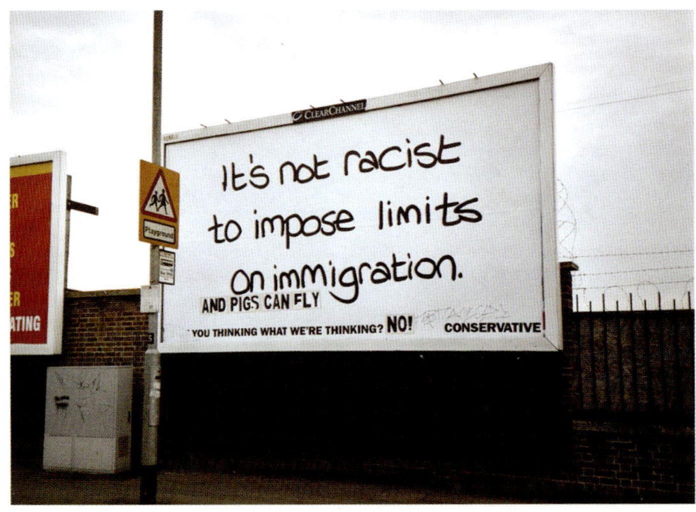

Clockwise from top left – 2005: Government = poverty | 2010: All politicians are greedy lying scum | 2005: It's not racist to impose limits on immigration | 2010: Don't vote Conservative |

Next page – 2005: Blair's mum, Blair's brother, a Blair clone [senior Conservatives Margaret Thatcher, John Major, Michael Howard]

Elections...

More original and subvertised billboards from 5 General Elections (1992 – 2010) at www.flickr.com/photos/donpedro

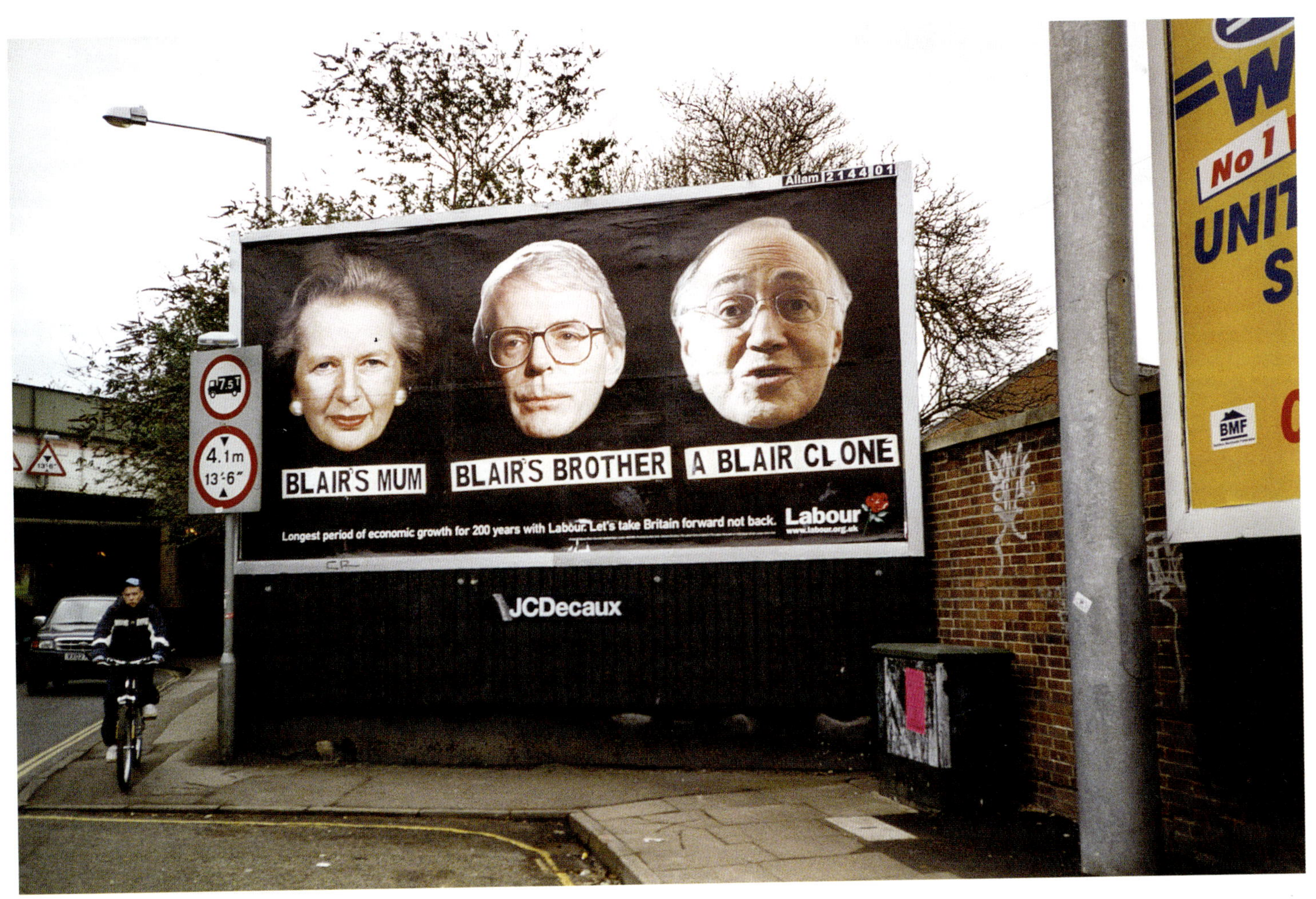

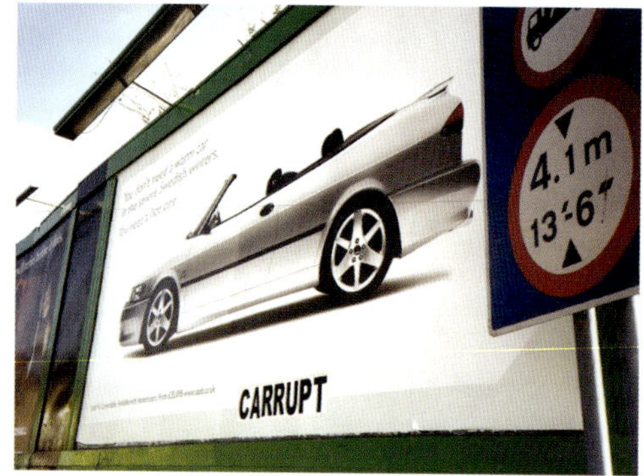

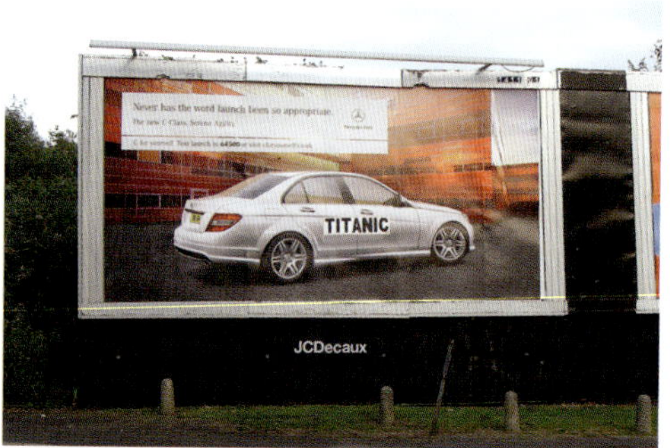

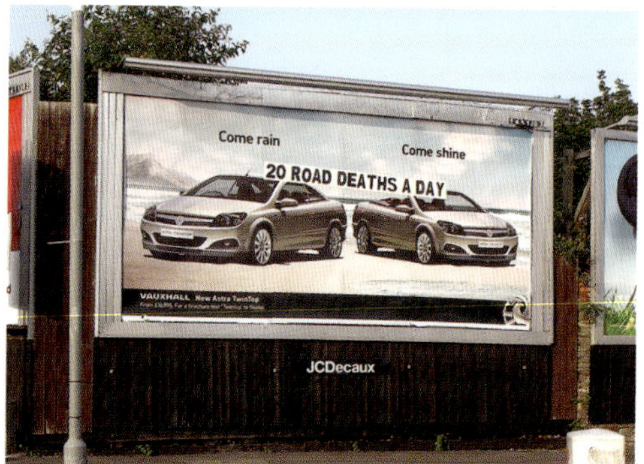

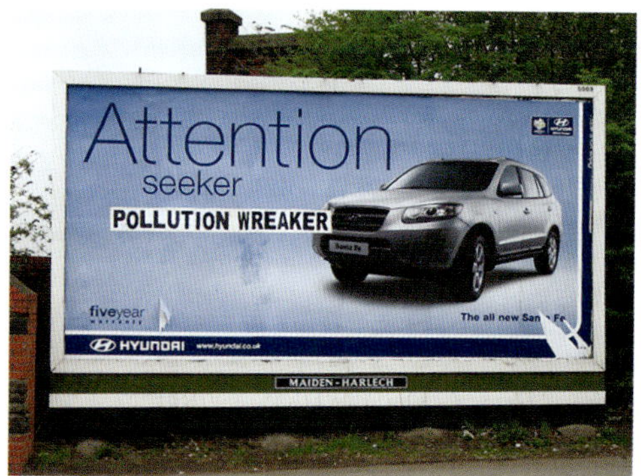

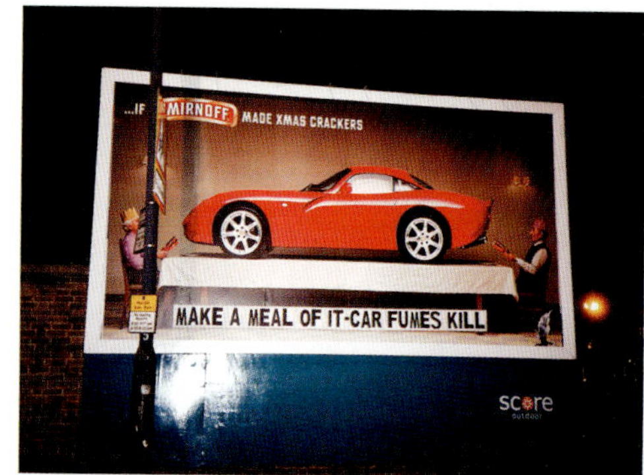

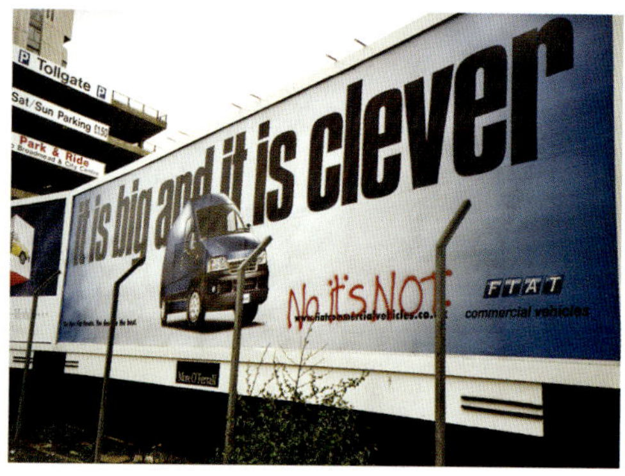

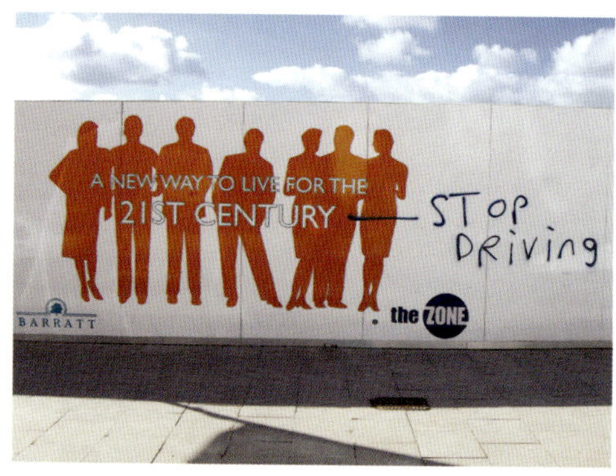

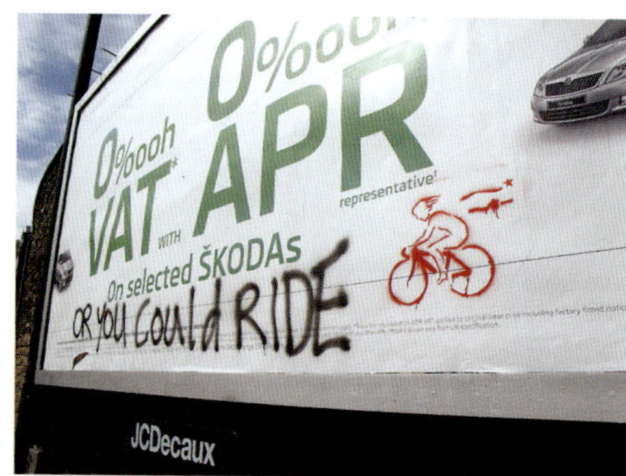

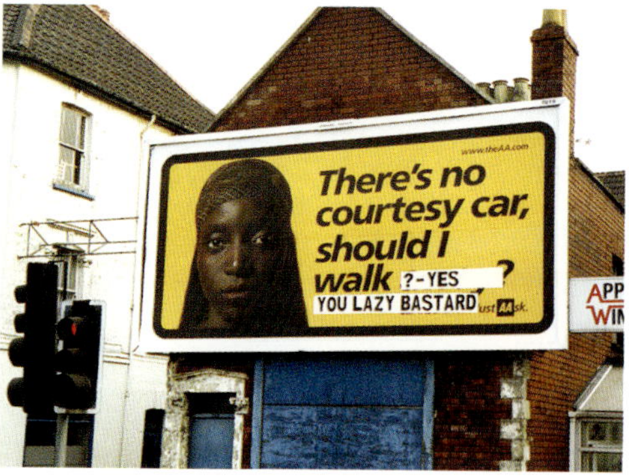

From top left – 2002: Carrupt | 2007: Titanic | 2006: 20 road deaths a day |
From middle left – 2006: Attention seeker pollution wreaker | 2001: Make a meal of it - car fumes kill | 2002: No it's not |
From bottom left – 2008: Stop driving | 2011: Or you could ride | 2003: There's no courtesy car, should I walk? Yes you lazy bastard |

Cars...

Cars have a symbolic quality - for some they're classically capitalist in their appeal to our aspirations and selfishness, whilst causing damage to our health and the environment. Billboards advertising cars are frequent targets.

It's estimated that over 600,000,000 passenger cars travel the streets and roads of the world today (Source: www.worldometers.info/cars). Along with light trucks they burn over 260 billion (US) gallons of petrol and diesel yearly (Source: Wikipedia).

Yet they're integrated into developed world economies and personal lifestyles to such an extent that moving to a world without them is very hard to imagine.

Leaving aside the amount of raw materials they require to manufacture, as long as they use fuel that is oil-based, cars are part of the problem.

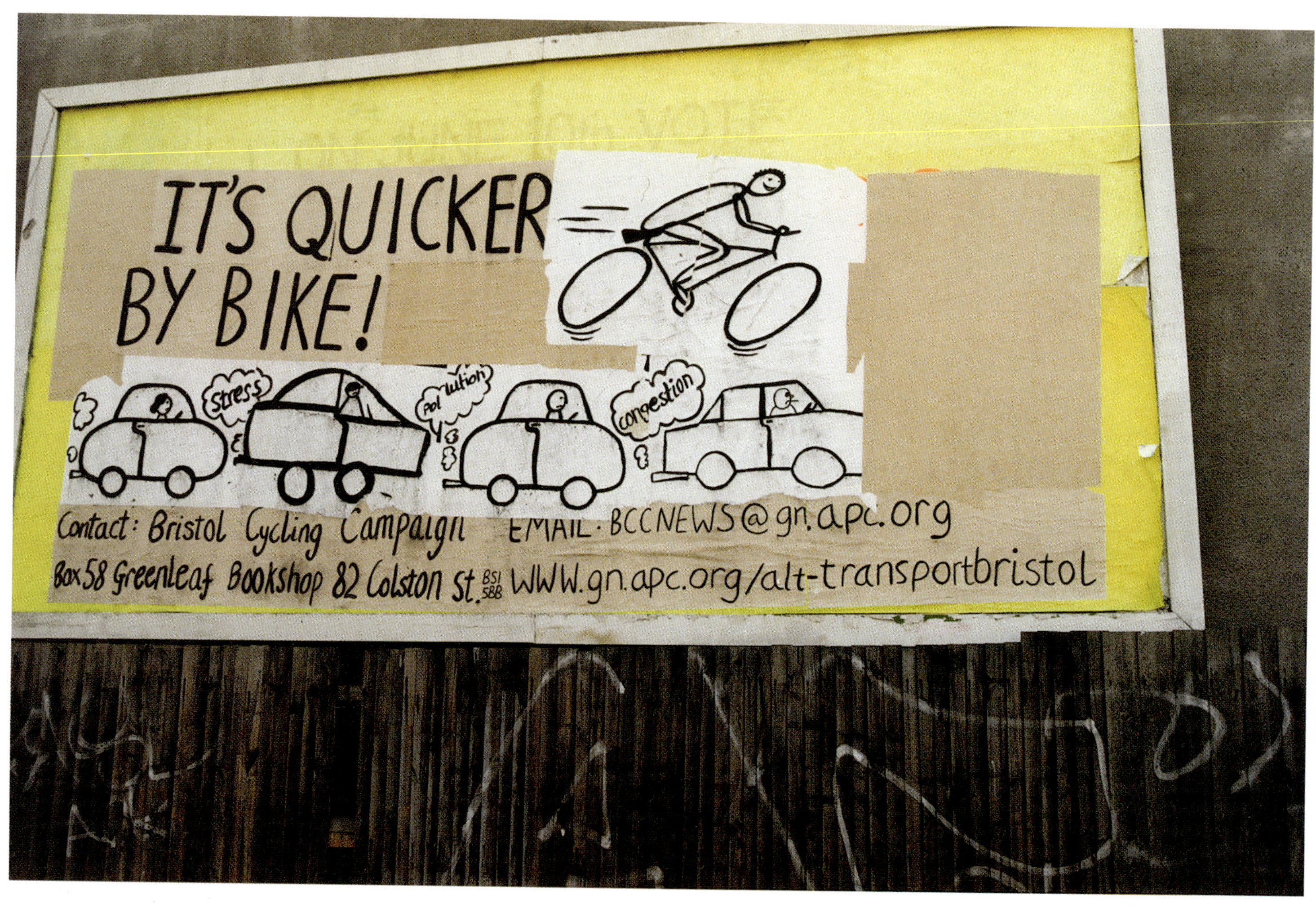

1999: It's quicker by bike!

Cars...

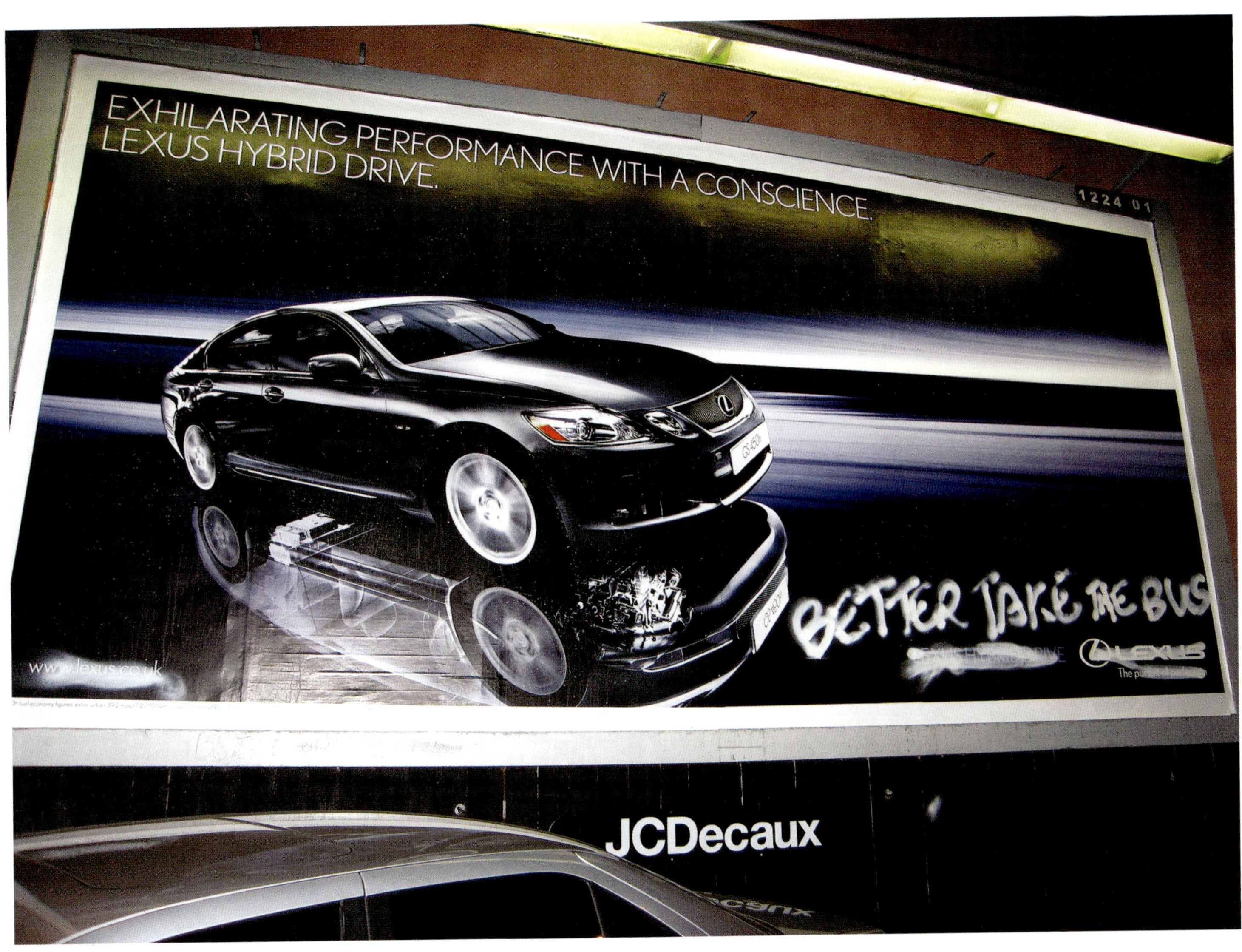

2007: Better take the bus

2005: The wheels on the buggy go round all day long, so…

Cars...

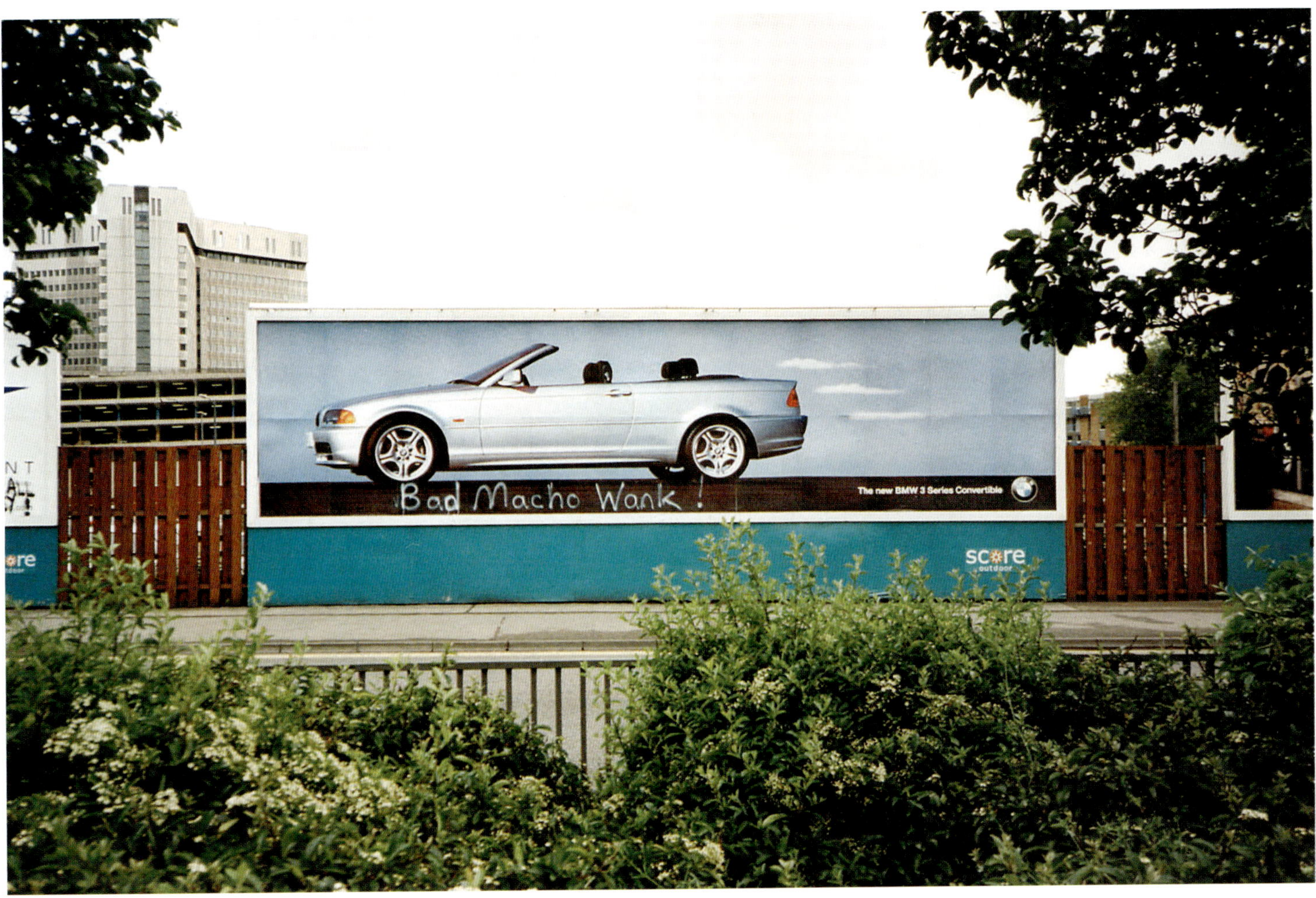

2000: Bad macho wank!

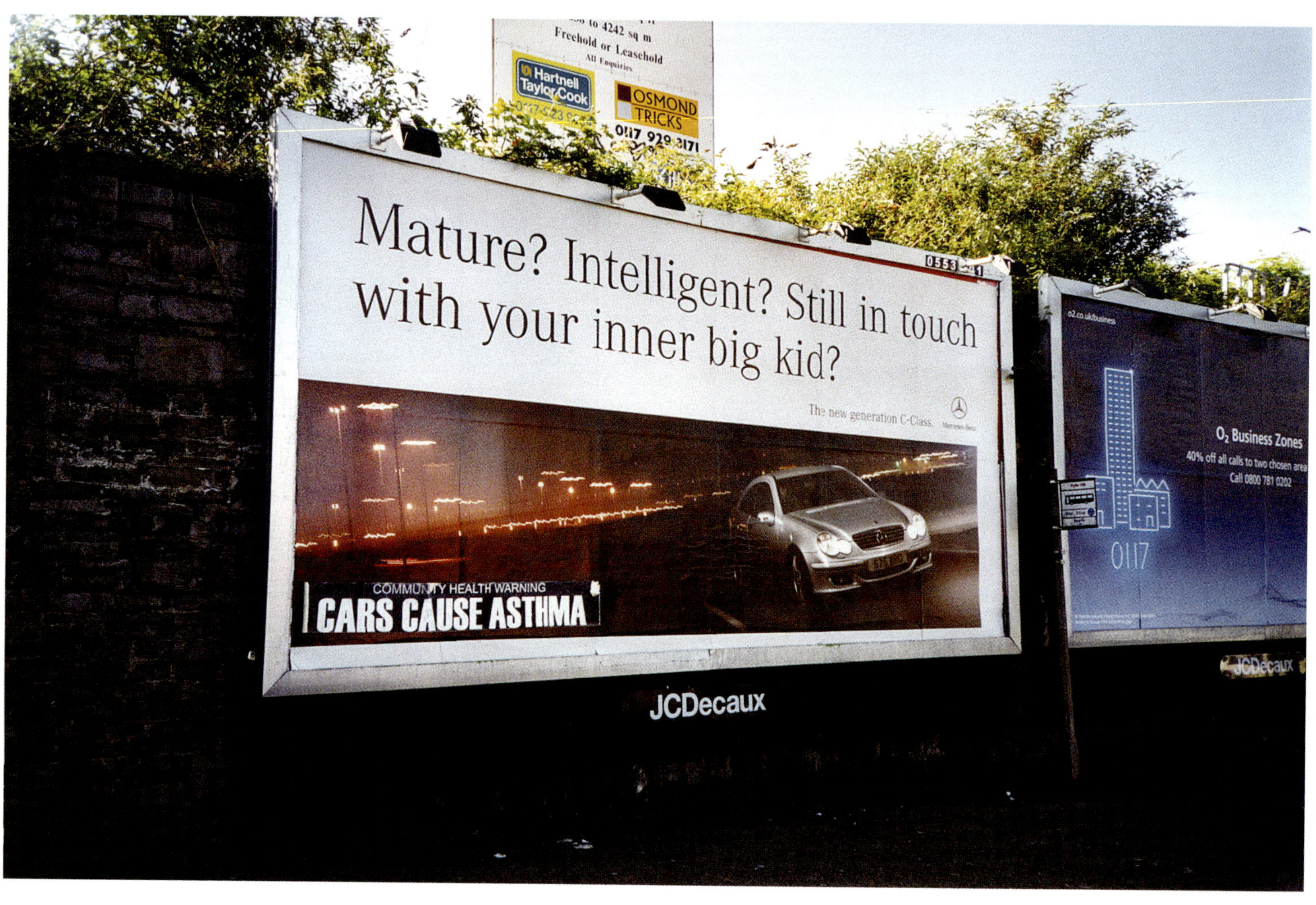

2004: Community health warning - Cars cause asthma

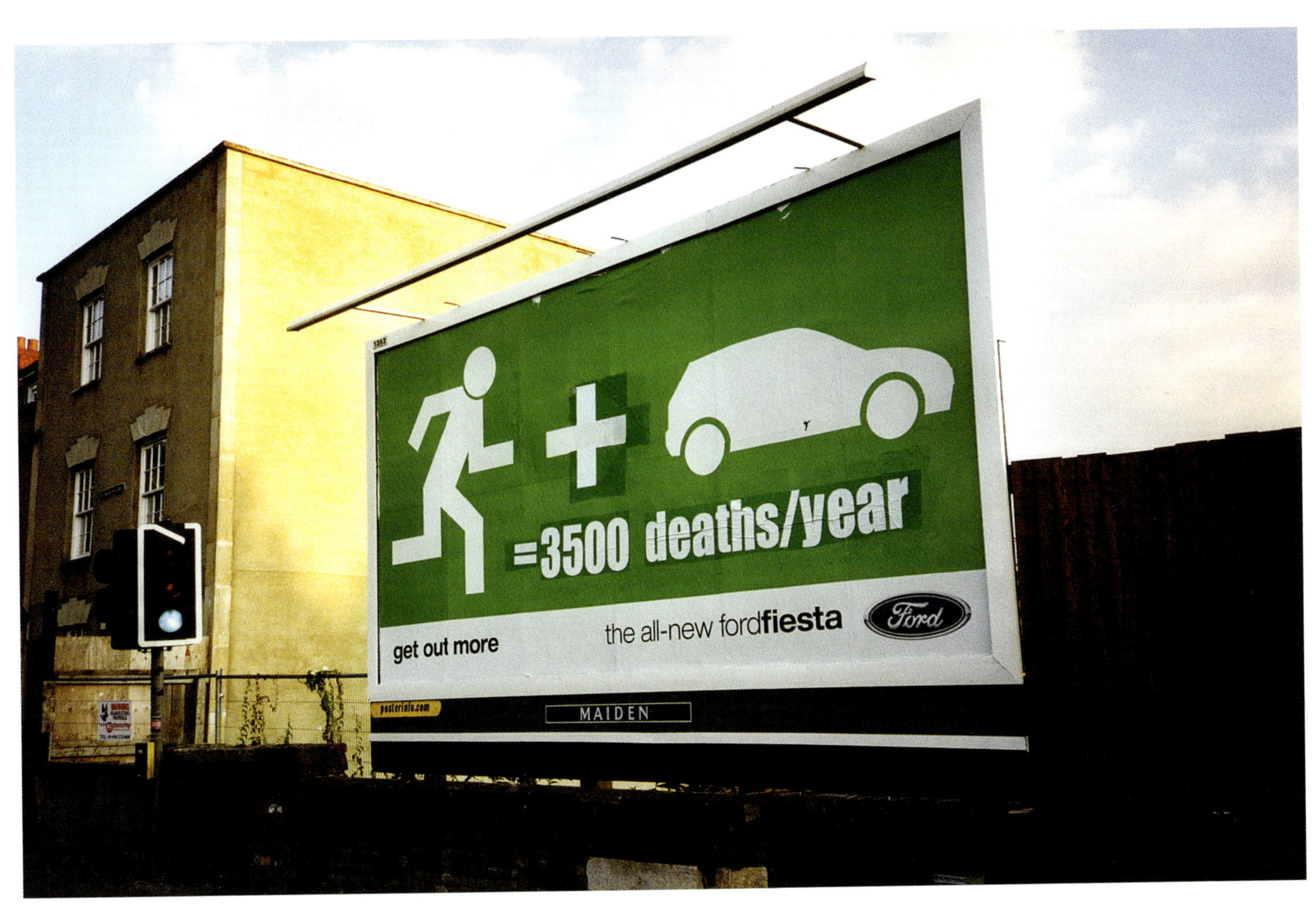

2002: =3500 deaths/year

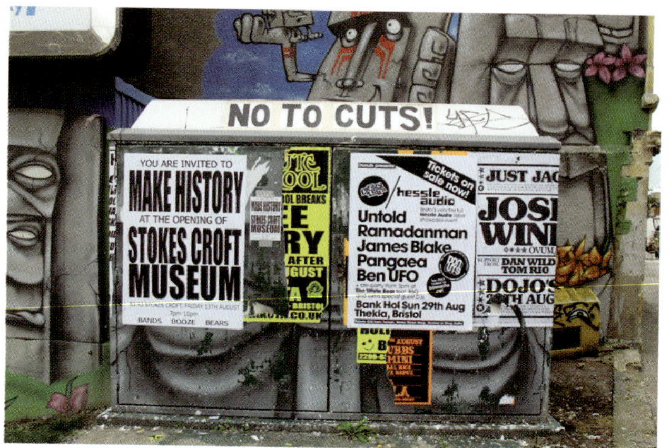
NO TO CUTS!
YOU ARE INVITED TO
MAKE HISTORY
AT THE OPENING OF
STOKES CROFT MUSEUM
BANDS BOOZE BEARS
Untold
Ramadanman
James Blake
Pangaea
Ben UFO
Bank Hol Sun 29th Aug
Thekla, Bristol
JUST JAC
JOSE
WIN
DOJO'S

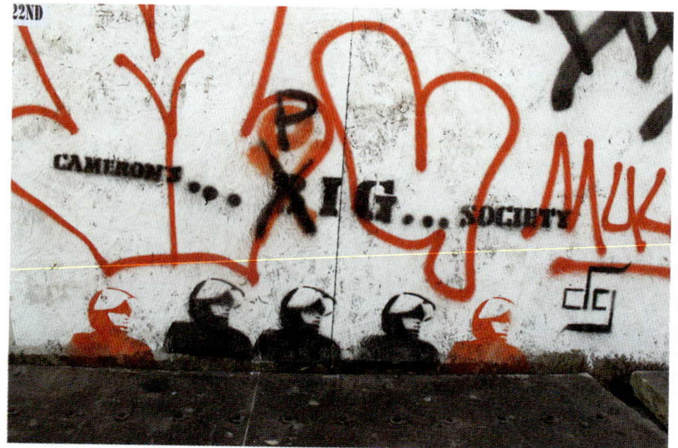
22ND
CAMERON'S ... XIG ... SOCIETY

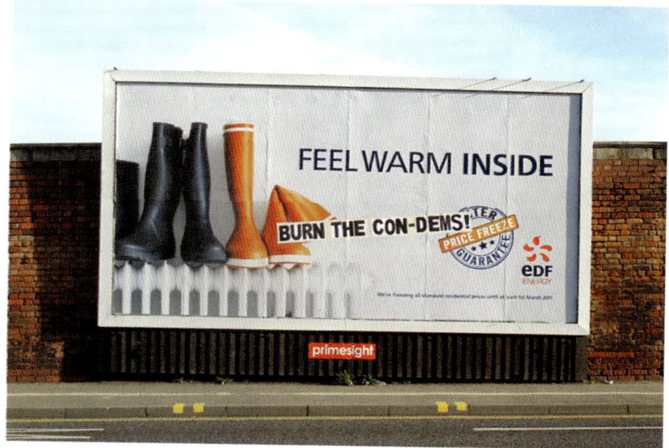
FEEL WARM INSIDE
BURN THE CON-DEMS!
WINTER PRICE FREEZE GUARANTEE
edf ENERGY
primesight

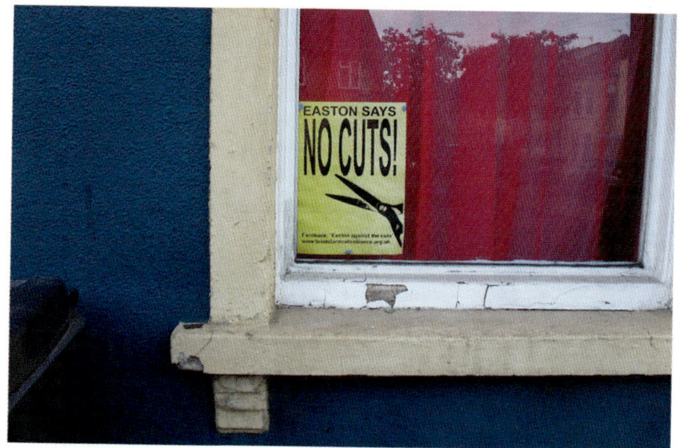
EASTON SAYS
NO CUTS!

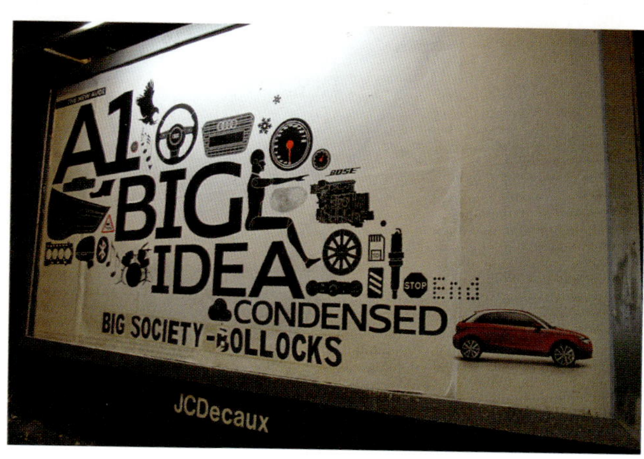
A1
BIG
IDEA
CONDENSED
BIG SOCIETY - BOLLOCKS
STOP End
BOSE
JCDecaux

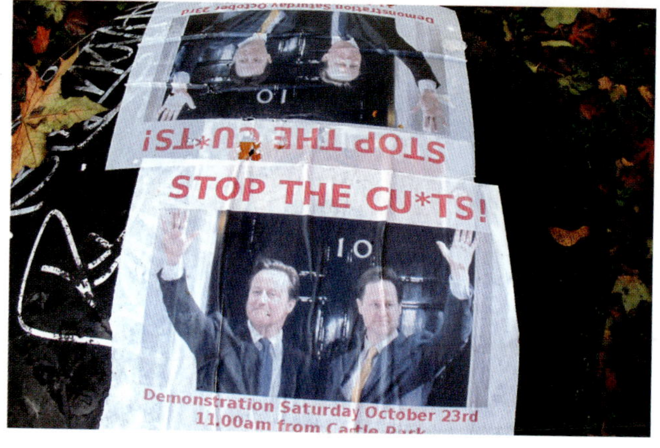
Demonstration Saturday October 23rd
STOP THE CU*TS!
STOP THE CU*TS!
Demonstration Saturday October 23rd
11.00am from Castle Park

Cuts and the coalition...

The Conservative and Liberal Democrat parties formed a coalition government in May 2010, and embarked on a huge programme of public spending cuts to address the country's budget deficit.

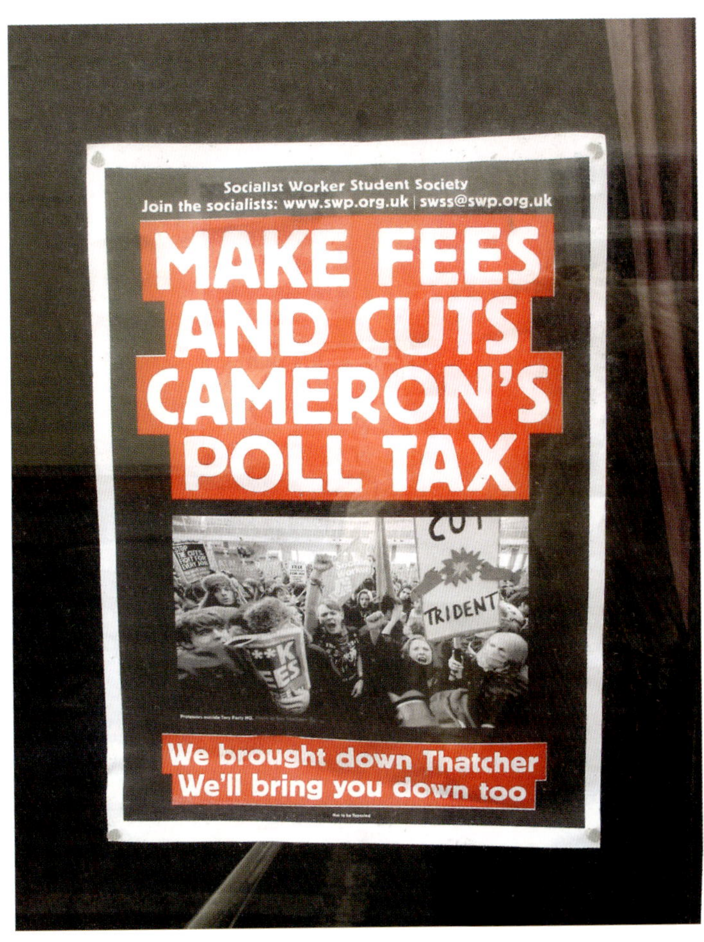

2011: Make fees and cuts Cameron's poll tax

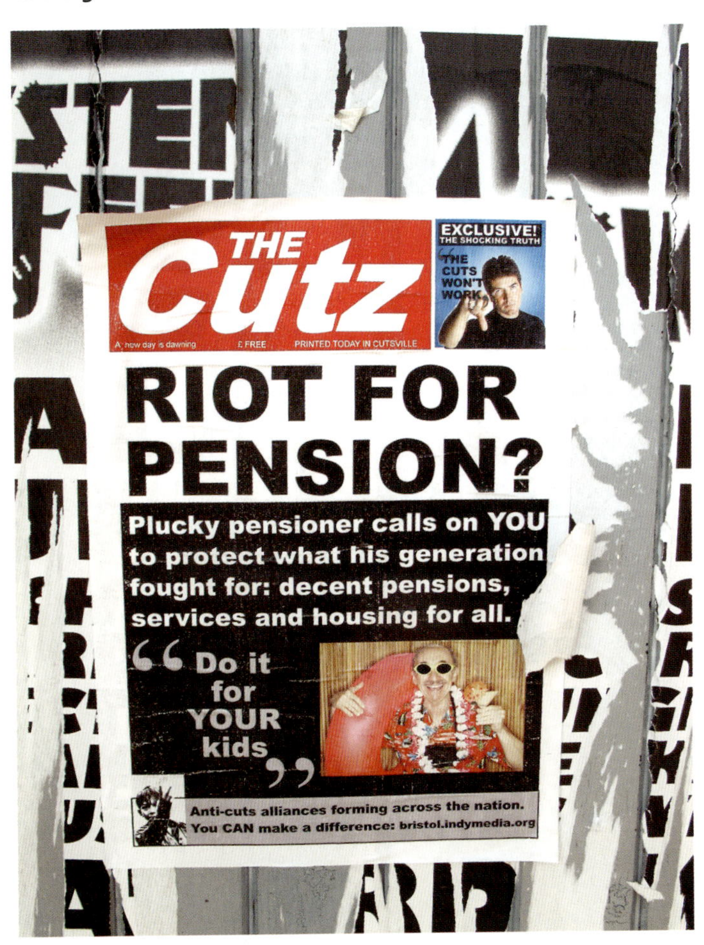

2010: The Cutz - Riot for pension?

Previous page, clockwise from top left - 2010: No to cuts! | 2011: Cameron's Pig Society | 2011: Easton says no cuts! Facebook 'Easton against the cuts' [www.bristoanticutsalliance.org.uk] | 2010: Stop the cu*ts! | 2010: Big Society - Bollocks | 2010: Feel warm inside - Burn the Con-Dems! |

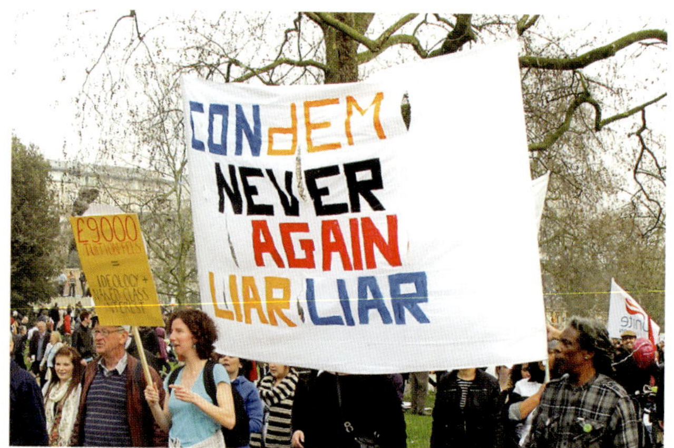
CONDEM
NEVER
AGAIN
LIAR LIAR
£9000

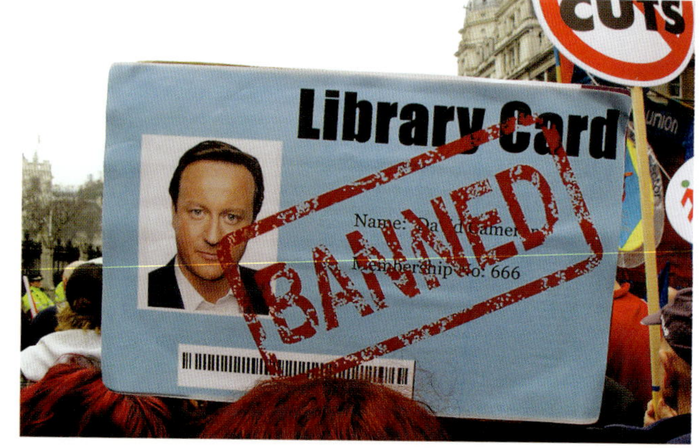
CUTS
Library Card
BANNED
Name:
Membership No: 666

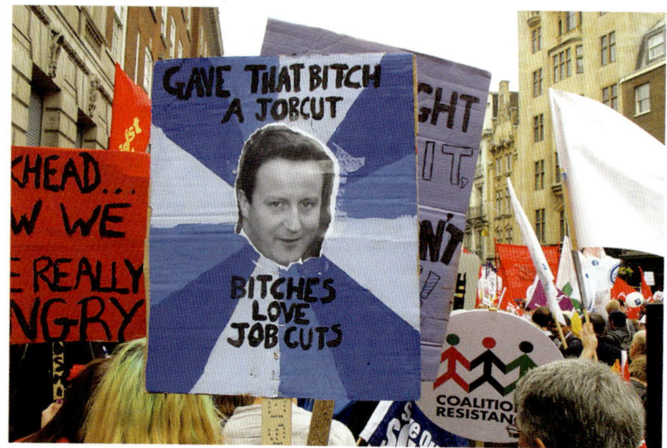
GAVE THAT BITCH
A JOBCUT
BITCHES
LOVE
JOB CUTS
HEAD...
W WE
E REALLY
NGRY
COALITION
RESISTANCE

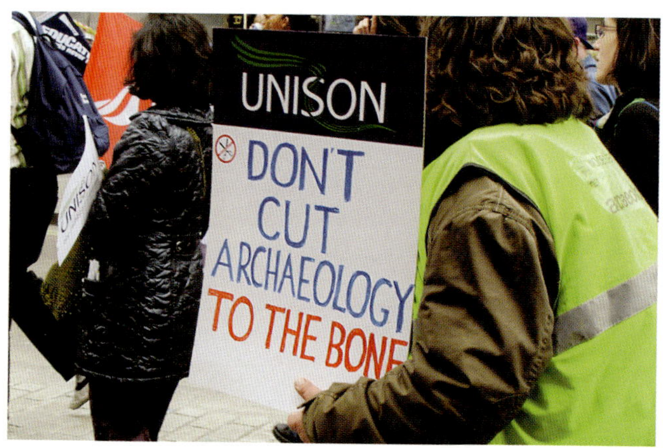
UNISON
DON'T
CUT
ARCHAEOLOGY
TO THE BONE

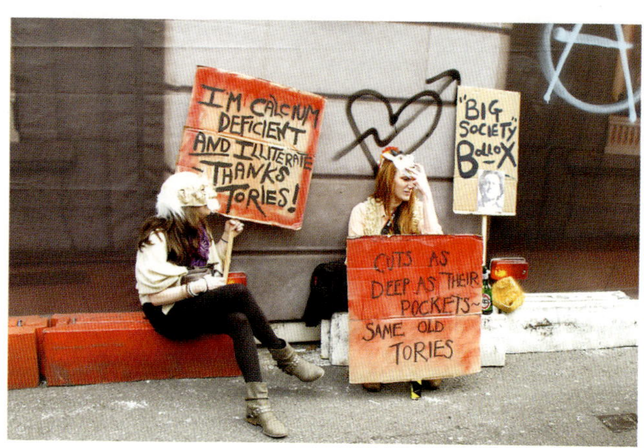
I'M CALCIUM
DEFICIENT
AND ILLITERATE
THANKS
TORIES!
"BIG
SOCIETY"
BOLLOX
CUTS AS
DEEP AS THEIR
POCKETS~
SAME OLD
TORIES

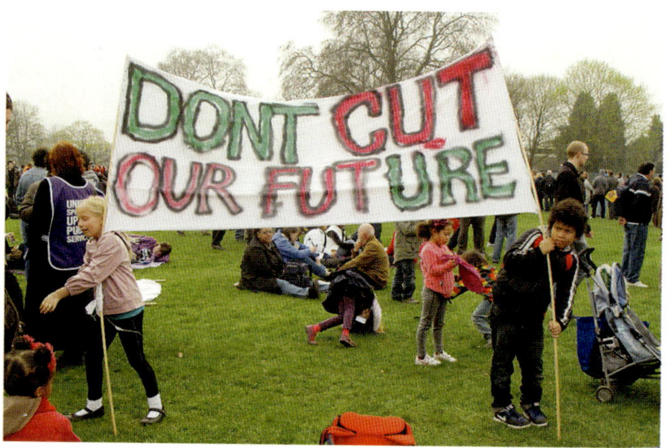
DONT CUT
OUR FUTURE

Anti-cuts demonstration...

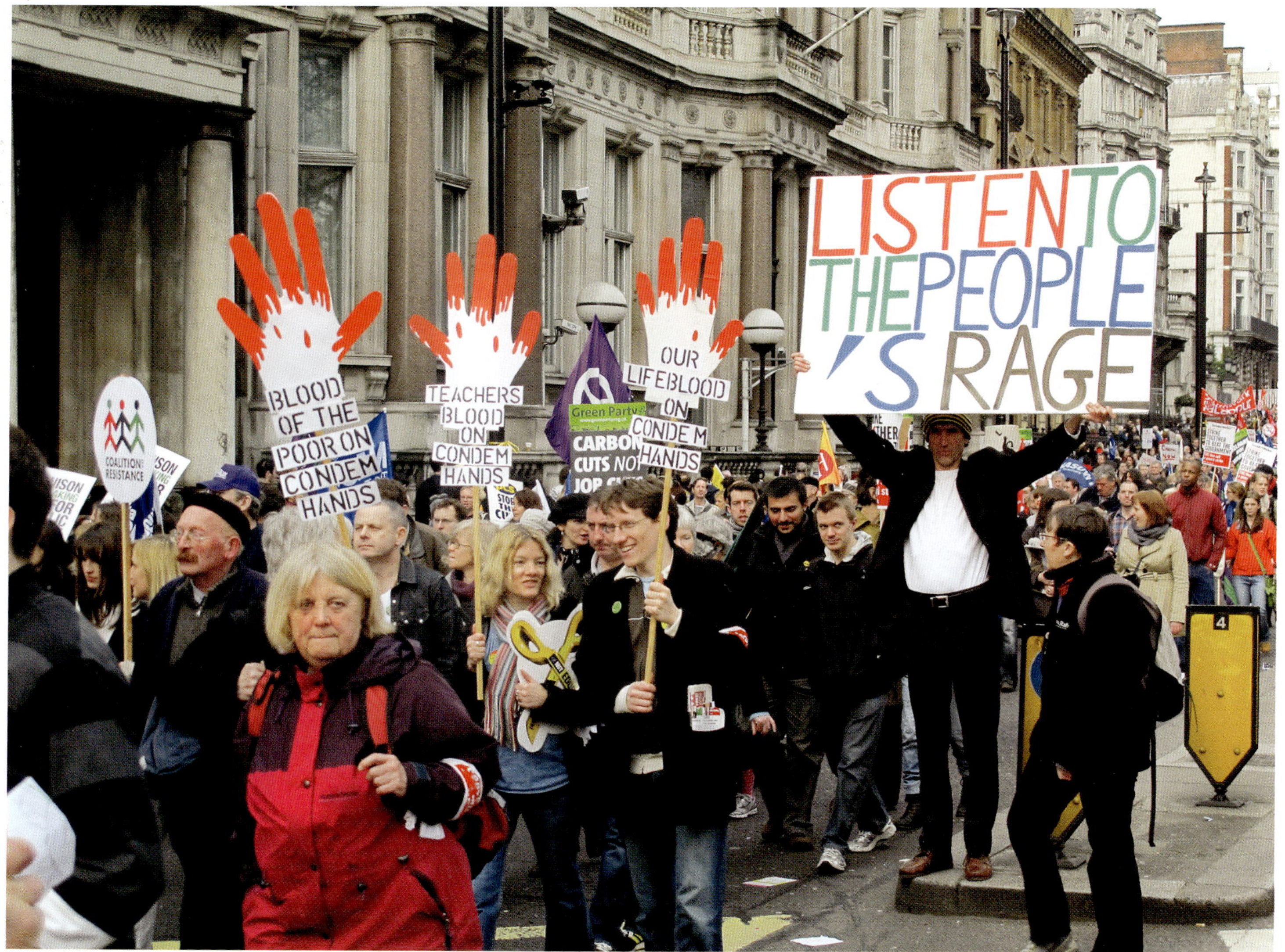

Previous page and next page: TUC anti-cuts march and demonstration, London, 26 March 2011.

Re: 'Gideon Scissorhands' on page 111... Chancellor George Osborne was christened Gideon. 'Edward Scissorhands' is a 1990 film whose leading character has scissors for hands.

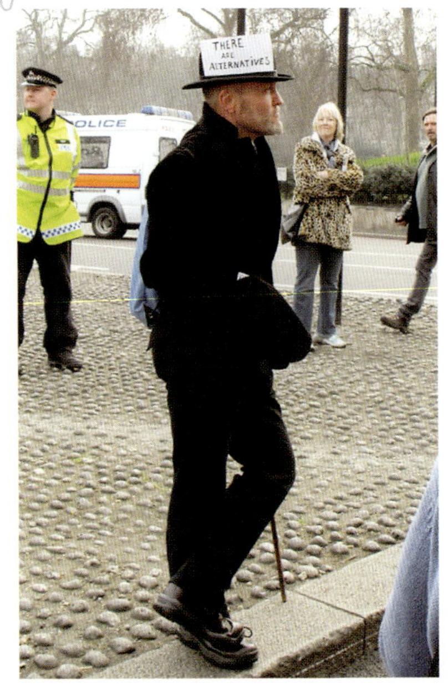

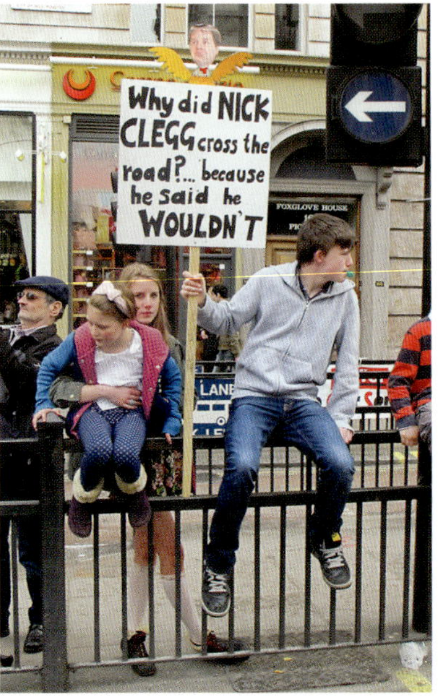

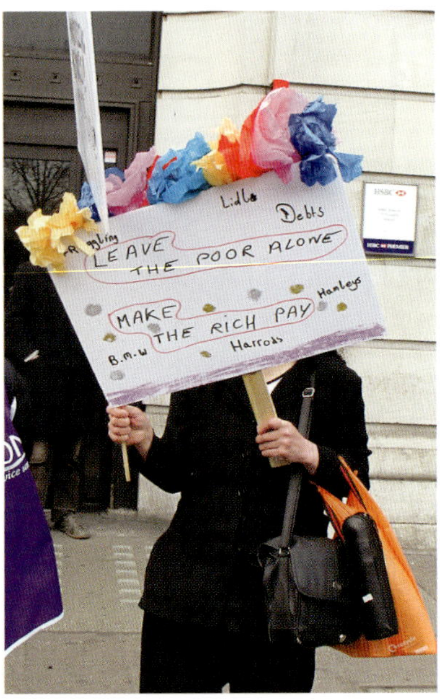

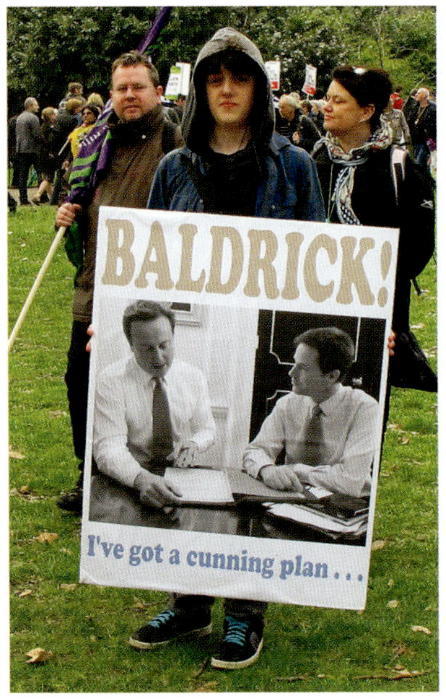

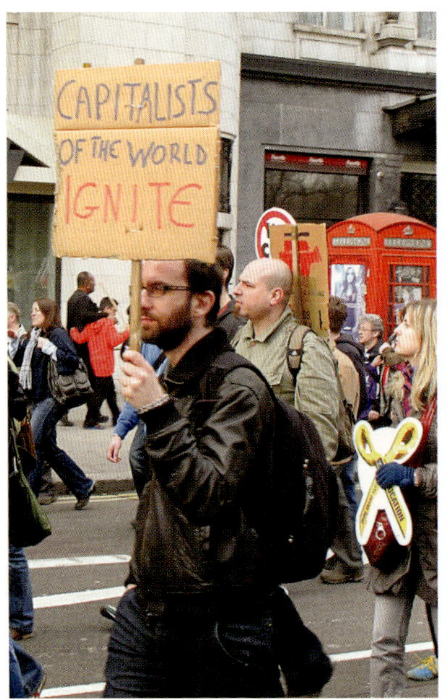

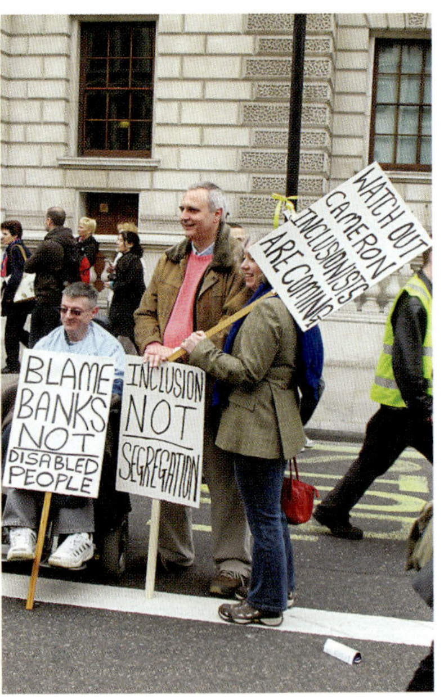

Anti-cuts demonstration...

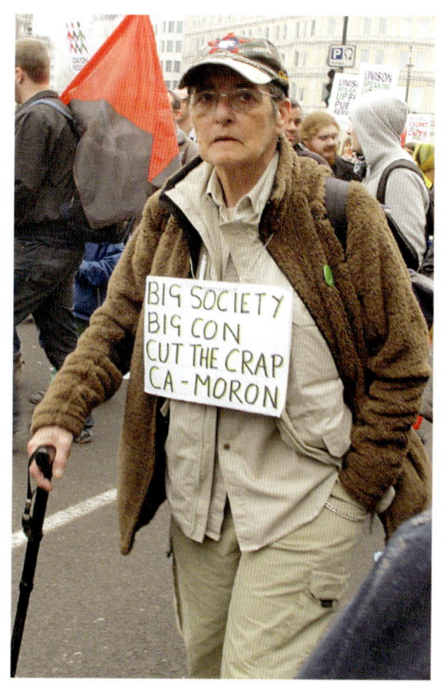
BIG SOCIETY
BIG CON
CUT THE CRAP
CA - MORON

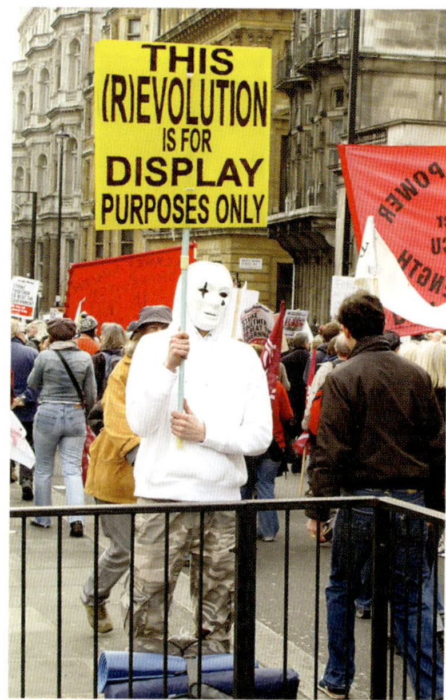
THIS
(R)EVOLUTION
IS FOR
DISPLAY
PURPOSES ONLY

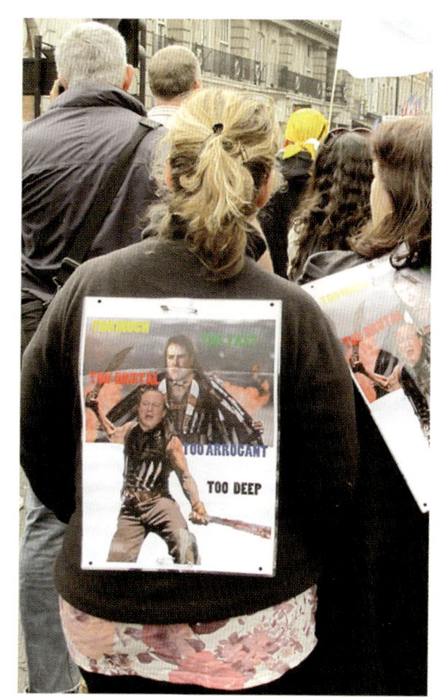
TOO ARROGANT
TOO DEEP

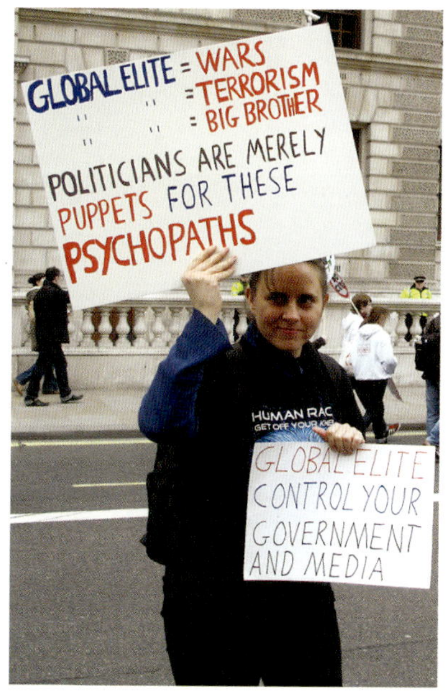
GLOBAL ELITE = WARS
= TERRORISM
= BIG BROTHER
POLITICIANS ARE MERELY
PUPPETS FOR THESE
PSYCHOPATHS
HUMAN RACE
GET OFF YOUR
GLOBAL ELITE
CONTROL YOUR
GOVERNMENT
AND MEDIA

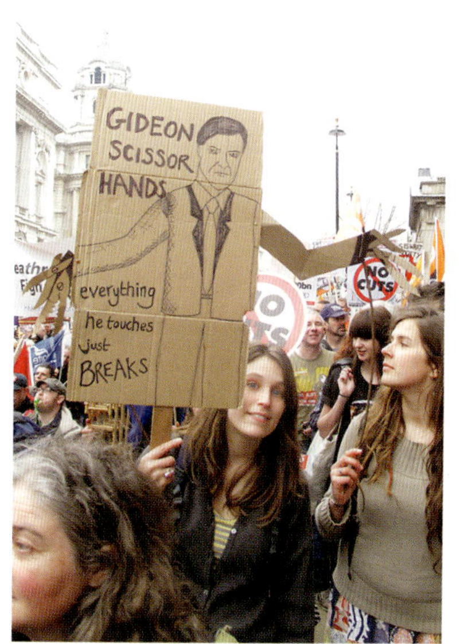
GIDEON
SCISSOR
HANDS
everything
he touches
just
BREAKS
NO CUTS

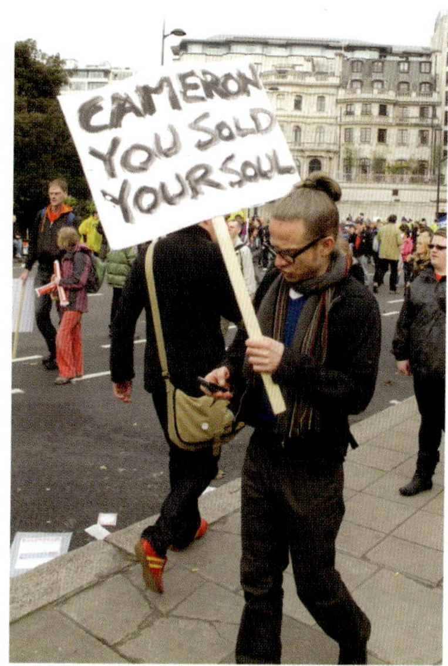
CAMERON
YOU SOLD
YOUR SOUL

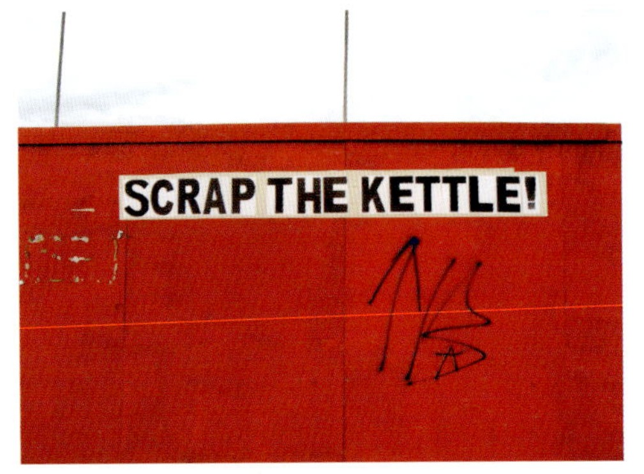

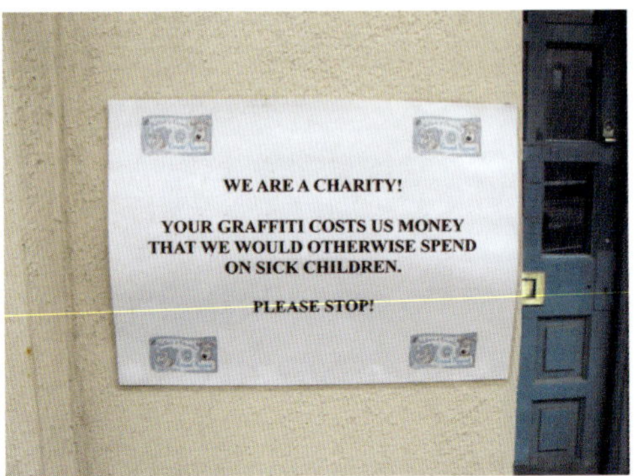

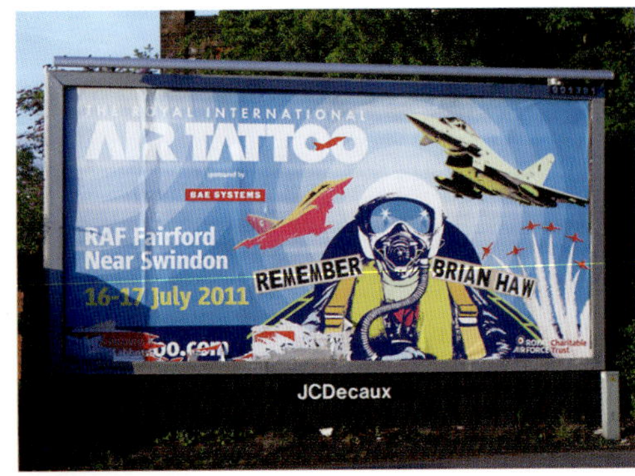

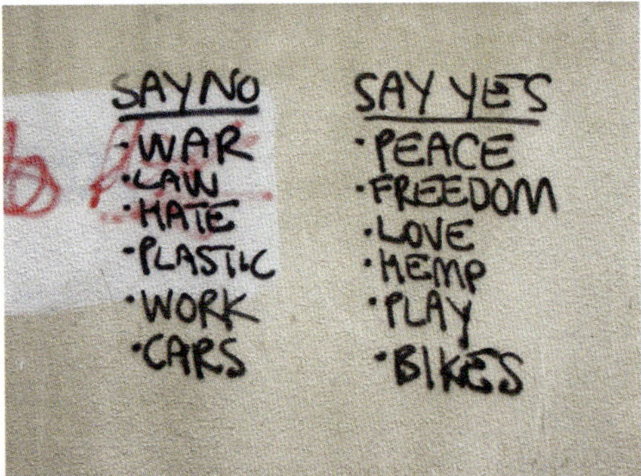

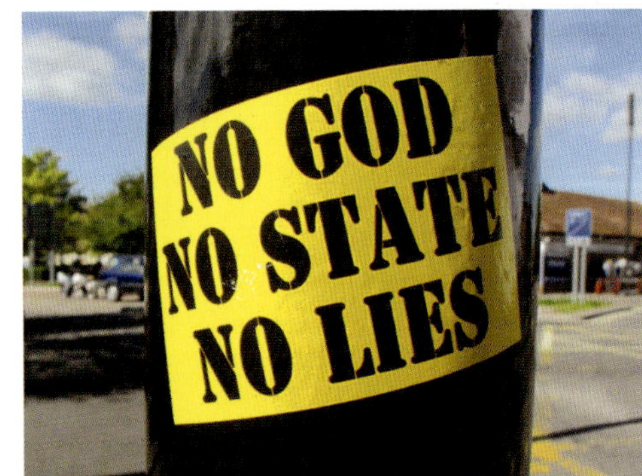

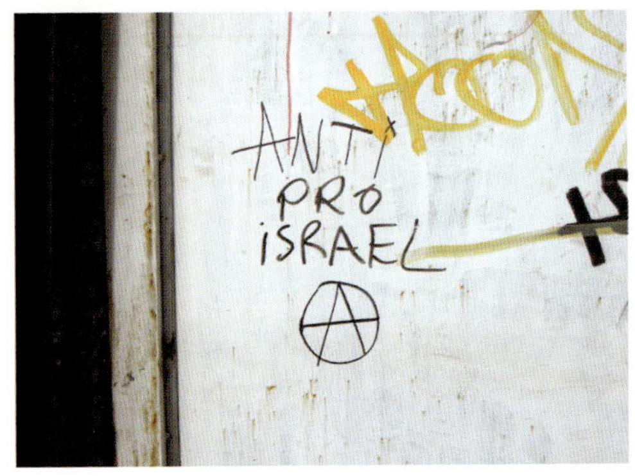

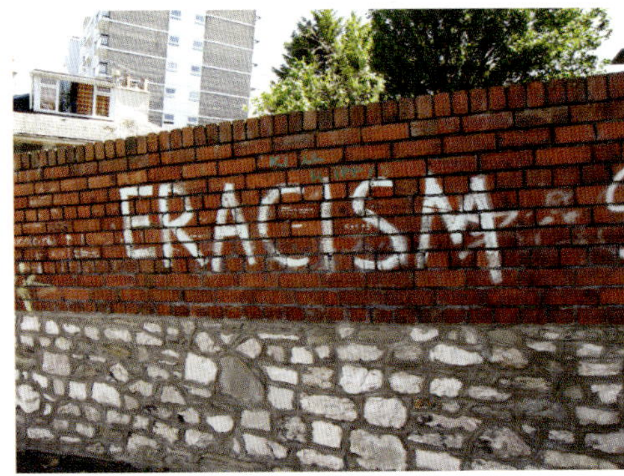

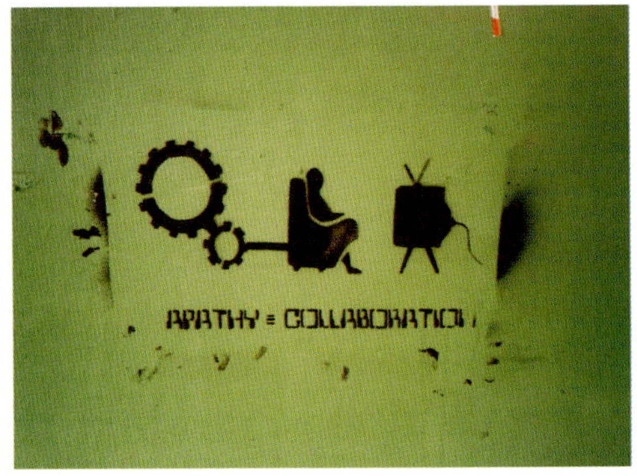

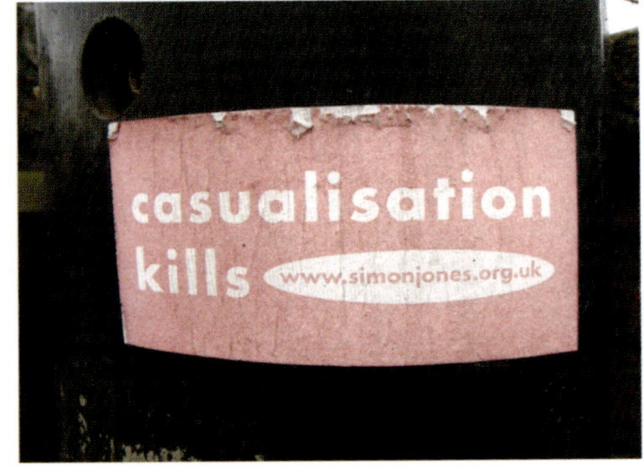

Top row from left – 2009: Scrap the kettle [The kettle is a policing method used during demonstrations] | 2008: We are a charity! | 2011: Remember Brian Haw [Peace campaigner who set up a camp in London's Parliament Square in 2001 in protest against UK and US foreign policy. He died in 2011] |
Middle row from left – 2007: Say no say yes | 2010: No God no state no lies | 2007: Anti pro Israel |
Bottom row from left – 2007: Eracism | 2002: Apathy = collaboration | 2010: Casualisation kills [www.simonjones.org.uk]

And the rest...

For the photos that don't fit neatly into a category.

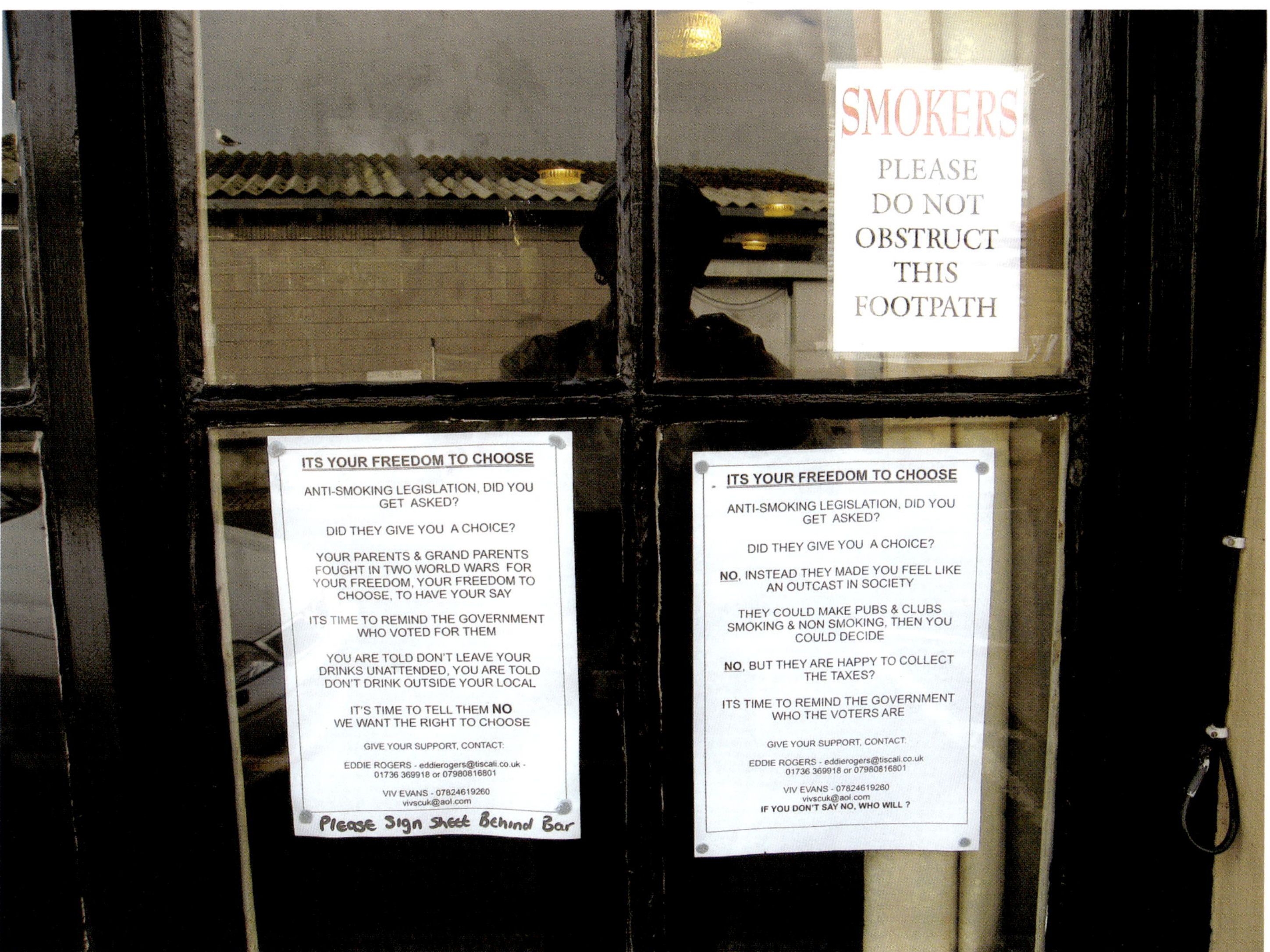

2007: Its your freedom to choose [The smoking ban in public places in England came into force on 1 July 2007]

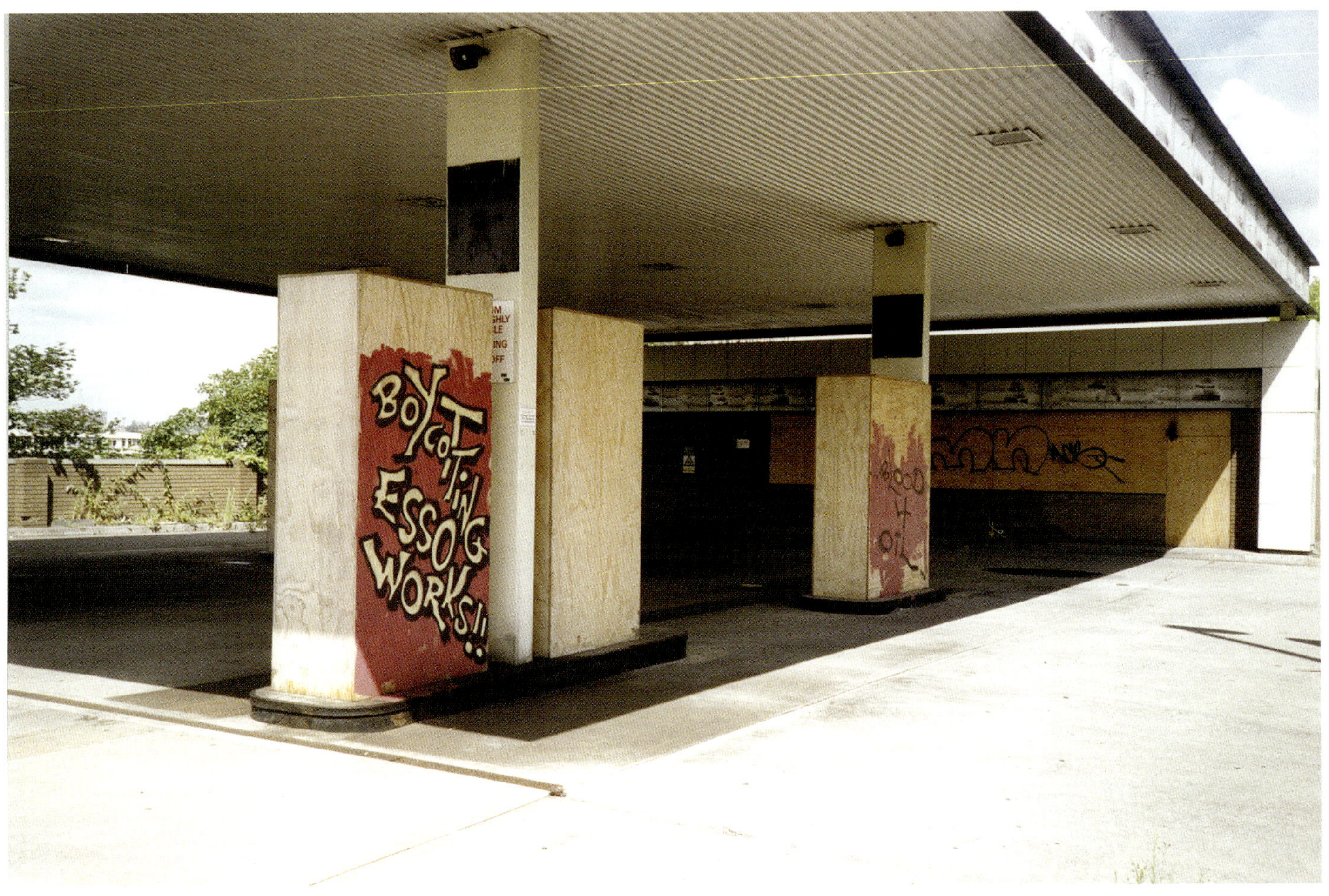

2003: Boycotting Esso works!!

And the rest...

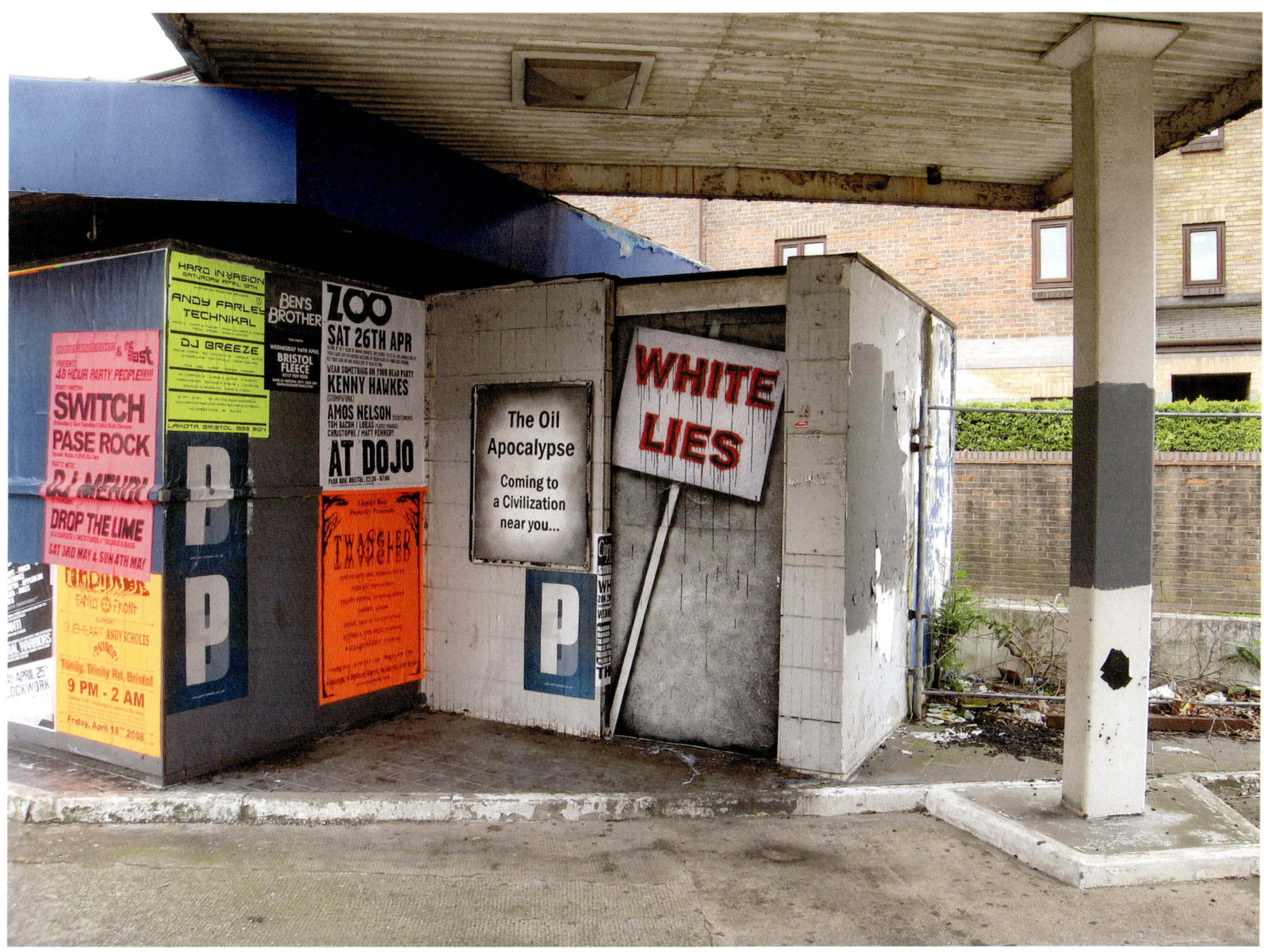

2008: The Oil Apocalypse - Coming to a Civilization near you...

[Our economies and way of life are extremely dependent on oil. However, as a finite resource, sooner or later supplies will dwindle, with more far-reaching consequences than most of us can imagine. Everything will change. Google 'peak oil', or see the film 'A Crude Awakening' to find out more]

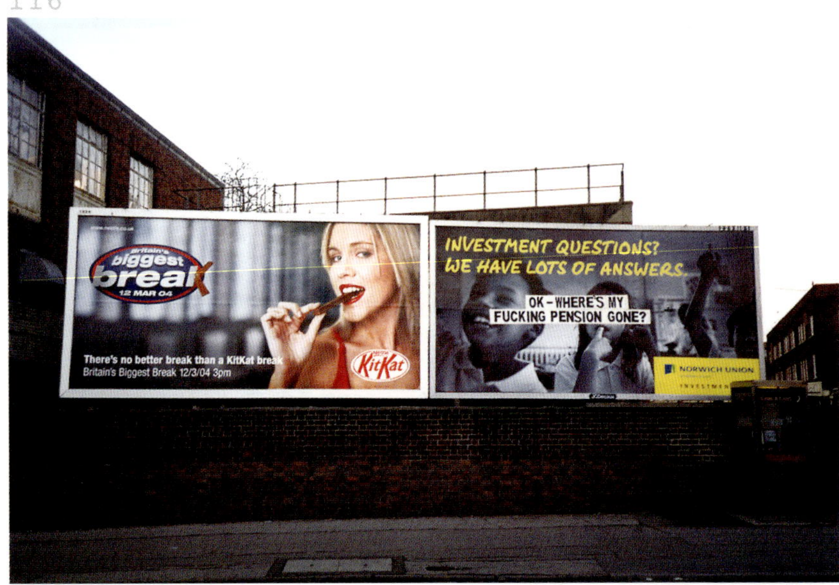

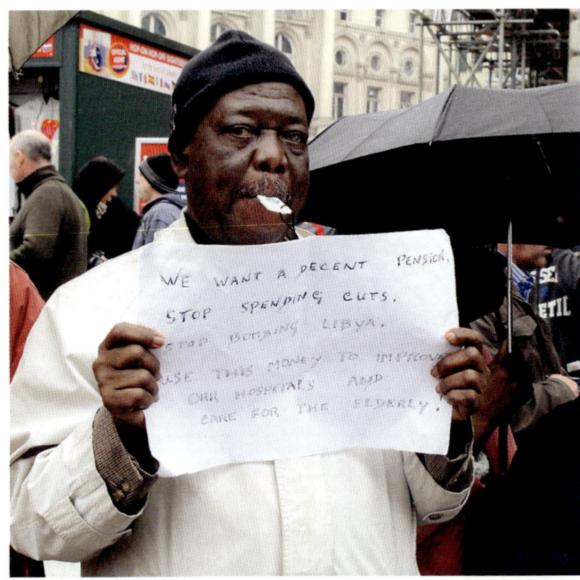

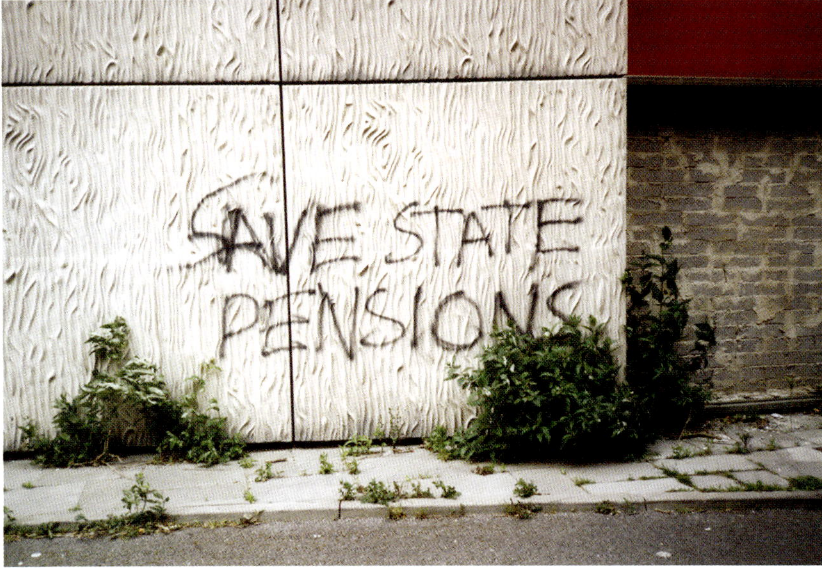

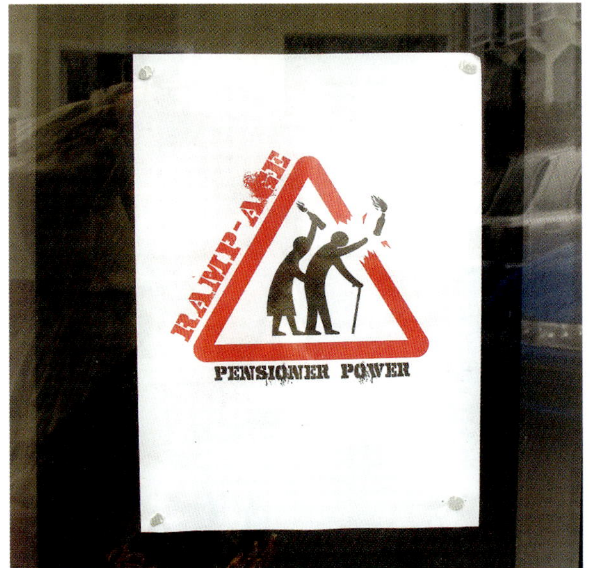

From top left. 2004: OK - Where's my fucking pension gone? [Pension funds are vulnerable if companies decide to use them to shore up their business, or if investments collapse. The Mirror Group under Robert Maxwell famously stole their employee's company pensions in 1999] | 2011: We want a decent pension stop spending cuts | 2011: Ramp-age - Pensioner power | 2005: Save state pensions |

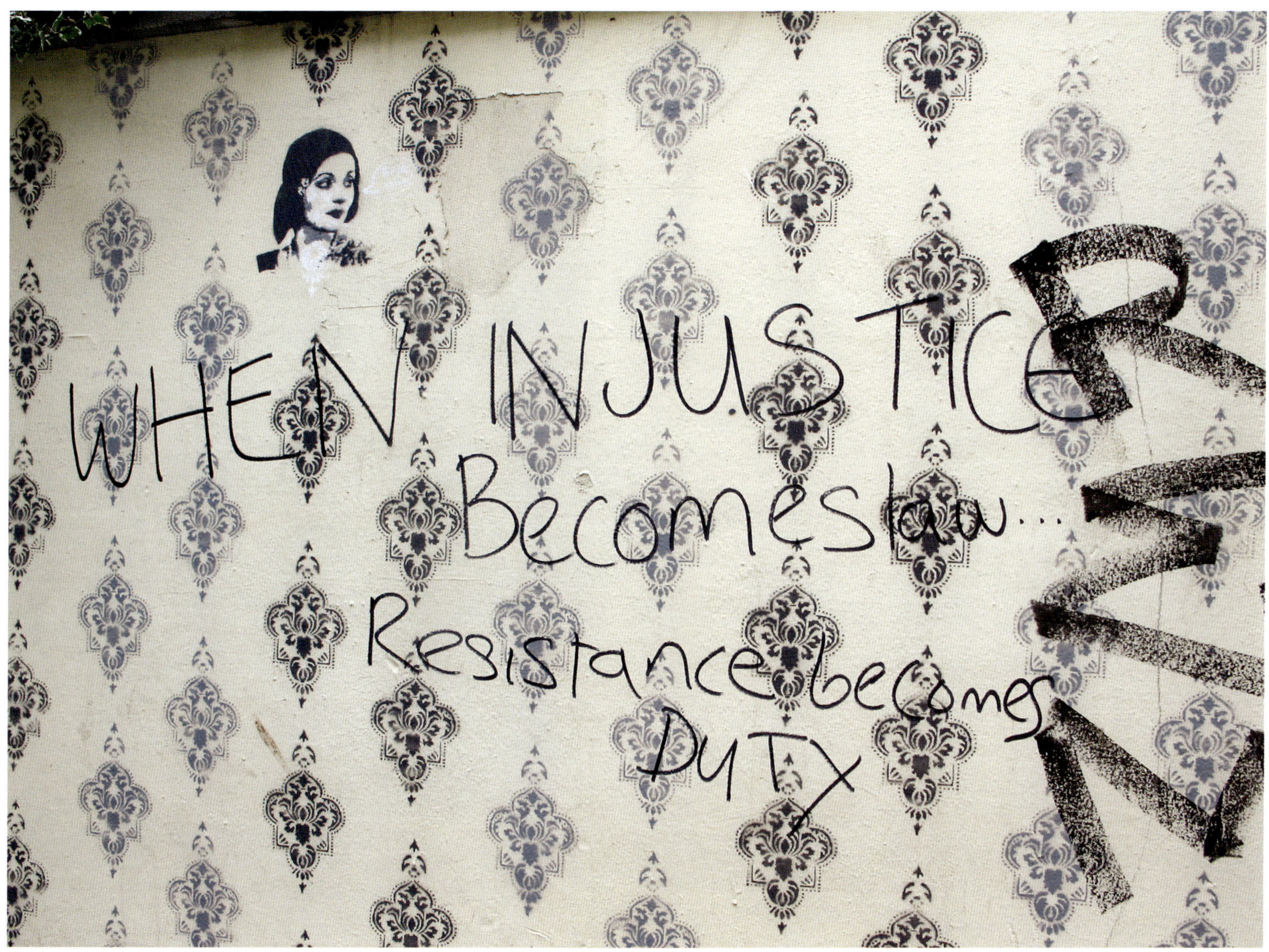

2011: When injustice becomes law resistance becomes duty

[Thomas Jefferson in 1787: "The spirit of resistance to government is so valuable on certain occasions, that I wish it to be always kept alive. It will often be exercised when wrong, but better so than not to be exercised at all."]

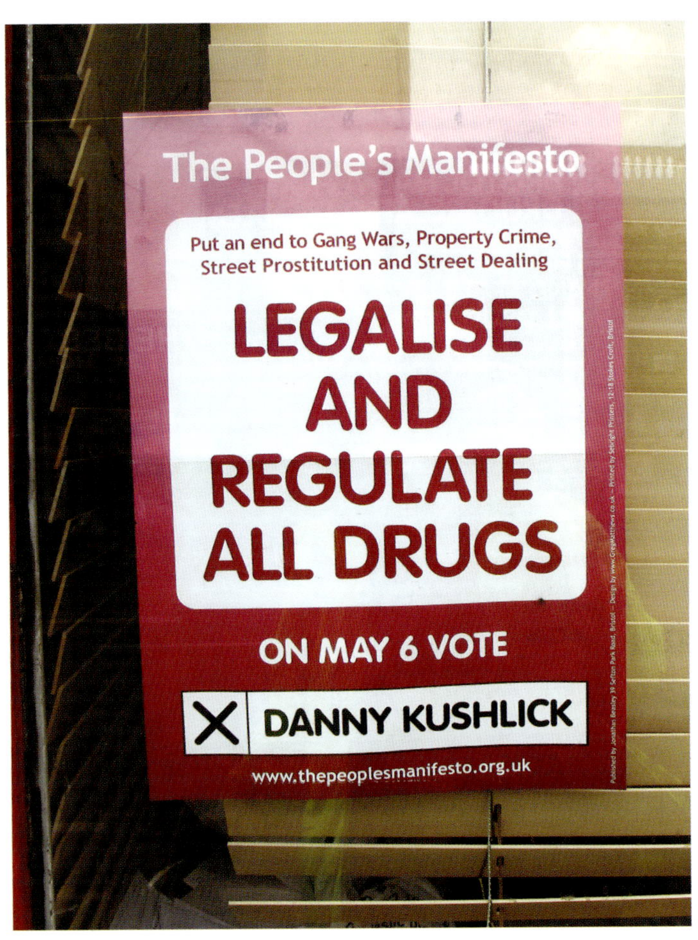

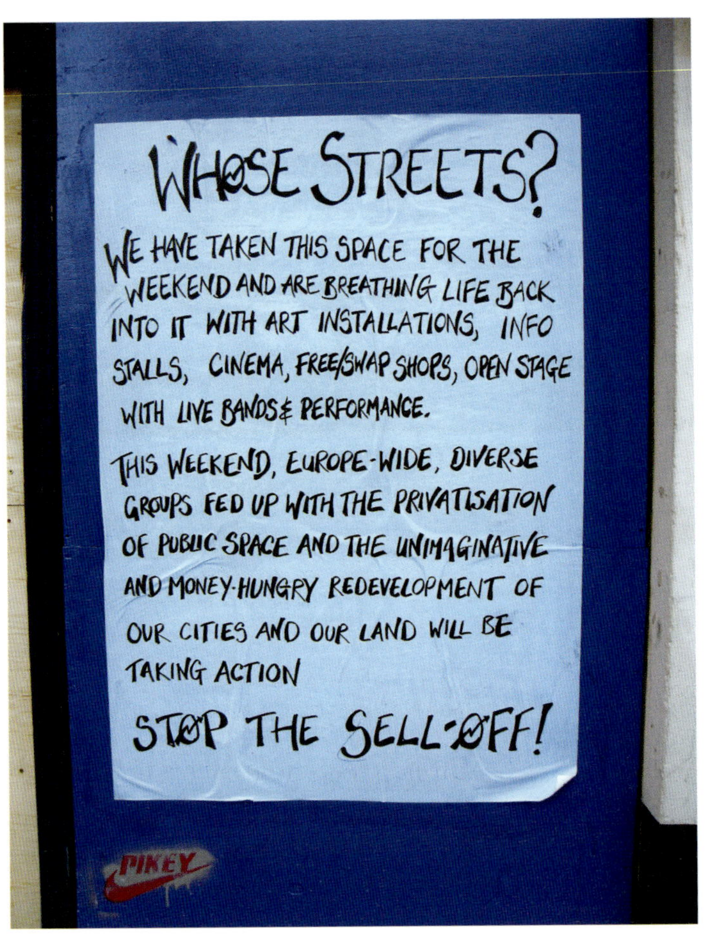

2010: Legalise and regulate all drugs
[www.thepeoplesmanifesto.org.uk]

2008: Whose streets?

And the rest...

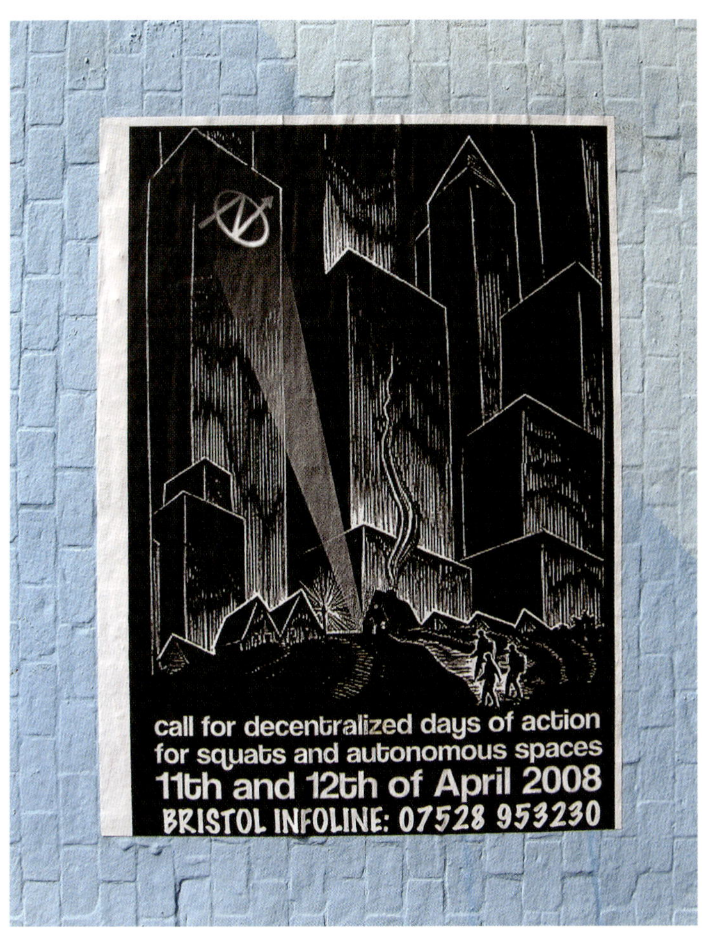

2008: Call for decentralized days of
action for squats and automomous spaces

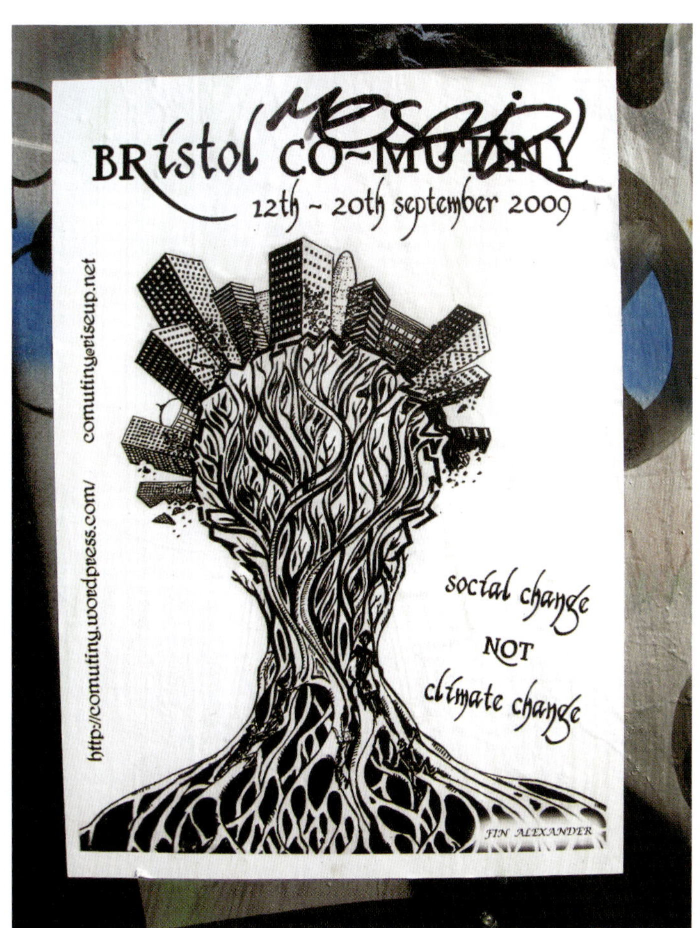

2009: Bristol Co-mutiny. Social change not climate
change [http://comutiny.wordpress.com/]

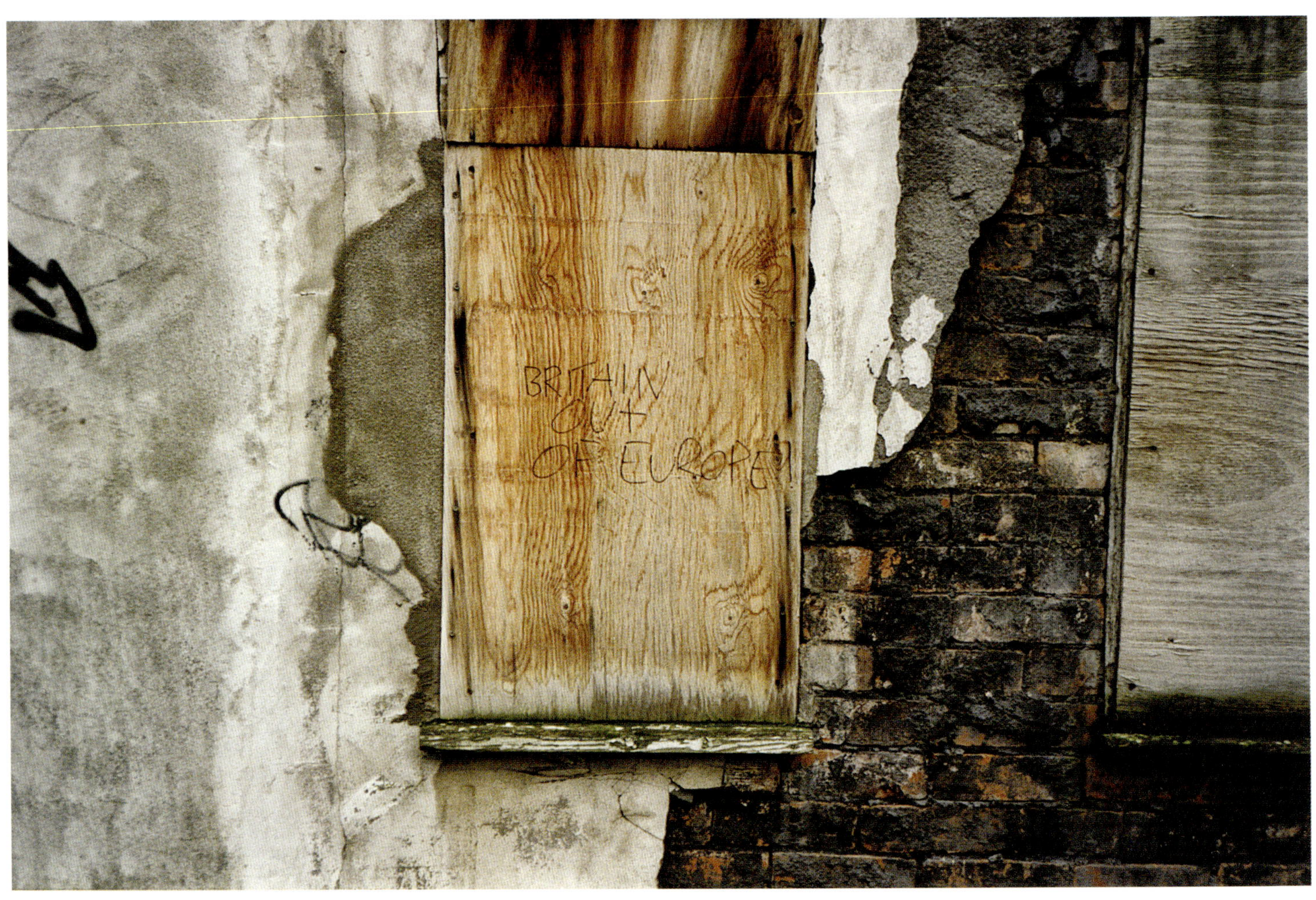

2001: Britain out of Europe

And the rest...

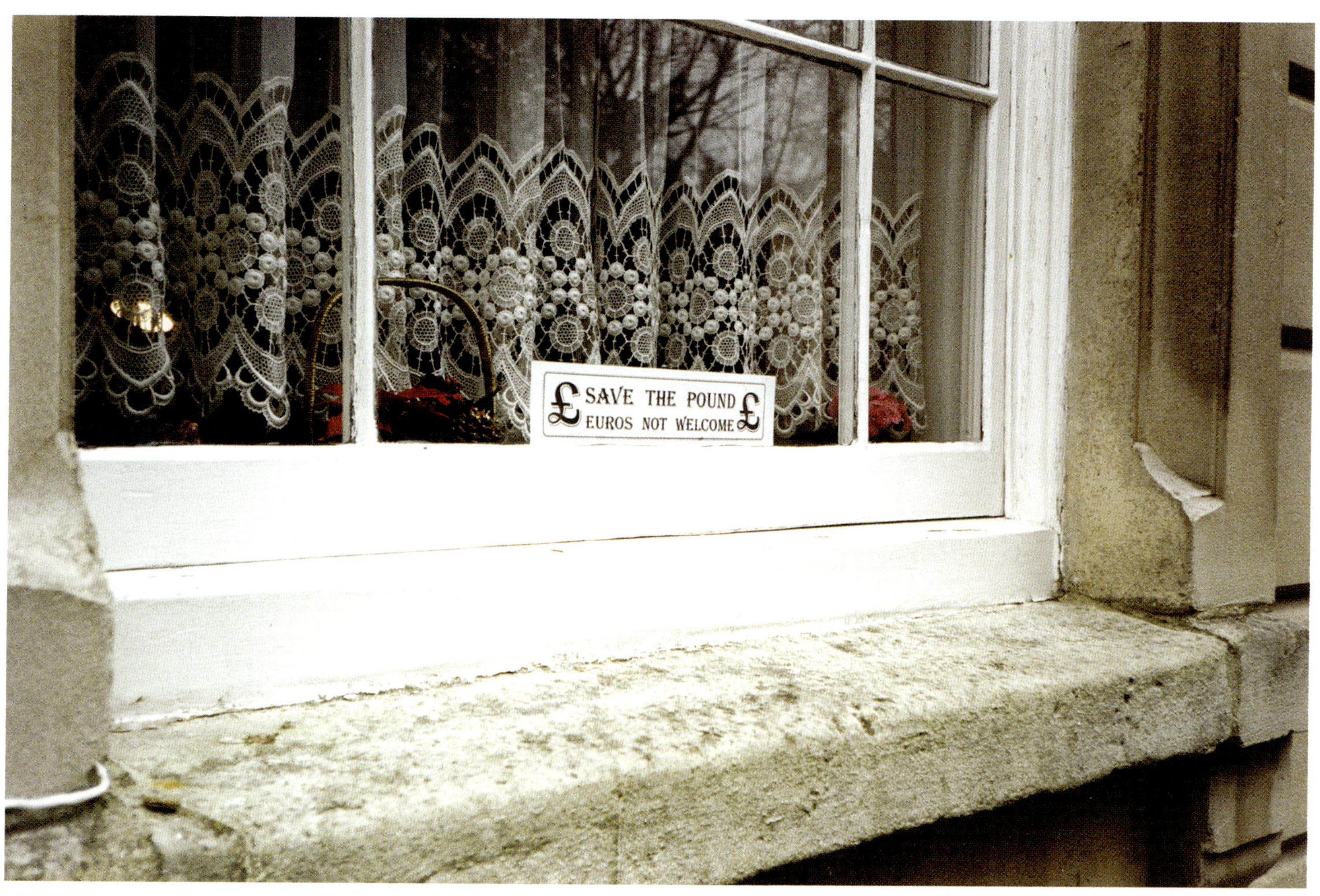

2002: Save the pound, Euros not welcome

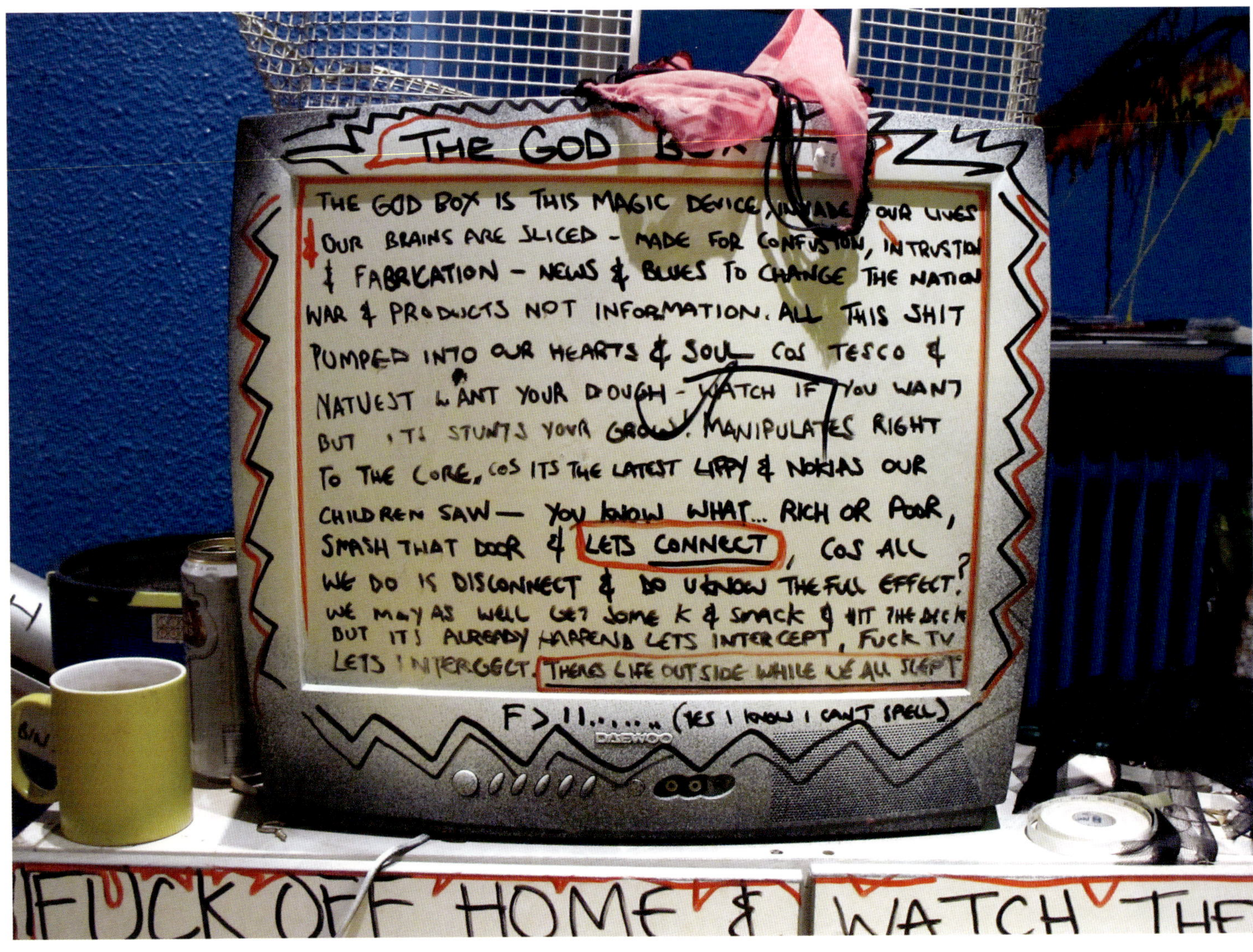

2011: The God Box [in a Temporary Autononomous Art exhibition]

And the rest...

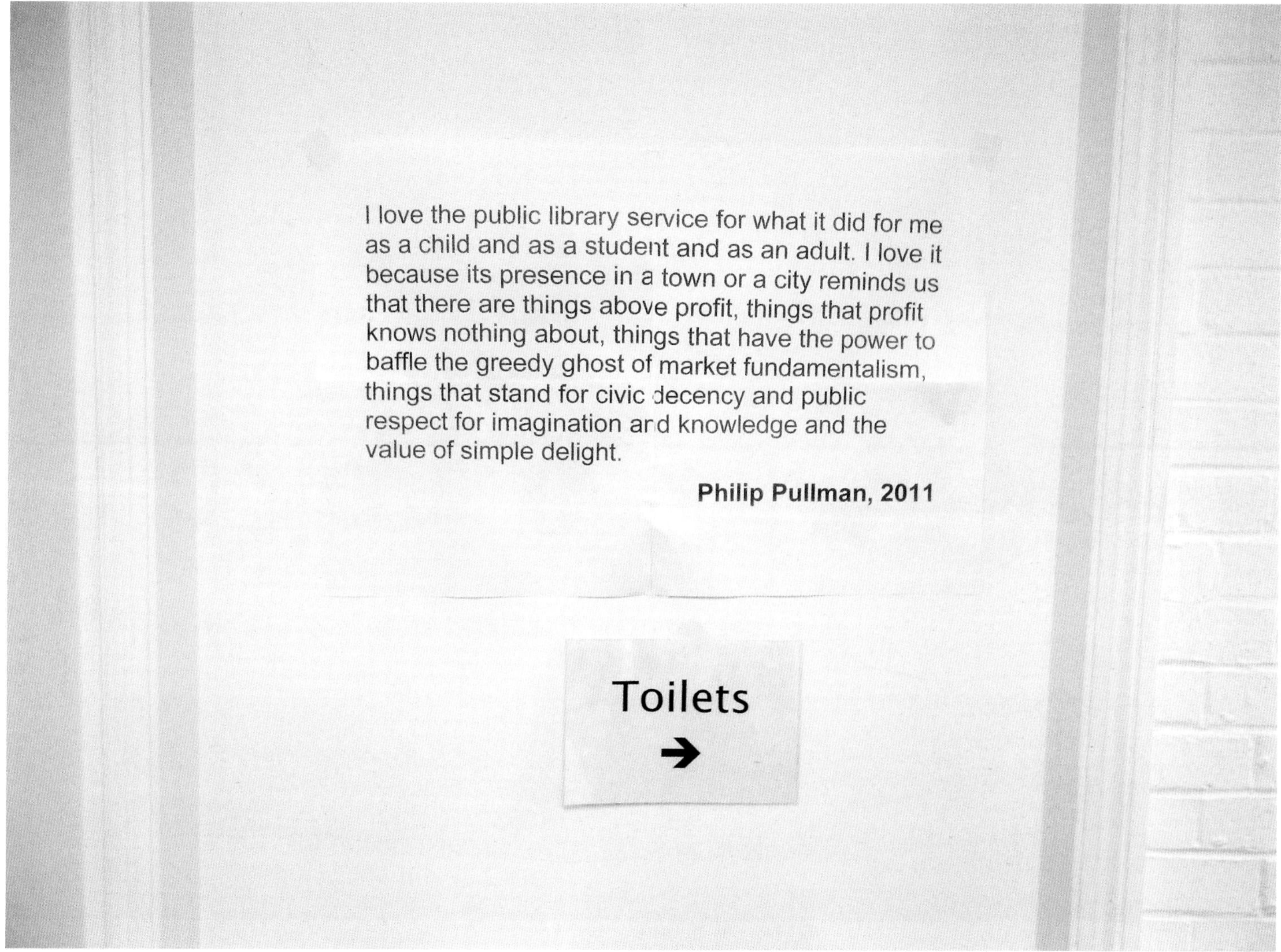

2011: I love the public library service...
[Author Philip Pullman defending libraries against local government expenditure cuts]

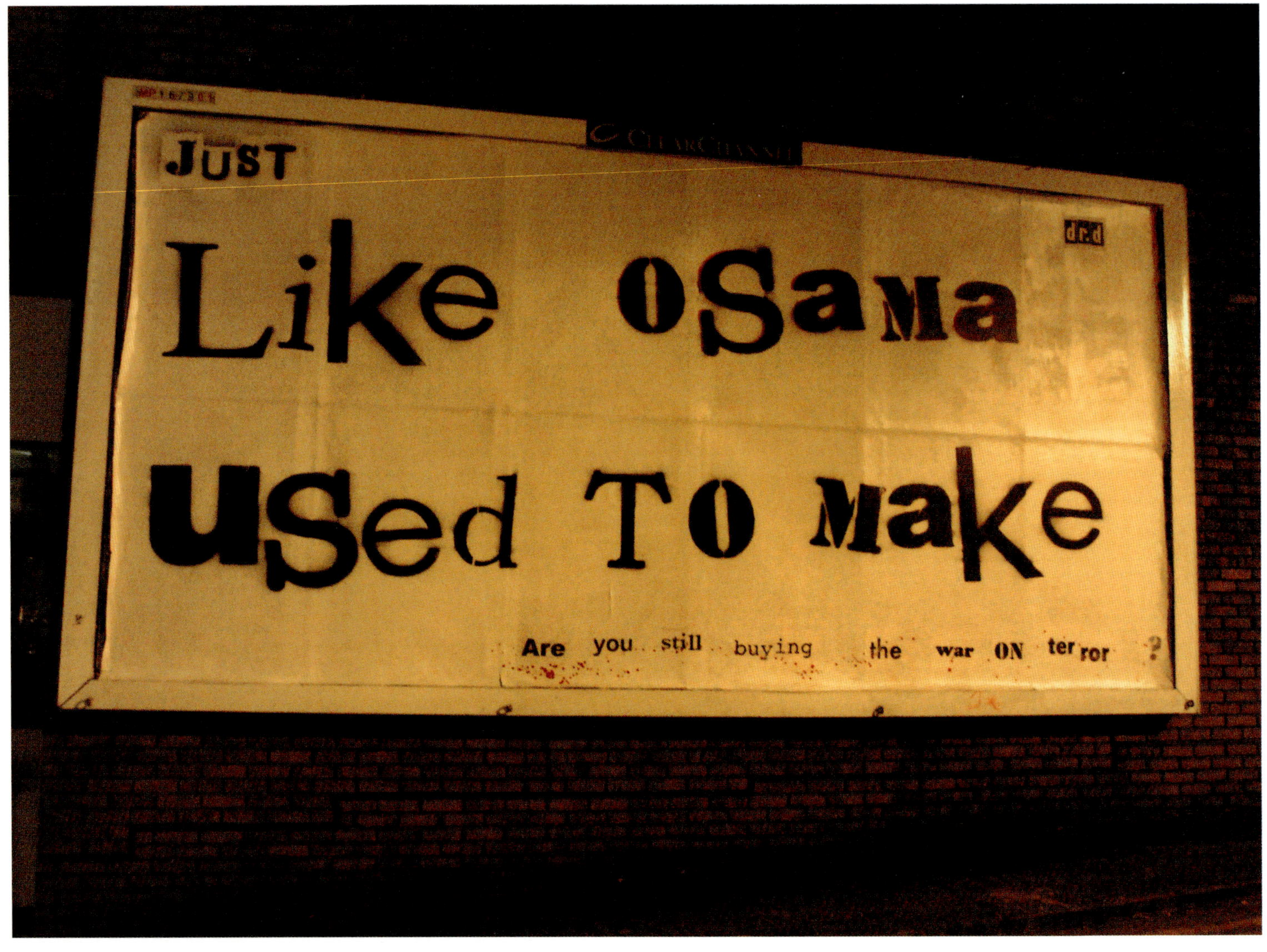

2007: Just like Osama used to make. Are you still buying the war on terror?

And the rest...

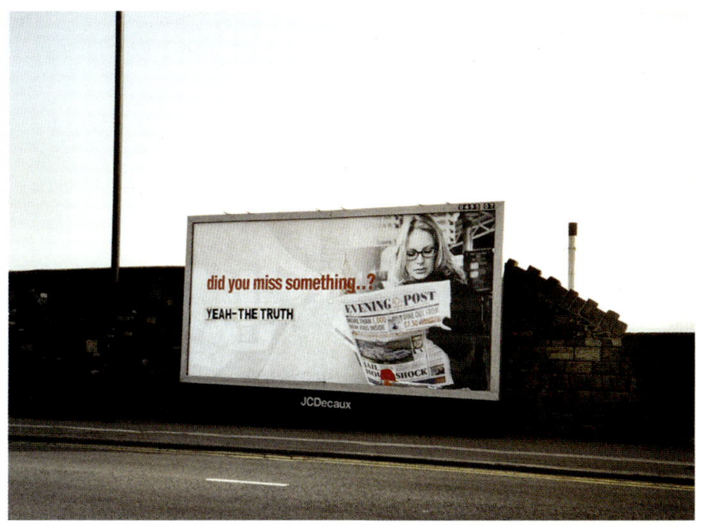

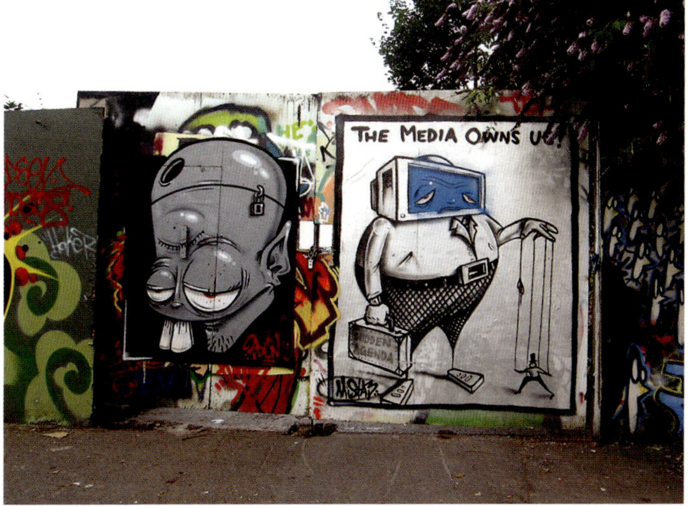

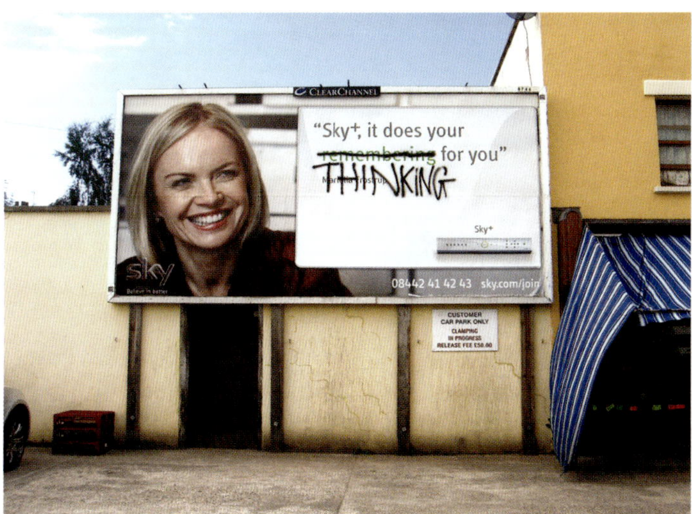

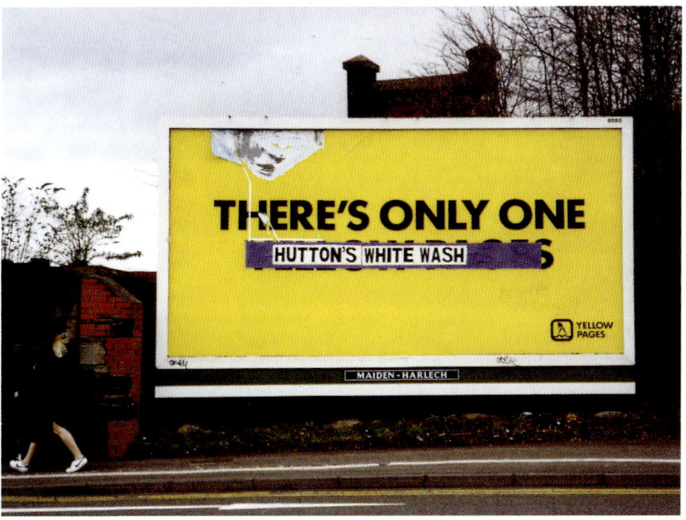

Clockwise from top left – 2003: Did you miss something? Yeah – the truth | 2008: The media owns us | 2004: There's only one Hutton's whitewash [The Hutton Inquiry was concerned with the death of David Kelly – a former UN weapons inspector named as the source of quotes made by the BBC to the effect that the Labour government sexed up its report into Iraq and weapons of mass destruction, a critical factor in parliamentary and public support for going to war with Iraq. It cleared the government of wrong-doing, but several national newspapers accused the inquiry of "an establishment whitewash"] | 2008: Sky, it does your thinking for you |

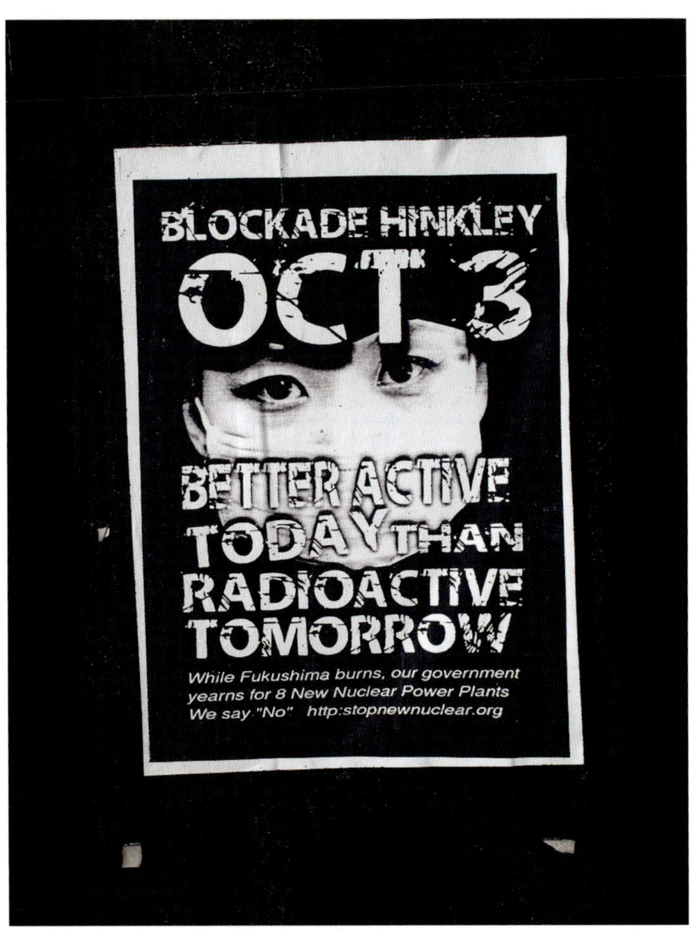

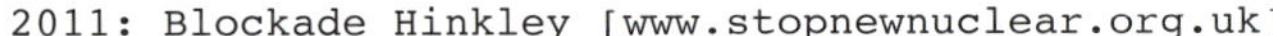

2011: Blockade Hinkley [www.stopnewnuclear.org.uk]

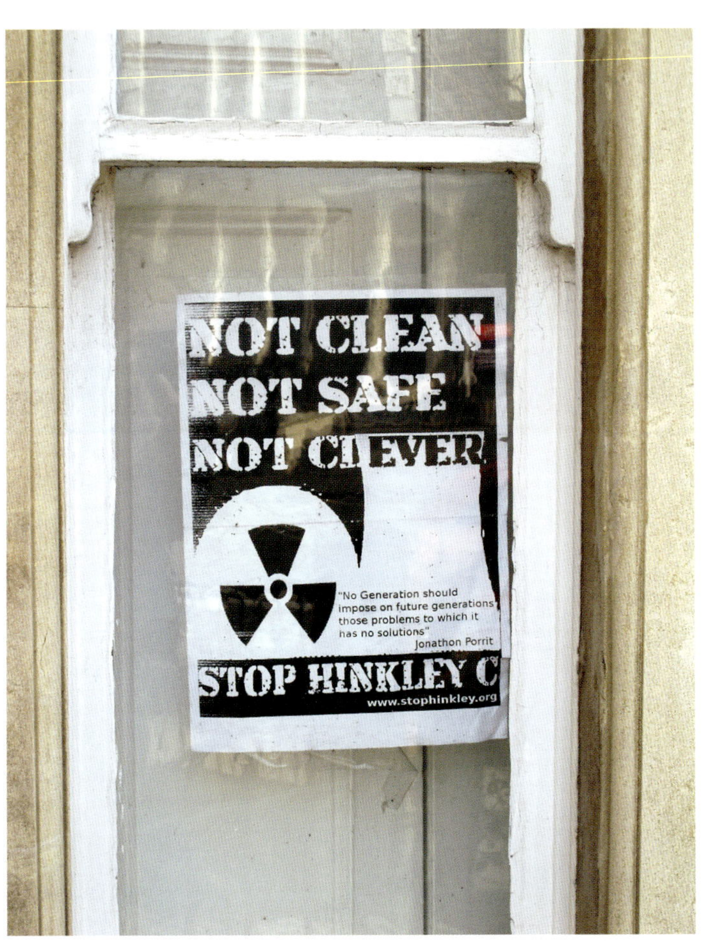

2011: Not clean not safe not clever [www.stophinkley.org]

[The nuclear debate was given fresh impetus by the melt-downs, explosions and spent fuel fires at the Fukushima power complex in Japan in 2011, which created a major disaster for public health and the environment as well as Japan's economy. The UK government is currently proposing to build 8 new nuclear power stations, the first at Hinkley Point in Somerset]

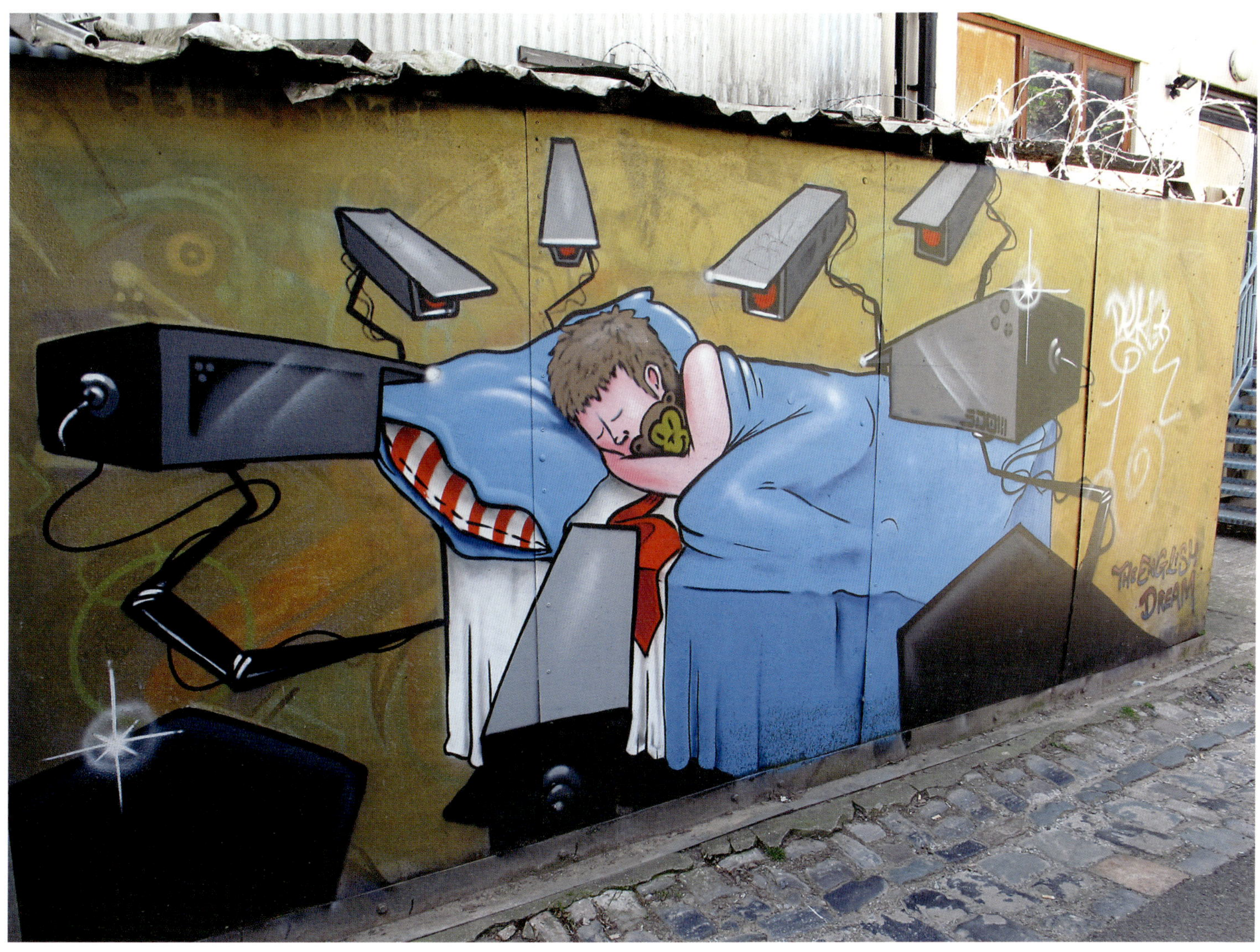

2011: The English Dream

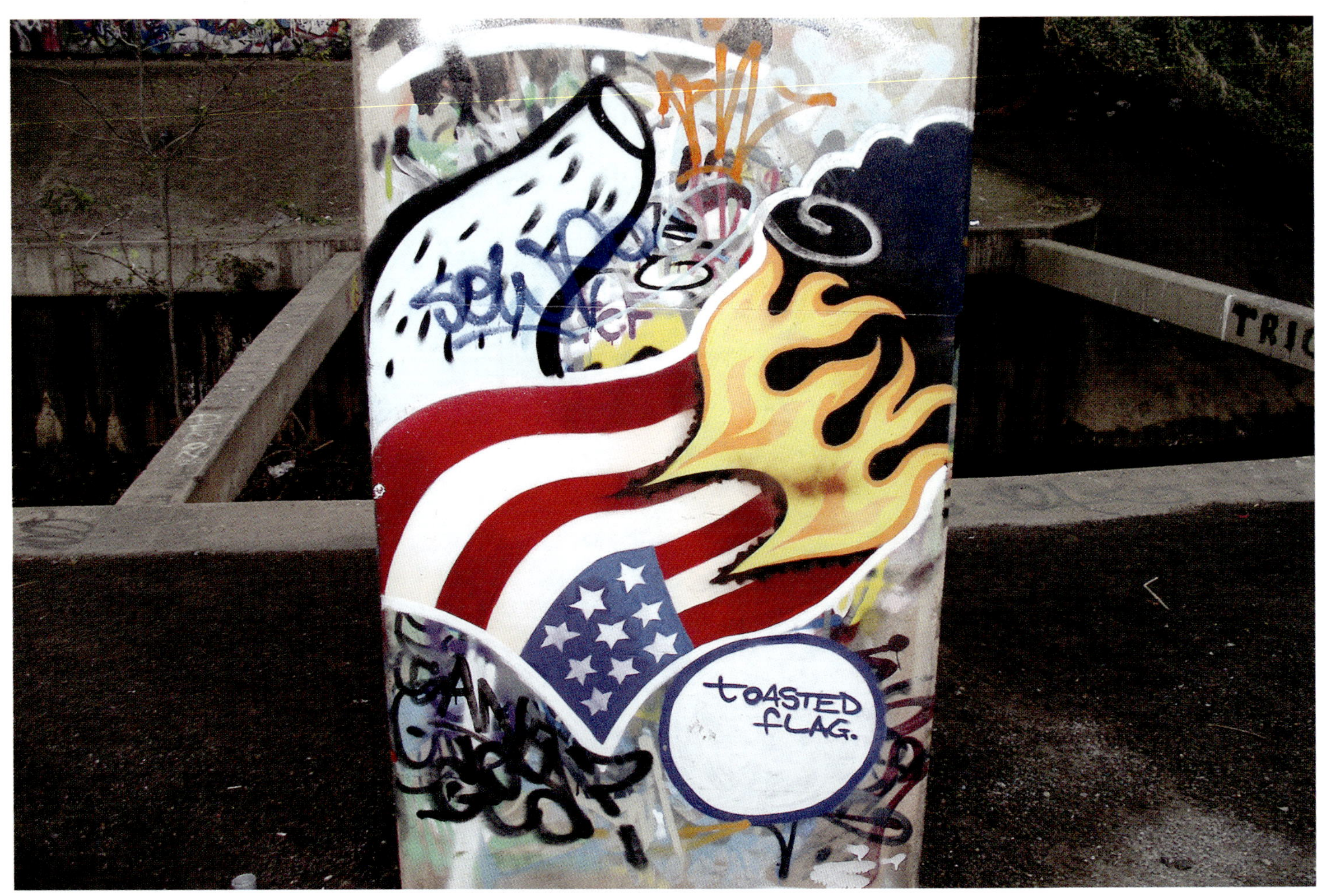

2005: Toasted flag

And the rost...

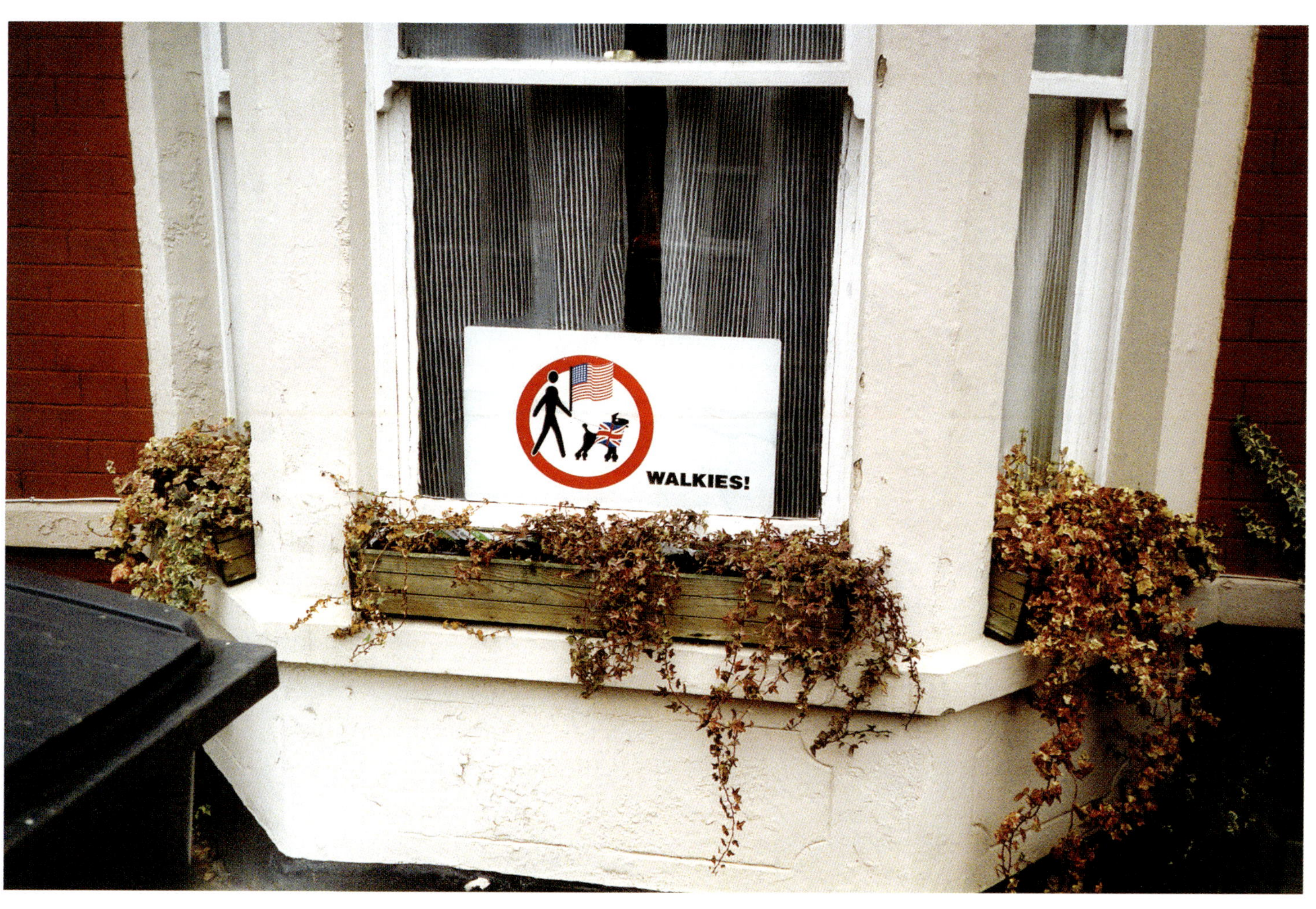

2003: Walkies!

Timeline of events...

2000

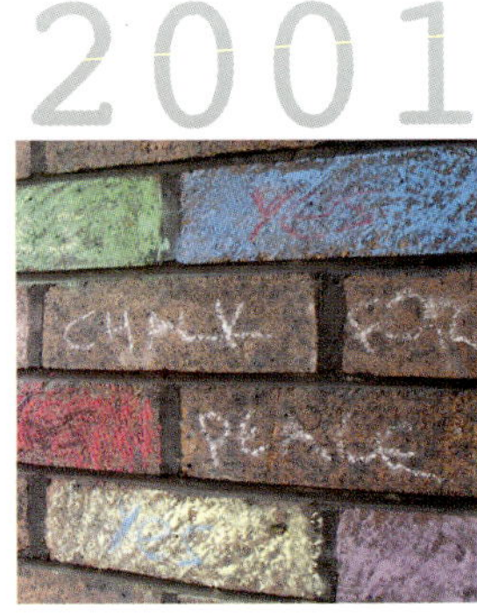

- George W Bush wins US presidential election after several Florida recounts
- Harry Potter & The Goblet Of Fire by JK Rowling becomes the fastest-selling book ever
- Human genome deciphered for the first time

2001

- Blair's Labour party wins a second successive general election victory
- World Trade Centre twin towers hit by hijacked jetliners
- Invasion of Afghanistan – the war on terror begins

2004

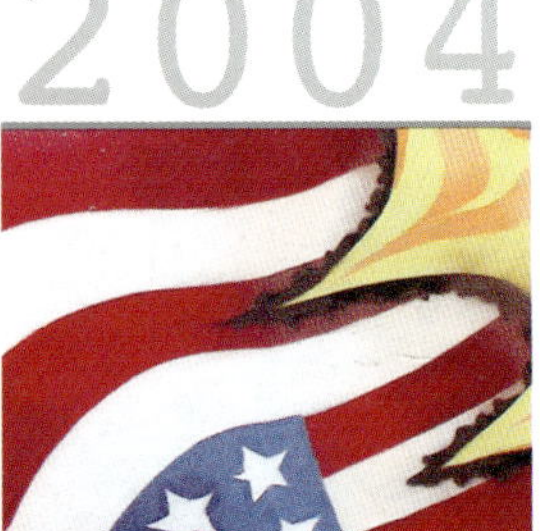

- George W Bush wins a second term in office
- Earthquake and tsunami in South East Asia kills over 230,000 people
- The Hutton Inquiry into the death of Dr. David Kelly is widely condemned as a whitewash

2005

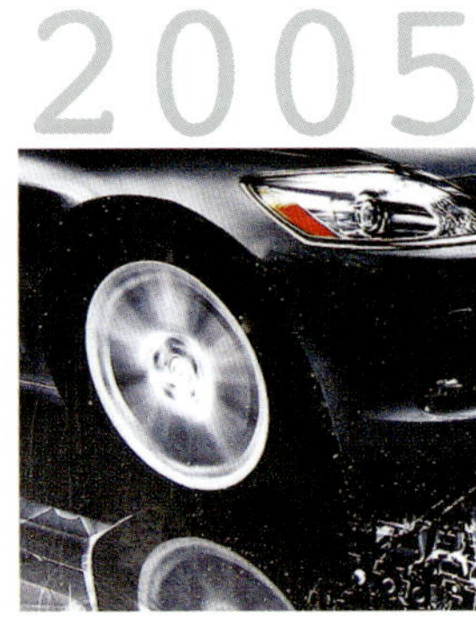

- Labour win a record third successive election victory
- MG Rover, the last British car manufacturer, goes into administration
- The Civil Partnership Act gives same-sex couples the same rights as heterosexual couples

2008

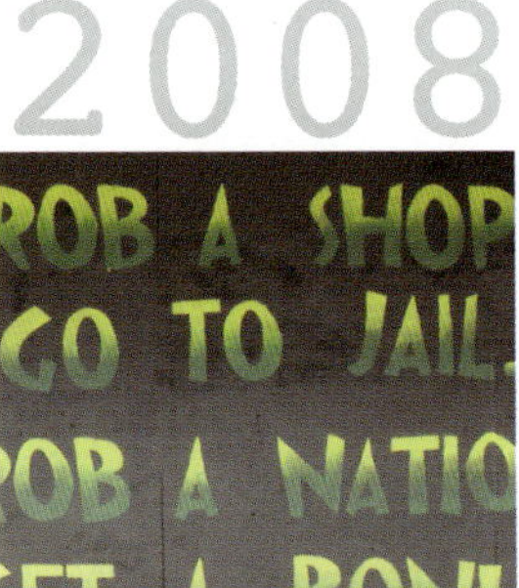

- The UK government bails out the banks with a £500 billion rescue plan
- Barack Obama elected President of the USA
- The last deep coal mine in Wales closes

2009

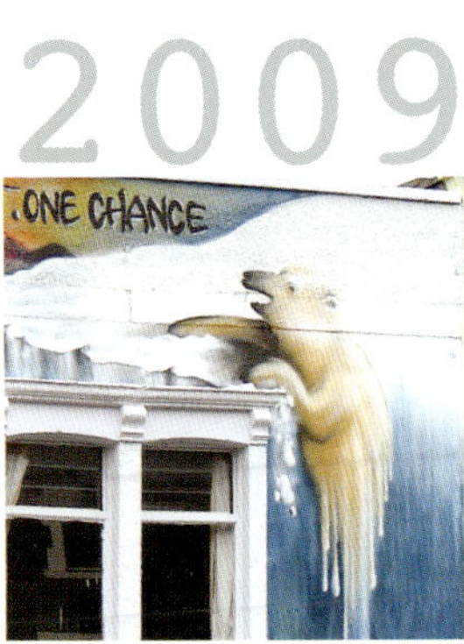

- The Telegraph publishes details of the MPs expenses scandal
- Copenhagen climate talks end in collapse
- The UK economy is officially in recession, and unemployment tops 2 million

2002

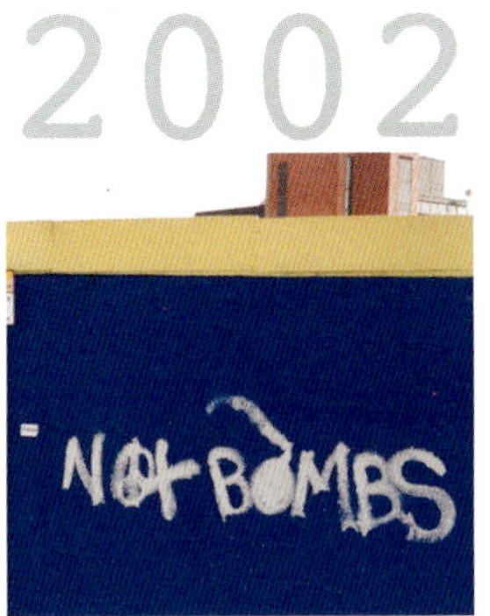

- Euro currency debuts
- BBC 6 Music is launched
- Estimated 40 million people now infected with AIDS/HIV virus worldwide
- UK government claim that Iraq could launch weapons of mass destruction in 45 minutes

2003

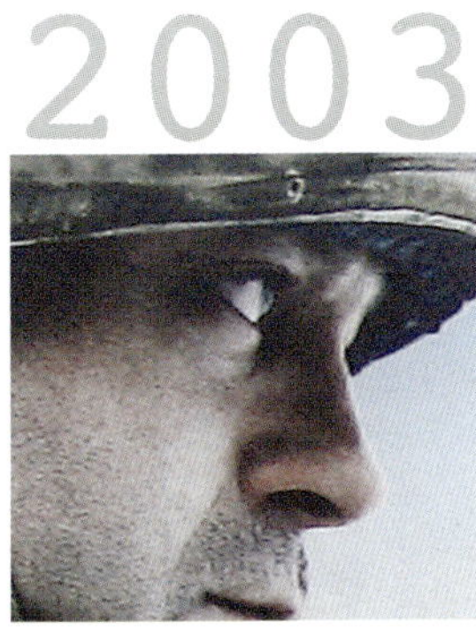

- The Iraq War begins as UK, US, Australian and Polish troops invade
- Police use the taser for the first time
- The UK has it's hottest summer for 13 years
- Dolly - the first sheep to be cloned (in 1996) dies

2006

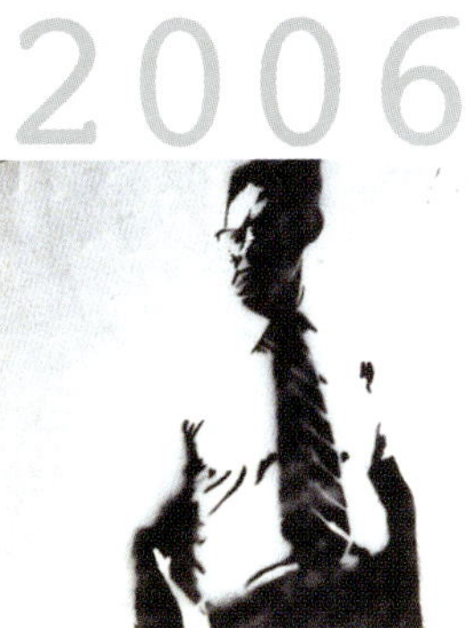

- Former Iraqi dictator Saddam Hussein executed
- Fathers 4 Justice campaigners invade the set of the National Lottery
- World population reaches 6.5 billion

2007

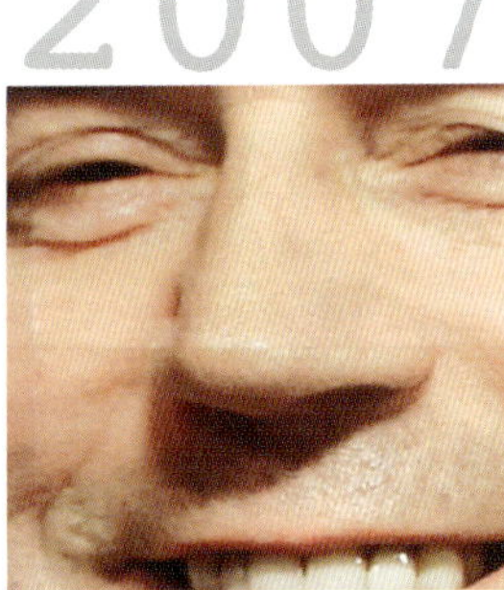

- The smoking ban in public places in England and Wales comes into effect
- Tony Blair resigns and Gordon Brown becomes Prime Minister
- Crash of stock markets worldwide, triggered by the crisis of USA sub-prime mortgage lenders

2010

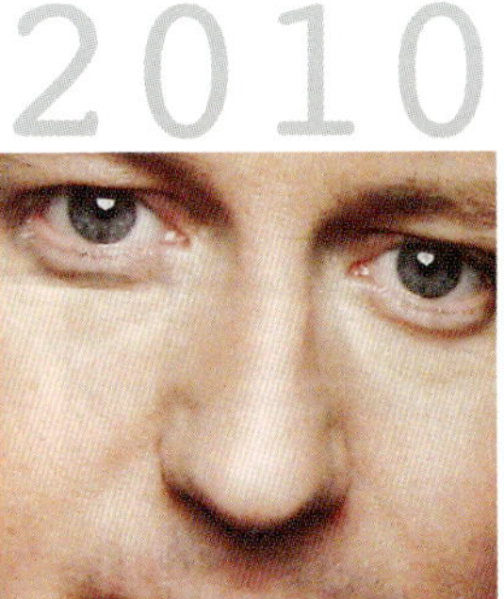

- David Cameron becomes the youngest prime minister since 1812.
- The death toll of British forces in Afghanistan reaches 300
- University tuition fees are capped at £9,000 in England.

2011

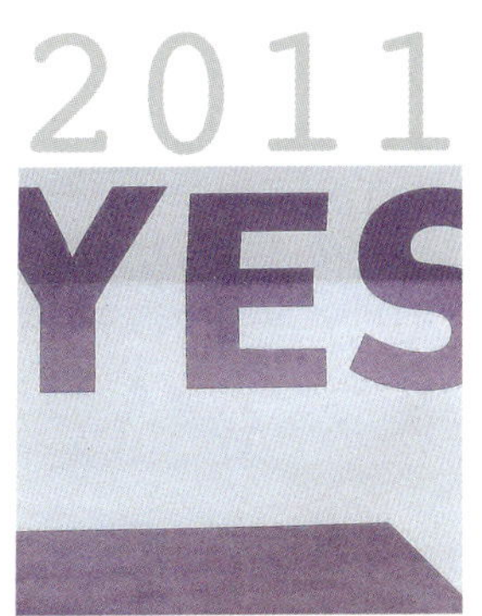

- A referendum on the alternative voting system fails to win popular support
- Fukushima nuclear reactor suffers melt-downs and explosions after an earthquake
- Summer riots take place in cities across England

First Edition of 500 copies published
2010 by Tangent Books ISBN: 978-1906477-38-7

This edition published 2011 by Tangent Books
ISBN: 978-1906477-53-0

Tangent Books
Unit 5.16 Paintworks
Arnos Vale
Bristol
BS4 3EH
0117 972 0645

www.tangentbooks.co.uk

Email: richard@tangentbooks.co.uk

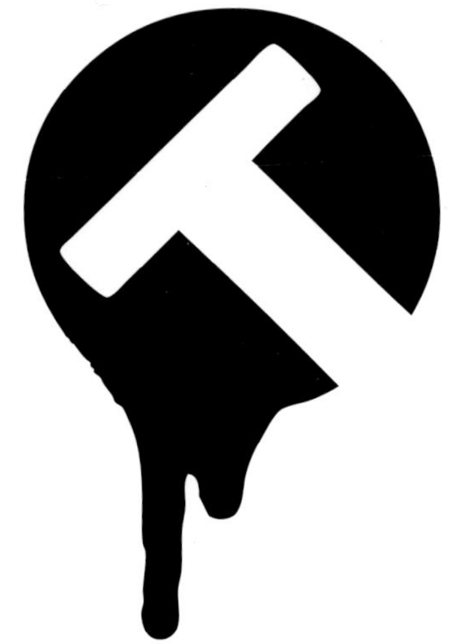

www.flickr.com/photos/donpedro

Layout: Outlaw Design www.outlawdesign.co.uk

Print Manager Jonathan Lewis (essentialprintmanagement@gmail.com)